THE
MORMONS

THE
MORMONS

By

Thomas F. O'Dea

THE UNIVERSITY OF CHICAGO PRESS

CHICAGO & LONDON

ISBN: 0-226-61743-2 (clothbound); 0-226-61744-0 (paperbound)

Library of Congress Catalog Card Number: 57-6984

THE UNIVERSITY OF CHICAGO PRESS, CHICAGO 60637
The University of Chicago Press, Ltd., London

© *1957 by The University of Chicago. All rights reserved*
Published 1957. Eighth Impression 1975. Printed in the
United States of America

To

GEORGIA

Preface

This book is a study of the Mormons by a non-Mormon. It is an attempt to say what Mormonism is as a religious movement and to explore what conditions and events, what kinds of human decisions and effort, have made it that. Moreover, it sets forth the religious world view of the Mormons, showing what Mormons believe and how they see the world, as well as the relationship of this world view to the conditions of life under which Mormonism originated and developed. Finally, it tries to point up particular problems and dilemmas that have attended the Mormon development.

It has sometimes been said that Mormonism is one of those complex human phenomena that are extremely difficult, if not impossible, to write about with anything resembling fairness and that this is especially the case for an outsider. Not unaware of the kind of problem such counselors of despair have had in mind, I have self-consciously tried to avoid those pitfalls I was able to see. I have striven throughout to combine intellectual objectivity with intelligent human sympathy. How well this has been done is a matter for the reader to judge for himself.

Not only is this a book by a non-Mormon about Mormons, but it is also a book by one whose background is largely eastern about a people who are westerners. I traveled around the globe in World War II and was later in Latin America, but unless one counts a week in California and an airplane ride across Arizona and New Mexico, I had never been in the West before I started the present work, which grew out of my concern with the sociology of religion. When my wife and I went to live among the Mormons in 1950, we were tenderfeet indeed. But since then we have come to know the Mormons in more than a bookish way and have come to feel at home in and to have a great affection for the West.

After a stay in Salt Lake City, we lived in a rural Mormon village for six months. Since then, we have come to know various parts of the Mormon country, and last summer I had the honor of being visiting professor of sociology at the Utah State Agricultural College at Logan, Utah. Whatever astigmatisms this book may reveal cannot be attributed to a lack of firsthand acquaintance, for I have tried to supplement the necessary library research with as much living experience as possible.

I would like to acknowledge my gratitude to all those who have helped me in the present effort—and they have been many indeed. First of all, I wish to express my thanks to Talcott Parsons, of the Department of Social Relations at Harvard University, under whose direction I wrote a thesis upon which a part of the present book is based; and also to Clyde Kluckhohn, John M. Roberts, and others of the Harvard Values Study Project with whom I was associated in part of this research. I owe a special debt of gratitude to the late Robert K. Lamb, of the Massachusetts Institute of Technology, who showed me aspects of my own research that I had not perceived myself. I also wish to express gratitude to A. L. Kroeber and Merle Curti, with whom I was associated at the Center for Advanced Study in the Behavioral Sciences in the academic year 1955–56, for reading and commenting upon drafts of some of my chapters. I am also grateful to Gordon W. Allport, of Harvard University, who gave a careful critical reading to one of the earlier drafts of one chapter, and to Evon Z. Vogt, with whom I did a comparative study referred to in the notes.

Especially are my thanks due to the large numbers of Latter-day Saints who were most co-operative in helping me. They are far too numerous to be listed here by name, but I would particularly like to mention the late Apostle John A. Widtsoe, who read an earlier draft of some of these chapters, and A. William Lund, Assistant Church Historian of the Church of Jesus Christ of Latter-day Saints.

There are several institutions without whose aid and co-operation this book could never have been written. In the first place, I wish to express my thanks to the Rockefeller Foundation (Social Science Division) for financial support of the research upon Mormon values on which my earlier doctoral dissertation and part of the present work are based. This research was part of the

Comparative Study of Values in Five Cultures Project of the Laboratory of Social Relations at Harvard University, to which and to whose directors gratitude is also due. Also I am indebted to the Massachusetts Institute of Technology and to John E. Burchard, dean of the School of Humanities and Social Sciences, and Howard R. Bartlett, head of the Department of Humanities, for the time and facilities afforded me both as a Carnegie Fellow in Sociology and as an assistant professor to continue this work. I must also express gratitude to the Center for Advanced Study in the Behavioral Sciences at Stanford, California, made possible by the financial support of the Ford Foundation, where as a Fellow I was able to pursue these tasks further. And, finally, I am grateful to Fordham University and to William R. Frasca and Rev. Joseph P. Fitzpatrick, S.J., for allowing me the margin of free time necessary to put this book in final shape in the past year.

Several libraries and their staffs have been extremely helpful: the Harry Elkins Widener and Houghton libraries at Harvard; the Yale University Library, and especially James T. Babb, librarian, and the staff of the Coe Collection of Western Americana; the Church Library of the Church of Jesus Christ of Latter-day Saints in Salt Lake City; the Boston and New York public libraries; and the Public Library at St. George, Utah, and its librarian, Mrs. Roxey Romney. I am also grateful to the late William Robertson Coe, who established the Coe Collection at Yale, for his personal interest in my work, and to his grandson, Michael Coe, who facilitated my use of materials contained in the collection previous to the completion of its cataloguing.

Thanks are due to the faculties of the three institutions of higher learning in Utah: the University of Utah, Brigham Young University, and Utah State University. I would also like to express thanks to Vincent Ostrom, of the University of Oregon, who discussed with me the complicated question of control of water in the West and gave me the benefit of his knowledge of this subject, and to Don A. Keister, of the University of Akron, who showed me material on the early history of Ohio in the Akron University Library.

Finally, I want to express my gratitude to Richard M. Packard, who encouraged me throughout this endeavor, and to my wife, whose constant help and co-operation made the completion of the task possible.

THOMAS F. O'DEA

Table of Contents

CHAPTER ONE

Who Are the Mormons?

11 million

The Church of Jesus Christ of Latter-day Saints, commonly called the "Mormon church," has over a million members, most of whom live in the intermountain West. Centered in Utah, with church headquarters in Salt Lake City, the Mormon area spreads over into Idaho, Oregon, Wyoming, Colorado, Arizona, New Mexico, and Nevada. Mormon settlements were also established in Mexico and Canada, and there are over two hundred and fifty thousand Mormons in California, many concentrated around Los Angeles and the San Bernardino Valley.

The Mormons were the first settlers in much of the West, having arrived in California by ship in 1846 and in Utah by wagon in 1847. A battalion of Mormons, five hundred strong, recruited under orders from President Polk, marched through what is now Arizona and New Mexico and arrived in California in January, 1847, thereby playing a major role in incorporating that area into the United States. Extending outward from Salt Lake City are small agricultural communities settled by Mormon pioneers and predominantly Mormon today, comprising a relatively homogeneous culture area between the mountain chains. In Utah the Mormons not only are the first settlers, surrounded by all those symbols of prestige that attend the descendants of pioneers in this country, but are also and have been from the beginning a large majority of the population. They feel the West to be their own peculiar homeland, prepared for them by the providential action of Almighty God, and its landscape is intimately associated with their self-consciousness and identified with their past.

Their ethnic composition is the result of the mingling of early American stock, from which their first adherents were drawn, with that of European converts—English, Scandinavian, and others —who came to join them in Illinois in the first half of the nineteenth century and in Utah in the second half. Thoroughly assimilated to a homogeneous group, they exhibit a high degree of self-aware-ness and display a special identity, recognized both by themselves and by their "gentile" neighbors.

From this Mormon country their influence has gone out even beyond the borders of the United States. They have produced figures of importance in public life, business, science, scholarship, and literature, both in the West and nationally. They continue to send out missionaries to other parts of the country, to Europe, and to Hawaii and Oceania, where they have had considerable success. Moreover, in recent decades there has been Mormon migration eastward, which has resulted in sizable and active Mormon groups in most large cities of the nation. The present position of Mor-monism in the West and in the whole country is a far cry from that of the despised and persecuted minority whose existence was considered a national problem and which was driven across the continent to the wastes of Utah in the middle of the last century.

Who are these Mormons? What do they believe? How did they come to be?

The Mormon church was founded in 1830 by a young man of twenty-six, who, together with his followers, offered claims to combine a restoration of primitive Christianity as it had been lived in the time of the Apostles with modern revelation from on high. The new religious group claimed nothing less than a reopening of the heavens and a resumption of divine revelation through the agency of its founder. This young man, whose name was Joseph Smith, Jr., was brought to the village of Manchester in New York State by his family when he was twelve years old. The frigid sum-mer of 1816—called locally "eighteen hundred and froze to death" —had driven them from Vermont, finishing off their long-declin-ing family fortunes. Both Vermont and New York were and had been the scenes of considerable religious agitation, and young Joseph could not have been untouched by the issues that were of central concern to his elders.

Writing later, in 1838, at a time when he was the head of a large religious movement, Joseph Smith described the effects of this environment upon himself. He declared that he was disturbed by the religious controversies that occupied the area in the 1820's. "In the midst of this war of words and tumult of opinions," he wrote, "I often said to myself, what is to be done? Who of all these parties be right? or are they all wrong together?" Troubled by these anxieties, Joseph Smith reported how he had recourse to the Bible. He was struck one day by the import of the first chapter, fifth verse, of the Epistle of St. James: "If any of you lack wisdom, let him ask of God, that giveth to all men liberally, and upbraideth not; and it shall be given him." Inspired by this passage, he "retired to the woods" to ask wisdom of God. Joseph Smith held that his petition was answered and that two heavenly personages appeared to him. They were, he said, the Father and the Son. They counseled him to join none of the contending denominations but rather to prepare himself for important tasks, the nature of which would be made known to him in the future.[1]

It was in this way, so Joseph Smith maintained, that there began a series of reported revelations, which included the miraculous discovery and translation of a set of gold plates. These plates Joseph claimed to have received from the spirit of Moroni, whom he and his followers referred to as an angel and who identified himself as the son of Mormon, the original compiler of the plates. They were turned over to Joseph's charge only after some four years of probation, during which he was tempted and tried, according to his own account. From these plates he claimed to have translated the *Book of Mormon*, which became the scripture of the new church, purporting to be a history of pre-Columbian America, its settlement by Hebrews, and their subsequent destiny and apostasy. This translation was said to have been accomplished by means of two special stones set in rims, making what must have appeared like strange spectacles, to which a breastplate was in some way connected. This curious instrument was called the "Urim and Thummim," a term of biblical origin referring to certain accouterments of the Jewish High Priest (Exod. 28:30; Lev. 8:8; Deut. 33:8; Ezra 2:63; Neh. 7:65).

Joseph declared that he was commanded by the angel Moroni not to show the plates to anyone at first and often, in fact, did not have them with him while translating. Various people said that they handled the plates, although they were covered at the time.

Emma Hale Smith, Joseph's wife, reported that she had lifted them wrapped in cloth in doing her dusting. Finally, however, he showed them, or rather had a heavenly personage show them, to his close associates, Oliver Cowdery, Martin Harris, and David Whitmer, possibly to allay their doubts as to the genuineness of his own calling. These three men signed a sworn affidavit declaring "with words of soberness, that an angel of the Lord came down from heaven, and he brought and laid before our eyes, that we beheld and saw the plates, and the engravings thereon." Somewhat later, Joseph himself is said to have shown the plates to eight others without any miraculous manifestations. These witnesses swore that "Joseph Smith, Jun., the translator of this work, has shown unto us the plates of which hath been spoken, which have the appearance of gold; and as many of the leaves as the said Smith has translated we did handle with our hands; and we also saw the engravings thereon." They added "with words of soberness" that they had "seen and hefted" the plates.

All three of the first group of witnesses apostatized, although Harris and Cowdery later returned. Likewise, three of the second group left the church. Yet the Mormons have maintained that all eleven of them remained steadfast to death in their testimony. No one has been able to upset this contention with convincing evidence, although it has not been unchallenged. Whitmer, who never returned to the church, continued to declare the genuineness of the testimony during his entire life and, before he died, wrote a pamphlet denying statements in the *Encyclopedia Americana* and the *Encylopaedia Britannica* to the effect that some of the witnesses had repudiated their testimony.

The new Mormon scripture gave prominence to several ideas that were filled with soon-to-be-delivered possibilities. It insisted that to "deny the revelations of God, and say that they are done away, that there are no revelations, nor prophecies, nor gifts, nor healing, nor speaking with tongues, and interpretation of tongues" is to reveal an ignorance and betray a denial "of the gospel of Christ" (Mormon 9:7–9). It promised that "signs shall follow them that believe" (Mormon 9:24). It also prophesied that its own message would be brought to the gentiles in the latter days and through them to the descendants of the apostate Hebrews— the American Indians—whose record it claimed to be.

The doctrines announced in the book and the problem of

whether to accept it as revelation or to dismiss it as a fraud, especially the latter option, gave sufficient grounds to set apart those who embraced the novelty and to separate them from the general run of their fellow citizens. This choice had indeed already made itself felt in a more personal form, before the completion of the book, in the question of whether or not to accept the pretensions of the prophet of Palmyra.

Thus was created both the doctrinal and the social basis for the organization of a new church. The inner urgings of the spirit characteristic of revivalistic Protestantism were transformed into latter-day revelation, and simultaneously the private interpretations and inspired utterances of enthusiastic religion were transmuted into the religious authority of a prophet who claimed direct communication with Almighty God. The exalted tension of religious expectation was about to claim fulfilment in a restoration of divine revelation and the confusion of denominational conflict to be clarified in the security of a revealed church. Mormonism claimed that God had intervened by special miraculous action in the history of America and of American religion and that Mormonism itself was the product of that very intervention, a divinely established vessel. What kind of person and place and what kinds of beliefs gave rise to such expectations and such convictions of fulfilment?

The Mormon prophet, who was born in Sharon, Vermont, in 1805, appears to have been an intelligent boy whose natural talents of leadership and love of adventure were confined by his lowly circumstances. Although he later represented himself as torn by religious turmoil at an early age, there is not much evidence for a precocious religiosity. While not unaffected by the religious tenor of time and place, he seems to have appeared to those who knew him as an agreeable and likable young man, somewhat of a ne'er-do-well, who did not associate with the most industrious youths of the village. He was a digger after treasure, an occupation that Yankees took from upland New England to New York, and in this activity his natural ability and his preference for romance over work led him to direct, rather than to do, the actual digging. He used a "peep-stone"—a sort of native crystal in the rough—in which he claimed he saw where treasure was hid, and he led his associates to it. Sometimes evil influences frustrated the diggers and had to be propitiated by the sacrifice of an animal and the sprinkling of its blood around the spot to be excavated. Nec-

romancy, midnight digging—in short, an innocent occultism—
seemed to occupy the youth. In this activity two characteristics
that were to stand out in his subsequent career made themselves
known—an ability to lead men older than himself and a fertility
of imagination.

The first official notice taken of Joseph Smith is said to be in
the record of a trial in Bainbridge, New York, in 1826. The immediate cause was his money-digging and his use of the "peep-
stone" for local farmers. The bill charged that "one Joseph Smith
. . . was a disorderly person and an imposter." Joseph later used
his peep-stone in the translation of his *Book of Mormon*, so that
even this activity was a sort of preparation for his prophetic
career. As time went on, many saw in him a disorderly person and
an imposter, but to others he became a prophet in converse with
heavenly powers. And to all he gave evidence of abilities which
few had surmised up to then.

The prophet was, like many of his fellow "Yorkers," of Yankee
stock. The Smiths had been in New England since 1638—Tops-
field, Massachusetts, and then upland Vermont—and the Macks,
the prophet's maternal ancestors, since 1669, in Lyme, Connecticut. Joseph Smith, Sr., had not done well, and the family was poor
and unsettled. In New York they did not choose to go to the
frontier but bought land at high prices in the settled area, attempting to make a new start in that part of the state soon to enjoy the
prosperity that the projected Erie Canal was to bring. The Mack
ancestry, of Scotch Dissenter stock, was not epileptic, as has been
charged, but Solomon Mack, the maternal grandfather of the
prophet, was a visionary who literally saw visions in his old age.
At the age of seventy-eight, he published a chapbook at his own
expense, containing his biography and some hymns. The immediate family of the founder seems to have been religious but non-
conformist, although his father is said to have been somewhat ir-
religious at times in his life. Lucy Mack, Joseph's mother, had an
eldest brother named Jason, who became a Seeker and who established a kind of communistic religious community in New
Brunswick made up of thirty poor families.[2]

The Smith family did not take hold well in their new situation,
although, as Cross noted, many an "honest and industrious farmer
followed their identical experience, pursued by bad luck or poor
judgment."[3] Yet they do seem to have been somewhat unusual in

their misfortunes. To improve matters, they engaged in digging after lost treasure, with the aid of supernatural devices. They are said to have been variously Methodists and Presbyterians in their religious affiliations.

The appearance of the Mormon church was neither unprecedented nor unique in many respects, for it was one of many religious bodies founded in the region south of the Great Lakes in the first half of the last century. It was, however, one of the very few that became an important factor in the history of the country. It bore within itself many of the marks of its place of origin, but almost from the start it manifested its own peculiar characteristics, setting it apart from American religious groups generally. The area of Mormon origin was west of the Catskills and the Adirondacks, where the moral intensity of the Yankee characterized the people. It was Frederick Jackson Turner who observed that the migrating Yankee was a reformer. He came from western New England, where democratic leanings in politics went along with dissent in religion and where moral earnestness and religious emotion kept evangelical enthusiasm alive well into the second quarter of the nineteenth century.

It was here that worldly prosperity, greatly augmented by the opening of the Erie Canal in 1825 and the concomitant population growth, was swiftly advancing society toward a preindustrial economic maturity based upon agriculture and trade. Mormonism arose in a region some 200 miles from Albany and less than 30 miles from Rochester, which was already a mart of trade and a center of religious fervor that had grown 512 per cent in population in the 1820's. Canandaigua, which had for some time been the center of the immediate district, was one of the two oldest towns in western New York and had well-established schools, libraries, and churches. It was, for that young country, a relatively sophisticated town, considered somewhat aristocratic, since it was the seat of wealthy landlords and their agents and had a strong Episcopal church.

Palmyra, 12 miles north, had become the chief local market since the opening of the canal, on which it was fortunate enough to be located. Between the two towns, halfway, is the village of Manchester, in the middle of western New York's richest soil area. In 1820 it boasted a school, produced wool, flour, and paper in local mills, and operated a blast furnace. Moreover, it possessed a library of six hundred volumes. The three towns and their immediate vicinities had attained a population of sixty persons per square mile by 1820, although 30 miles to the south was land that had been cleared hardly a decade.

In order to grasp fully the circumstances under which Mormonism arose, it is necessary to consider both the religious condition of the time and the psychological makeup of the people. Western New York was the scene of the most intense religious concern that the country has ever seen, before or since. Religion had early given way to indifference in many American communities after the passing of the first generations of settlers, and in the eighteenth century there were large numbers of unchurched people in the American Colonies. In the Puritan settlements, church membership had always been an exclusive matter, secured only with difficulty. Out of one hundred and one colonists who had arrived at Plymouth on the "Mayflower," only a dozen were members of the first church. In the Massachusetts Bay Colony about one-fifth were professing Christians. To the obstacles raised by high standards must be added the unsettling experiences of migration. Especially as settlement went westward, migration removed the emigrants from many of the older cultural restraints and set them down in a wilderness that was almost a *tabula rasa*. Moreover, the association of Calvinism with the rising middle classes influenced the formation of its religious outlook and left by the wayside those poorer groups who found unsatisfying the religion of businessmen and university-educated ministers. To all this must be added something of the spirit of revolt carried here from Europe. Colonial churches were often the products of political and religious revolution in the mother country. Although new authorities had been established, that they were established against pope, king, and bishop could not be conjured away. All these factors tended toward a progressive loss of religious vitality.

Toward the end of the eighteenth century, new ideological elements complicated the picture. Anticlericalism among the believers was matched by a positive tendency toward unbelief. Political radicalism and associated religious skepticism, together with the spread of so-called "natural religion," threatened the older orthodoxy. Moreover, religious innovation—such as denial of the dogma of the Trinity—began to make headway. Thomas Paine's *Age of Reason*, an example of cruder lower-middle-class "infidelity," was known all over the new republic by the end of the century, and small indeed was the hamlet where it had not penetrated.

Such deterioration called forth two strong reactions, each of which was fostered and organized by the clergy. First came the Great Awakening of the 1740's. Starting from many local sources and becoming a continental movement of great dimensions, it swept the country, and penitence, conversion, and religious enthusiasm seemed to penetrate all classes of the population. Yet this fervent revival of religion died down in time and in many places left spiritual deadness in its wake. Temporal crises usurped Colonial attention, and in the period of the Revolutionary War and immediately afterward religious conditions and the state of morals have been described as reaching the lowest ebb in our national history.

The response was the Second Great Awakening, affecting most religious groups. This new spirit spread through the West, where the state of religion in a newly settled region had been considered most deplorable. There the camp meeting became a standard feature. Emotional religion came to characterize the movement in that area, and extremes of what were called "bodily exercises"—in which persons swooned, barked like dogs, and fell down in fits of uncontrolled jerks and kicks—were common. This revival was a national movement, although eastern enthusiasm was calmer and more restrained, and it led to a restitution of American religion, the importance of whose effects can hardly be overestimated.

When New England, aroused by this second great revival movement, spilled out its urge to brotherhood in missionary activities beyond its own borders and went "over into Macedonia," western New York received special attention. Perhaps no soil was ever better prepared for the seed, for the migrating Yankee had taken a background of revivalistic religion with him, although with many it may have lain dormant, awaiting the reawakening. Indeed, western New York, as time went on, seemed to develop an intensification of one side of the New England character. Having revolted from the bleaker teachings of the older Calvinism, the New Englanders in the newer region, where old communal inhibitions were removed, were given to the development of peculiar "isms" of a religious or related nature. In such isms there is often to be found unmistakable evidence of the degree to which the older and explicitly repudiated Calvinism had influenced their fundamental outlooks and responses.

These people were, of course, credulous by sophisticated standards, but they were not docile: they demanded experiential proof for ideas as they understood such proof, and they were quite capable of carrying to extremes their long-ingrained tradition of dissent. They were, moreover, inclined toward individualism. Nonconformity, unrestrained by the older religious notions and by the churches of the standing order, was seen in terms of a moral imperative when it was believed to be dictated by conscience. Such nonconformity was combined with a Puritanical and typically New England regard for the community morality when that morality was accepted—and accepted it had to be unless conscience dictated otherwise. There resulted a character structure that blended curiosity, hardheadedness, and skepticism with credulity, combined individualism with community-mindedness; and joined action to introspection to create a "quarrelsome, argumentative, experimenting brood."[4]

It must not be imagined that this part of the country was either a frontier outpost or a region lacking in the ordinary educational accomplishments of the day. The region of western New York State where Mormonism arose was the kind of middle-class Yankee agrarian society that sent its children to school to learn the three R's. This education was given to girls as well as boys, and, in fact, women were gaining more leisure here, as elsewhere, for concerns and interests of their own, interests that often turned to religious matters. Western New York sent more of its children to school than did the eastern part of the state. It was an area judged to be more youthful but "less isolated and provincial, more vigorous and cosmopolitan, than Vermont."[5] Throughout western New York religious enthusiasm was highest in Yankee, rural, prosperous, and relatively sophisticated areas, and it was precisely in such an area that Mormonism arose. Moreover, the lack of docility that characterized these people was to be seen in their political attitudes. Although local factors ranged them on the side of the Whigs, they were generally as egalitarian and democratic as any Jacksonian. It was the representatives from western New York who forced through an extension of suffrage in the state constitutional convention of 1829.

It was into this region that the Second Great Awakening sent its forces in the 1820's: Bibles, tracts, periodicals, and itinerant preachers poured into the area. The result proved not to be disappointing. The opening of the canal was one catalyst, precipitating the religious outburst that followed 1825. Another was the "Morgan incident," which involved the alleged kidnapping and murder of an ex-Mason to prevent lodge secrets from being betrayed. The consequent excitement reached a fever pitch, and its effect upon this aroused section of the country is difficult to overestimate. A third disturbing element was the preaching of Charles Finney, whose unorthodox Presbyterianism and so-called "New Measures" set the country aflame and whose followers spread, as their leader had done before them, what was perhaps the most sensational and unrestrained evangelism ever to engage the blazing spirits of Yankees and Yorkers.

The sowers of the wind had not long to wait. From about 1825 to 1850 the zeal of sensationalistic evangelism and emotional conversion seared western New York and gained for that region the name of the "Burned-over District." It was the peculiar genius of the people of the area that everything they touched went to extremes. Temperance was embraced, and it came to mean total abstinence, including abstinence from wine and beer and, some suggested, from tobacco, tea, and coffee. Abolition became the demand that slaves be freed immediately, and all churches and Christians who stopped short of demanding immediate manumission were branded as blackest sinners.

Western New York experienced a kind of apotheosis. The latent implications of ideas that had been proclaimed by the great Reformers and had been restrained by social taboo, educated sensibilities, Christian inhibitions, or political repression were now given open expression and enthusiastic acceptance. Luther had proclaimed the priesthood of believers, declaring that "all Christians are truly of the spiritual estate, and there is no difference among them, save of office," and had characterized any notion of the indelibility of priestly ordination as "mere talk and a figment of human invention." The Westminster Confession, that cold and harsh credo of the conservative wing of English-speaking Presbyterianism—the type that the Baptists accused of "priestcraft"—declared: "The authority of the Holy Scripture . . . dependeth not on the testimony of any man or church; but wholly upon God (who is truth itself) the author thereof. . . . Our full persuasion and assurance of the infallible truth and divine authority thereof is from the inward work of the Holy Spirit, bearing witness by and with the Word in our hearts." The assembly of divines who drew up this statement in 1643 were attempting to prepare a new Puritan establishment for the English Commonwealth. They soon saw their efforts frustrated by some of the implications of their ideas, and, instead of an established Puritanical church, there followed a proliferation of separate sects.

Yet in Europe these implications usually did not find uninhibited expression; there Protestantism settled down, and success brought conservatism. In America the situation was somewhat different. Here a more left-wing Protestantism achieved a partial victory. Dissent, enthusiasm, and emotional expression, antiauthoritarianism, anticlericalism, and experimentation with new theological ideas characterized much of the American scene. These tendencies reached a kind of acme of expression in the burned-over district, where native sensibilities were becoming immune to the kind of shock that accompanies religious innovations in more conservative communities. There was hardly possible any kind of religious novelty that might not be given a hearing in that region, where the fires of evangelical fervor dissolved much of traditional restraint for many and even the authority of Scripture for some.

From "inward light of the Holy Spirit," as conservative Protestants conceived it, to emotionally induced conversion, such as prospered in the great revivals, is not a long step when conditions are conducive, and in western New York they were conducive indeed. From such inner guides to truth understood in terms of the general framework of the Christian tradition to idiosyncratic interpretation outside that tradition is a longer step, but in the atmosphere of time and place it, too, was taken by large numbers. Out of the emotional fervor of the revivals came antinomianism and perfectionism, which in their most extreme form led to the Oneida Community and the sexual communism of the justified.

Moreover, what has been called "ultraism" flourished. This term refers to the individualistic insistence upon the dictates of an eccentric conscience, often going over into a kind of one-ideal reformism, seeing in the one ideal that was aggressively advocated the only important human problem or the answer to all human difficulties. Such extremes led many away from traditional religion. Millerites prepared for the end of the world; Universalists gave up older theological positions for a rational liberalism; some people embraced utopian socialist doctrines and became followers of Fourier; Swedenborgianism gained adherents; and Mesmerism became a popular and serious concern. Some people went in a fundamentalist direction, others followed liberal rationalist lights. Both groups found some *rapprochement* in spiritualism, which also began in this region and closed the cycle in mid-century.

It was almost as though much of the religious experience and moral history of America had been transported to western New York, there to undergo a forced growth in most unusual circumstances. Mormonism arose early in the cycle, but it was a legitimate product of the intensified experience of the region. As such, it inherited from its background certain attributes that had come to characterize American religion in its long and fitful history, and these attributes were to be woven into the fabric of Mormon beliefs and to be brought by the Mormon converts out of New York and made the basis of a Mormon commonwealth.[6]

In order to understand the outlook of Mormonism, it is important to examine briefly the chief contributions to Mormonism from its religious background in western New York. We begin with two seemingly contradictory, but actually complementary, tendencies. The first was a result of the notion that accepted and even expected the establishment of new religious groups based upon novel claims or emphasized distinctions. From the start of the Reformation such tendencies had found encouragement, though often not officially. The new churches of the Reformation were, as a matter of fact, less successful in maintaining unity than was the older Catholic body, and, as time went on, numerous sects made their appearance. The more extreme sects often made claims of special revelation or of interpretations supported by visions and other unusual and supernatural phenomena. In western New York the idea of religious innovation and the establishment of new religious bodies came to receive wide acceptance. Revivalism tended to foster innovation and division.

However, at the same time, revivalism also fostered a desire for and a tendency toward unity. The first three decades of the nineteenth century saw the foundation of many interdenominational agencies—Bible societies, missionary societies, temperance groups, and others. This tendency toward the unity of Christians found more explicit expression in the foundation of a group that called itself "Christian," embraced a radical congregationalism in church government, and adopted no hard-and-fast dogmas—all in the attempt to bring frontier Christians together in one church. The founders of this group were Barton W. Stone, the great revival preacher, and his associates. A similar development was the founding of the Disciples of Christ by Alexander Campbell and his followers, advocating a literal understanding of the New Testament or what they called the "restoration of the ancient order of things." This movement joined with the Stonites, and the united body, with no central directing agency, used both names, Disciples and Christians.

This ecumenical desire to see a united church found expression in the Mormon claim to be a divine restoration of the ancient church and therefore to present an unquestionable basis for uniting all genuine Christians. Furthermore, the Campbellite idea of restoring the New Testament order is to be seen in the basic Mormon understanding of Mormonism itself as just such a restoration. In fact, one of Campbell's associates, Sidney Rigdon, the chief revival preacher of northern Ohio, became one of the first important converts to accept the Mormon innovation.

Another important idea in the air when Mormonism arose was that of religious socialism or "communitarianism." This ideal derived from the ideas and aspirations of the radical sects of the Protestant Reformation, many of whom found such practices to be implied by the description of the primitive church at Jerusalem in the Acts of the Apostles, where it is said that "all that believed were together, and had all things common." Such groups found in a simple communism a way out of spiritual and material oppression. A group of this kind arose in Zurich in the first days of the Reformation, but Zwingli considered its communism to be a sin, thus foreshadowing the reception that many such groups would experience from more conservative brethren. These communitarians often developed an ethic of brotherhood and mutual aid and added to their dependence on inner light as a source of religious authority a hope for social regeneration, which often involved chiliastic expectation of an immediate Second Coming of the Lord.

At the time that Mormonism was founded, there were such communitarian groups in the region. The Shakers, so important in transmitting the radical tradition of the left wing of the Reformation from Europe to America, had difficulties in the new country, difficulties which transmuted their hopes for an immediate Second Coming into religious socialism. This group, followers of Mother Anne Lee, who claimed to be a second incarnation of the Godhead (this time of its feminine aspect), came to America in 1774. Between 1787 and 1826 the Shakers, who called themselves "The United Society of Believers in Christ's Second Appearing" or "The Millennial Church," established twenty communities in the United States. All but two of them were still in existence in the latter year, when another was established at Sodus Bay on Lake Ontario, in New York, 30 miles from Palmyra.

The year after the Shakers adopted communism (1787) saw the rise in central New York of the sect led by Jemima Wilkinson (or Wilkerson), a woman of Quaker background, who held that after her conversion a new spirit inhabited her body and that she was chosen to proclaim "News of Salvation to All that would Repent and believe in the Gospel." She founded the "Community of the Publick Universal Friend" on Seneca Lake, which, like the Shakers, emphasized celibacy and communism. Her appearance there was not without a real effect in the area.

Such communitarian ideals were to have considerable influence upon the Mormon ethic, as the new church turned its attention to economic matters. Yet that ethic shows the result of an even more important tendency displayed by American religion in the period before the new church was established. Perhaps the most striking development and one that takes on the appearance of a long-term trend is the growing recognition of free will and the efficacy of human effort.

Early American religion had derived largely from Calvin. Calvinism, whatever its tendency, emphasized the awful sovereignty of Almighty God and the vitiated condition of sinful human nature. Man could do nothing to improve his spiritual condition; he was either of the elect or of the damned. Yet Calvinism was a religion of activism and, from the beginning, was embraced precisely by those social classes whose way of life demanded active participation in the productive work of the world. The New England Puritan was also a man of action, despite his deep concern with theological problems. Calvinism, with its emphasis upon activism and upon the aloneness of the individual and its insistence upon the more arduous virtues of work, honesty, thrift, sobriety, and prudence, certainly appealed to the rising middle classes. Yet these groups were concerned with life in the world, and that life required great expenditure of human energy. The classes that embraced Calvinism by devoting themselves to trade and industry were to transform man's material environment. Obviously, such men needed to believe that human effort was efficacious. A theology that portrayed man as incapable of doing anything for himself did not meet their needs. H. Richard Niebuhr has observed that the doctrine of predestination, which in its Calvinist form seemed to imply a fatalistic position of man in the world and to deprive him of genuine constructive freedom, "was hard to reconcile with the native interests of the bourgeois mind and suffered an early eclipse wherever the trading class was dominant."[7]

One way in which striving was justified in the minds of Calvinists was through the development of a doctrine of evidences. The Calvinist was to know his eternal condition by his inner state. If he felt securely of the elect, it was taken to mean that he had received grace and was saved. But dependence on such subjective states was a source of great uncertainty, and in the face of that metaphysical anguish, men looked for other signs. Actions were watched as signs of election or perdition, and, in time, worldly success came to be interpreted as the product of good character. Good character indicated that one had received grace and was of the fortunate few who were elected for everlasting bliss. While such a doctrine of evidences would have seemed blasphemous to Calvin, it seemed to his middle-class, Bible-reading followers natural enough that those with whom the Lord was, would, like Joseph of old, be prosperous men. As a result of this development, effort, practically speaking, was enjoined as a source of evidences, while theoretically it was seen as the result of spiritual regeneration, which was God's work alone. In this form, striving was justified, while the conviction of special election provided the morale-building notion that God and history had chosen one as an instrument to accomplish appointed tasks.

Yet such qualifications of the older view were not enough; men rebelled both overtly and covertly against the orthodox idea. In 1603 Jacobus Arminius, an eminent Protestant theologian at Leyden, attacked the Calvinist theory, accusing it of making God the author of sin. He set forth anti-Calvinist ideas—not unlike those defined by the Catholic church at the Council of Trent—

denying that human nature had been completely incapacitated by sin and affirming free will. He was to have great influence, and he gave his name to an important trend in Protestant thought. Arminianism had considerable effect in America, especially among the Methodists, who were everywhere opponents of Calvinism.

In addition, the revival movement contributed to the increasing conviction that man could do something for himself. Revivalist preachers stressed the use of human means that might be conducive to religious conversion. To recommend the use of means available to the ordinary man is to encourage the belief that man can accomplish something toward his eternal salvation. Furthermore, Colonial churches had themselves adopted means to encourage the halfhearted. In Connecticut the revivalists, while not denying the orthodox position, stressed man's ability and his responsibility in regard to his spiritual condition and conveyed the idea of human freedom to their listeners. "Works"—the doctrine that man can merit some reward from God—was given a new emphasis, and predestination was allowed to slip into the background.

From the period of the Great Awakening of the 1740's, numerous revolts against Calvinism marked the American religious scene, thus giving open expression to the acceptance of man's freedom and responsibility. If the bourgeois classes of Europe found the old doctrine harsh, how much more so would those of the new continent, for since "the days when the fleet of Columbus sailed into the waters of the new world, America has been another name for opportunity."[8] In Boston, in the period during and after the Revolutionary War, a cultured burgher class went over first to Episcopalianism, then to Arminianism, and ended in Unitarianism. Their poorer relations, who shared with them both the Puritan past and the liberalizing tendencies of the present, went over to Universalism. The differences between the former (who followed Charles Chauncy and Henry Ware) and the latter (who were led by Murray and Ballou) were social and cultural rather than matters of theological principle, "the Universalists holding that God was too good to damn man; the Unitarians insisting that man was too good to be damned."[9]

In Rhode Island, one branch of Congregationalism followed Samuel Hopkins in a religion of "disinterested benevolence," deserting the strict Calvinism of Jonathan Edwards in which they had originated. Southern New England also saw the rise of

Taylorism. Taylor rejected the older views and declared that human depravity consisted in "the free choice [by man] of some object other than God, as his chief good." Such liberating theological ideas were carried further in Connecticut by Horace Bushnell. Perry Miller has traced a line from Jonathan Edwards to Ralph Waldo Emerson, showing the departure of New Englanders from Calvinism. A parallel line may be traced from Edwards to Bushnell and the Social Gospel. The first line is manned by rebels, the second by the orthodox, but both mark out routes by which men traveled away from Calvinism. Analogous lines may be found in the Freewill Baptists and in the New School Presbyterians.

The West also revolted against the denial of human freedom. It was a rebellion of western democracy against an aristocratic theology that seemed to imply the existence of a small elite of chosen men, a proclamation of pioneer self-help and effort against the notion of election, and a victory of yeoman convictions of human worth over the older doctrine of depravity. Kentucky was influenced by American and English Unitarianism. The Methodists were strong in the West, and they were convinced antipredestinationists. The Baptists remained, on the whole, professing Calvinists, but in their revivalism they developed a democratic, unlettered, emotional religion that implied freedom and individualism. In the evangelism of Finney that shook western New York and in his later Oberlin theology, human worth was strongly affirmed, and it was declared that "the sinner's cannot is his 'will not.' "

American life had demanded recognition of the meaningfulness of human striving and the freedom and worth of the individual. The history of American religion in the two centuries before the formation of the Mormon church had witnessed a large-scale desertion of Calvinist pessimism and the recognition of the efficacy of human effort. Mormonism was to make that optimistic estimation of man and his prospects a central part of its basic beliefs.

Mormonism had, then, inherited from its background four major tendencies—sectarianism, ecumenism, communitarianism, and the recognition of human freedom and striving—and these were to leave a permanent mark upon its doctrines. Closely related to the last of these religious tendencies and equally important in its effect upon the new group was the widespread secular optimism that characterized American psychology at the time. The belief in and

confidence of quite ordinary men engendered by American experience and nurtured by religious and secular doctrines became a central strand in Mormon religious values. The continuing westward expansion, which was pushing the frontier toward the Pacific, and the concomitant progress of American industry and invention, which had wrought a revolution in manufacturing, mining, transportation, and communication and even agriculture, were two important dimensions of the situation in which the new Mormon church saw the light of day.

When Joseph Smith was born in 1805, there were seventeen states in the federal Union, and Ohio had just been admitted some two years earlier. Two years later, Robert Fulton's steamboat made its first successful round trip between New York City and Albany. In 1844, when Joseph Smith was killed, the Union was composed of twenty-six states, and in 1845 Florida and Texas were admitted, followed in 1850 by California. The year 1844 also saw Samuel Morse's electric telegraph operating between Washington and Baltimore, while nine years later, in 1853, the Baltimore and Ohio Railway entered the state of Ohio. In the meantime, road-building and the construction of canals were pursued with great enthusiasm and were vastly expanded. Before Joseph Smith was born, Jefferson had won an important election; before he was twenty-five years old, Jackson had won another. Expansion, the rise of the common man, the call of manifest destiny—all these were in the air when Mormonism was born. Such a spirit could not help affecting the new religious movement.

To establish securely the new Mormon church, in order that it might become the vehicle for continuing and developing these ideas and values and so that it might reduce some of them to practice, required more than the rediscovery of a book, even a miraculously translated one like the *Book of Mormon*. It demanded the belief in contemporary revelation, to give form and meaning to the claim of a resumption of direct converse between God and man. Moreover, it required that such contemporary converse be channeled through and identified with the Mormon prophet.

When the wife of Joseph's scribe, Martin Harris, destroyed the first 116 pages of his translation in a fit of spite, what appeared at first to be a crisis of threatening proportions turned out to be just the occasion necessary. In dismay over his loss, Joseph thought of asking God's advice, a solution as pregnant with possibilities as the

Book of Mormon itself. The result was two revelations that warned him of transgression and suggested that he translate other plates for the first section of the book. This turn of events set a weighty precedent. Before latter-day scripture was quite born, latter-day revelation through the agency of a modern prophet had sprung full grown from the head of Joseph Smith.

Further revelations followed in 1829. Joseph used revelation to solve problems as they arose, including the problem of meeting challenges to his own leadership. How to understand what the newly discovered scripture implied with regard to baptism offered another difficulty. Again Joseph appealed to heaven. This appeal eventuated in what Mormons call the "divine restoration of the Aaronic priesthood." Joseph and his associates claimed that John the Baptist came to them and, acting under the direction of the Apostles Peter, James, and John, ordained them to the "Priesthood of Aaron, which holds the keys of the ministering of angels, and of the gospel of repentance and of baptism by immersion for the remission of sins." The Mormon church, in a sense the first fruits of the Burned-over District's zealous harvest of innovations and its most impressive and lasting product, was ready to begin its dramatic and tempestuous career.

Early in 1830 the *Book of Mormon* was published by the Wayne *Sentinel*, Thurlow Weed of the Rochester *Anti-Masonic Inquirer* having turned down the job, pronouncing it "a jumble of unintelligent absurdities"[10] after reading a few chapters. In April, 1830, Joseph Smith announced to the little group of followers whom he had gathered about himself a revelation that contained words proclaiming the "rise of the Church of Christ in these last days . . . by the will and commandments of God." The revelation designated two men as those to whom these commandments were given, "Joseph Smith, Jun., who was called of God, and ordained an apostle of Jesus Christ, to be the first elder of this church," and "Oliver Cowdery, who was also called of God, an apostle of Jesus Christ, to be the second elder of this church, and ordained under his hand."[11] The revelation continued for 84 verses, giving detailed instructions with respect to baptism, the Lord's Supper, the duty of those who were to serve as elders and in such lesser positions as teachers and deacons, as well as the duty of members.

This foundation was followed on the day appointed by the formal incorporation of the church, six men having been involved,

as required by New York State law. At the first meeting after incorporation Joseph Smith gave another revelation, stating that he should "be called a seer, a translator, a prophet, an apostle of Jesus Christ, an elder of the church through the will of God the Father, and the grace of your Lord Jesus Christ," and added that the church should "give heed unto all his words and commandments which he shall give unto you as he receiveth them . . . for his word ye shall receive, as if from mine own mouth, in all patience and faith." Joseph Smith claimed for himself the office of the Lord's chosen spokesman.

A new scripture miraculously translated from plates of gold! A new prophet called and designated by God himself and speaking in his name! A new church restoring by divine appointment the ancient order of things! Such were Mormonism's answers to the confusion and contention that characterized religious concern in western New York. The basic ideas and values that the new movement inherited from its cultural background were to infuse the teachings that its prophet was to develop to meet the requirements of the exciting career upon which it was now embarked. Mormonism was to transform these ideas and values and to innovate as fearlessly as it went on as it had at its inception. Joseph Smith had started his followers on the path that would lead them through great suffering to great accomplishment and himself to the leadership of a dynamic religious movement and to violent death. Throughout its history, as in its very origin, Mormonism was to be both typical of the larger American setting in which it existed and at the same time peculiarly itself, with its own special idiosyncratic emphases and interpretations. Even when most at odds with its fellow Americans, it was to be typically American, and it was always to feel and express this curious combination of typicality and peculiarity.

In 1855, eleven years after Joseph Smith had died, the victim of his enemies' brutal aggression, an important Mormon leader wrote these words of memorial:

> The United States of America was the favoured nation raised up, with institutions adapted to the protection and free development of the necessary truths, and their practical results. And that Great Prophet, Apostle and Martyr—
>
> ### JOSEPH SMITH
>
> was the Elias, the Restorer, the presiding Messenger, holding the keys of the *"Dispensation of the fulness of times."*[12]

The *Book of Mormon*

The New Scripture and Its Manifest Meaning

The *Book of Mormon*, which, according to Mormon belief, was miraculously translated from plates of gold by Joseph Smith, claims to be the record of the aboriginal inhabitants of the Western Hemisphere and covers a period of a thousand years, from 600 B.C. to A.D. 400. It is made up of fourteen books and an editorial note and fills 522 pages in the current edition of the Utah church. The first two books, I and II Nephi, cover a period from 600 to 545 B.C. and tell how Lehi, a descendant of Joseph who was sold into Egypt by his brothers, together with his wife Sariah, his four sons—Laman, Lemuel, Sam, and Nephi—and their families and followers, left Jerusalem shortly before the Babylonian captivity and, led by the Lord in a ship which Lehi had built at his command, arrived at a land of promise across the sea. The rebellion of Laman and Lemuel and their people is punished by their being cursed with a dark skin, and from these Lamanites the American Indians are believed to have descended.

Next follow four short books—Jacob, Enos, Jarom, and Omni—which bring the chronology up to 130 B.C. and tell of the land of Zarahemla, which had been settled by other Hebrews who had left Judah when Zedekiah (II Kings 25:1–7) was carried away captive to Babylon. Then follows the editorial note called the "Words of Mormon," which was supposed to have been written in A.D. 385 by the compiler.

Next are the three main books—Mosiah, Alma, and Helaman—which develop the history of the Nephites, the descendants of

Lehi's faithful son, from 145 to 2 B.C. Here are found the rule and preaching of Benjamin and Mosiah, the wars with the Lamanites, the persecution of true religion, the founding of Alma's church, his high priesthood and chief judgeship, the second Alma as high priest and chief judge, the preaching so reminiscent of revival exhortation, the conversion of Lamoni, the appearance of Korihor the Anti-Christ, the threat from secret organizations (which, it has been suggested, represent the Masons), the admonitions of Alma, the prophecy of Samuel the Lamanite, and much else. This record is continued in III and IV Nephi, which describe the coming of Christ to this continent after the Resurrection and the flourishing of the Church of Christ among both Nephites and Lamanites during a period of peace and righteousness, bringing the story up to A.D. 321. The Book of Mormon follows, recounting how sin and apostasy follow the period of virtue and relating the final struggle between the Nephites and Lamanites, in which the former are wiped out in punishment for their sins and in fulfilment of prophecy. This battle takes place at the Hill Cumorah, where Joseph Smith was later given the gold plates, which had been stored there by Moroni.

At this point the narrative is interrupted by the Book of Ether, which gives the history of the Jaredites, a people whose discovery by the Nephites was reported in the Book of Omni. Jared and his people had come to the new world in saucer-like submarines at the time of the Tower of Babel and had been destroyed because they would not repent of their iniquity. It is here that the word "Deseret" is used and translated to mean "honey bee." This word was later proposed by the Mormons as the name for the state of Utah. Finally, there is the Book of Moroni, a kind of postscript in which Moroni, who later is said to have given the plates to Joseph Smith, describes ritual practices and gives doctrinal instruction.

This work, which is sacred to the Church of Jesus Christ of Latter-day Saints and which ranks with the Bible as holy scripture in its eyes, has been variously explained by non-Mormons. Some have denied the authorship of Joseph Smith and attributed it rather to his first important convert, the Campbellite preacher Sidney Rigdon, who is alleged to have reworked a romance of Solomon Spaulding. While some reputable scholars have given this theory serious attention,[1] it actually arose out of anti-Mormon animosities and was an attempt to discredit the early Mormon movement. The theory is supported by a tenuous arrangement of circumstantial evidence and an even more questionable analysis of internal content. Few, if any, scholars take it seriously today. Writers have also attempted to explain the origin of the work on the basis of abnormal psychology. This kind of theory was put forward by I. Woodbridge Riley in 1902 and was accepted by Eduard Meyer in his *Ursprung und Geschichte der Mormonen*, published in 1912.[2] Such an approach sees Joseph Smith as a visionary whose bad ancestry and epilepsy made it possible for him to see visions to be accounted for in medical terms, while their concrete religious content is explained as a reflection of the cultural setting. Such theories are, at best, learned conjectures, and, as one fashion succeeds another in psychological theorizing, they take on a very dated appearance. The real problem in the present case is the lack of factual basis for the medical explanations, for we have little or no evidence of the hereditary or other abnormalities and nervous instabilities and none at all of the epilepsy upon which such explanations are based.

There is a simple common-sense explanation which states that Joseph Smith was a normal person living in an atmosphere of religious excitement that influenced his behavior as it had that of so many thousands of others and, through a unique concomitance of circumstances, influences, and pressures, led him from necromancy into revelation, from revelation to prophecy, and from prophecy to leadership of an important religious movement and to involvement in the bitter and fatal intergroup conflicts that his innovations and success had called forth. To the non-Mormon who does not accept the work as a divinely revealed scripture, such an explanation on the basis of the evidence at hand seems by far the most likely and safest.[3]

The manifest theme of the book is the arrival and settlement of Hebrews on this continent before the Christian Era, a theme that serves the obvious purpose of explaining the origin of the American Indian, a subject upon which there had been much speculation. The presence of Indian mounds and palisades in western New York and Ohio had increased interest in the subject. Yet the explanation offered by the *Book of Mormon* was not new. It was the conjecture most widely entertained at the time, and it had been the opinion of many clergymen since Cotton Mather that Hebraic origin must explain the genesis of human existence on these shores. Many books had been written on the subject, and recently there had been published another, one quite possibly known by Joseph Smith.⁴ This work, written by Ethan Smith and entitled *View of the Hebrews: or the Ten Tribes of Israel in America*, was published in 1823. It contained "all the items of three generations of specious scholarship and piecemeal observation on this subject."⁵ It also contained Caleb Atwater's description of Indian mounds in Ohio and one of Central American ruins by Von Humboldt. It was a source of genuine information as well as of erroneous inference on the subject of Indian origins.

To the popular notions of Hebraic genesis, the *Book of Mormon* added nothing new except the very important claim of presenting original written remains, and these on the basis of miraculous intervention. It is this aspect of the book rather than the novelty of its hypothesis that explains its appeal, limited though it was at first. Yet the manifest theme of Hebraic origins of the Indian had an important influence upon Mormon thinking and even upon Mormon destiny. From the first, the new church conceived as part of its task the reconversion of the Indians that they might once again become a "white and delightsome people" (II Nephi 30:6). A generally favorable attitude toward the Indians has marked the Mormons ever since. Moreover, since the church moved west almost immediately and sent out missionaries to the aborigines shortly after its founding, this Mormon attitude antagonized fellow whites on the frontier. The suspicions aroused by the Mormon attitudes toward the Indians were an element in the hostilities between the Saints and their gentile neighbors in Missouri in the 1830's, and in Utah in the 1850's the Mormons and the Indians felt themselves allies in a struggle against the United States.

The "explanation" through divine revelation of the origin of human culture on these shores and the content of that explanation itself—that the Hebrews had been led here by God—could not but mold a reverent attitude toward this land. The *Book of Mormon* thereby became more than an explanation, it became a dedication. The popular beliefs in the special character of this continent reflected the utopianism of generations of immigrants, whether explicit, as in John Winthrop's establishment of Zion on Massachusetts Bay, or implicit, as in the aspirations of the thousands of indentured servants who signed up for seven years' labor prefatory to achieving yeoman status in the new West. The romantic nationalism of the new republic and the optimism and expectation that characterized the third decade of the nineteenth century were full of promise to the common man. The *Book of Mormon* enshrines these sentiments in an American scripture. In the golden bible brought forth by Joseph Smith, a prophet of old calls this continent "a land which is choice above all other lands" (II Nephi 1:5) and declares that "there shall none come into this land save they shall be brought by the hand of the Lord" (II Nephi 1:6). The ideology of immigration has been consecrated and transformed into prophecy. Moreover, "it shall be a land of liberty" (II Nephi 1:7). The *Book of Mormon* also consecrates the democratic sentiments that had run so deeply in revival religion and pervaded so much of political life at the time. In content as well as origin, the *Book of Mormon* was an American document.

The Basic Themes of the Book

More profound, if less palpable, than the theme of Hebrew origin and American peculiarity is a second theme that is bound up inextricably with the first, the theme for which the first may indeed be said to serve mainly as scaffolding. It is this second theme that explains how the book could have become the scripture of a new church; for, indeed, New Yorkers in the 1830's were not so concerned with the mystery of Indian origins as to be converted to a new religion on the basis of a solution of this problem. Neither were the English and Scandinavian converts of the next decade, although the emphasis on America as a land of promise must have played an important role, especially when Mormon efforts to build their holy city were giving tangible form to such hopes. It is this second theme that has received least attention from non-Mormon commentators, who have often found in superficial peculiarities and literary awkwardness the chief objects of their attention. Indeed, the *Book of Mormon* has not been universally considered by its critics as one of those books that must be read in order to have an opinion of it. The *Book of Mormon* is concerned fundamentally with the problem of good and evil. It is a story of backsliding and repentance and of apostasy, which projects before its reader the religious sentiments and ideology of western New York and, indeed, of much of postrevival America in the second quarter of the nineteenth century. As such, it is an almost completely neglected primary source for the intellectual history of the common man. Its fundamental theme combines the concomitance of righteousness and prosperity of the later Calvinism with the call to repentance and humility of revivalistic Christianity, without either the stress on human depravity of the former or the excessive emotionalism of the latter. It suggests over and over again a cycle that begins with virtue and prosperity and leads to pride and inequity, to social divisions and arrogance, to sin and decadence, and thence to the Lord's chastisement. This, if it does not end in destruction, is followed by repentance and the reinstatement of righteousness, which lead to prosperity and a recapitulation of the theme.[6]

In the second Book of Nephi, Joseph Smith attempts to give a philosophical explanation of the problem of evil and discourses upon the necessity of opposition in all things. The rest of the work, however, is based implicitly upon another theory of evil. With the shrewd realism of the common man and that insight into the inner state of personal inclination which revival religion had fostered, evil is seen to be the result of the pride and worldliness that come from economic and social success. For, behind the "costly apparel" (Alma 1:27, 4:6) of the well-to-do, the religion of the poor suspects corruption; beneath inequity, it is surmised, must lurk iniquity. Yet, as the sects of the lower classes in Europe often transmuted their resentment into an ethic, unostentatious and ascetic, of brotherhood and fellowship, so does the *Book of Mormon* also present an ethic of aiding the poor and unfortunate which makes a man his brother's keeper and cautions explicitly against considering the poverty of the poor the fruit of iniquity; it thereby rejects the other side of the Calvinistic linkage of virtue and prosperity which in itself is one of the book's chief themes (Mosiah 4:17–20).

The central theme of the books of Mosiah and Alma, the largest and most central of the work—and, indeed, that of the *Book of Mormon* as a whole—may be summed up in one verse from Alma: "Thus we see how quick the children of men do forget the Lord their God, yea, how quick to do iniquity, and to be led away by the evil one" (Alma 46:8). Yet, as we have seen, righteousness will lead to worldly prosperity—"inasmuch as ye shall keep the commandments of God ye shall prosper in the land" (Alma 36:30)—which leads to "being lifted up in their hearts, because of their exceeding great riches" and thence to failure "to walk uprightly before God" (Alma 45:24). This cycle from virtue to prosperity, from prosperity to pride, from pride to a fall, and thence to repentance, which reinstates righteousness to start the cycle over again, gives many opportunities for prophets and preachers to arise and call the people to repentance. The central message of the book is repentance,[7] and the work is full of slightly concealed revival meetings, as in Jacob's words to the people of Nephi (II Nephi, chaps. 6–10); Nephi's commentary upon Isaiah (II Nephi, chaps. 25–33); Benjamin's exhortation to his people and their conversion (Mosiah, chaps. 1–6); the preaching of Abinadi (Mosiah, chaps. 11–17); the preaching of the two Almas (Mosiah, chap. 18, and Alma), of Amulek (Alma, chaps. 9–14), and of Samuel the Lamanite (Helaman, chaps. 13–15), to name the most obvious examples. Indeed, at one time "Alma did speak unto them, when they were assembled together in large bodies, and he went from one body to another, preaching unto the people repentance and faith on the Lord" (Mosiah 25:15), a scene strongly reminiscent of the camp meeting. Yet the revivalism of the *Book of Mormon* is the more dignified revivalism of New England and is not marked by the "jerks," "barking," and other bodily exercises of the frontier variety. In only one instance does it approach excess, when three converts swoon (Alma 19:6, 13, 14).

The doctrine of the book is wholeheartedly and completely Arminian. It tells men that "because that they are redeemed from the fall they have become free forever, knowing good from evil; to act for themselves and not to be acted upon . . ." (II Nephi 2:26); and that they are "left to choose good or evil" (Alma 13:3).[8] Men, says the *Book of Mormon*, will be judged by God according to their works—"Ye must stand before the judgment-seat of Christ, to be judged according to your works" (Mormon 6:21).[9] This doctrine proclaims that "whosoever will come may come and partake of the waters of life freely; and whosoever will not come the same is not compelled to come; but in the last day it shall be restored unto him according to his deeds" (Alma 42:27). While the salvation of men is through the merits of Christ, these merits are available to all who repent. The Atonement was for all men, and grace and mercy are available to all.[10]

Much can be seen in the *Book of Mormon* of the implicit mentality of the popular Protestantism of the time. For example, the story of the first Alma (Mosiah, chaps. 23–24) is, in a very profound sense, the history of sectarian, left-wing Christianity, as seen by itself, projected into an ideal or mythological representation. The persecution of the prophet Abinadi, his burning by the king and the established church in a scene recalling the deaths of Ridley and Latimer under Mary Tudor (Mosiah 17:13–15), the secession of Alma and his founding of a church that bore all the marks of sectarian regeneration, and its final exodus into the wilderness, where (reminiscent of John Winthrop) the regenerate founded a free colony and where (anticipating what had come only much later in Massachusetts) they established republican government—all this must have sounded deep resonances in the minds of those whose forebears had left England in the reign of the Stuarts (Mosiah, chaps. 11–18).

The *Book of Mormon* is an ideal projection of left-wing Protestantism in another sense. All the Nephite prophets, from Lehi in 600 B.C., who was "a visionary man" (I Nephi 2:11), to Moroni, who tells us that by the power of the Holy Spirit we may know all things (Moroni 10:5), spoke, like Alma, "according to the Spirit which testifieth in me" (Alma 7:26), when indeed they did not converse with angels, with Christ, or with the Father himself.[11] Moreover, by this revelation and prophecy they spoke and taught "with power and authority from God" (Mosiah 18:26). Yet nowhere in the *Book of Mormon* does this abundance of inspiration and revelation and following of the Spirit "wheresoever it leadeth" get out of hand. Nowhere are the elect plunged by such criteria into controversy, with brother pitted against brother, each claiming divine sanction for his doctrine. Contention there is within the church of God, but good and evil are easily discernible at all times, and the Holy Spirit is never confused with impulses of human or demoniacal origin. Complete freedom of inspiration and interpretation combines easily with revealed authority, the inspirations of all showing remarkable unanimity. Moreover, this absolute freedom of revelation expresses itself in an authoritarian church structure whose rulers are priests who have been called by God and who are the revelators of his word. Hence there is no splintering; instead, the ecumenical aspirations of sectarianism find expression in a united church. That this sectarian utopia could not exist in the real world the Mormon prophet learned at once, when he had to restrict the prophetic gifts of his associates. At no point does this emphasis upon the inner workings of the Spirit verge toward—let alone become—antinomianism. There is again and again in the *Book of Mormon* strong insistence upon keeping the commandments of God—"I know if ye keep the commandments of God ye shall be saved" (Mosiah 12:33).[12] "This life became a probationary state" (Alma 12:24).[13] As we have seen, righteousness is understood to mean keeping the commandments of God and is rewarded by worldly prosperity—"inasmuch as ye shall keep the commandments of God ye shall prosper in the land" (Alma 38:1).[14] There is not the slightest trace of that development which came to be known as "perfectionism" and which, as typified by Noyes and the Oneida Community, held that the saved could not sin. The *Book of Mormon* tells the repentant and regenerate that they must endure "to the end."[15] The shrewd realization of how likely men are to fall, of their susceptibility to the temptations of pride, together with the call for them to repent, is central to the whole work.

Those who have made sport of Joseph Smith's attempt to imitate the English Bible have often failed to note the intellectuality of the *Book of Mormon*. There is nothing obscure or unclear in its doctrine. Even the notion of prophecy and revelation, so central to it, leads to intellectual clarity. The revelation of the *Book of Mormon* is not a glimpse of higher and incomprehensible truths but reveals God's words to men with a democratic comprehensibility. "Plainness" of doctrine—straightforwardness and an absence of subtle casuistries—was for its rural audience a mark of its genuineness. The book insists that the age of miracles is not over: "O all ye that have imagined up unto yourselves a god who can do no miracles, I would ask of you, have all these things passed, of which I have spoken? Has the end come yet? Behold I say unto you, Nay; and God has not ceased to be a God of miracles" (Mormon 9:15, 19). These miracles, which join wonder to plainness, follow upon faith, and faith is facilitated by the plainness and straightforwardness of doctrine which the Nephite prophets favor and with which they favor their congregations.[16] The intellectuality of the *Book of Mormon* is to be seen in its recognition of currents of thought other than and antagonistic to its own point of view, and especially in its awareness of current skepticism and rationalism. In the Book of Helaman both the Nephites and the Lamanites show tendencies then to be found in the towns and villages of western New York. They depend "upon their own wisdom saying: Some things they [the prophets] may have guessed right, among so many; but behold, we know that all these great and marvelous works cannot come to pass, of which has been spoken. And they began to reason and to contend among themselves saying: . . . if so, and he be the Son of God, the Father of heaven and of earth, as it has been spoken, why will he not show himself unto us as well as unto them who shall be at Jerusalem?" (Helaman 16:15–18). In the Book of Alma (Alma 30:15–18) the arguments of the atheists and scoffers are summed up: "Behold ye cannot know of things which ye do not see; therefore ye cannot know that there shall be a Christ . . . it is the effect of a frenzied mind; and this derangement of your minds comes because of the traditions of your fathers . . . whatsoever a man did was no crime . . . when a man was dead, that was the end thereof."

In contrast to the extremes of religious enthusiasm that were soon to follow upon the revivals preached by Finney and his associates later in the decade, the intellectuality of the *Book of Mormon* and its appeal to its adherents as a reasonable answer to problems of existence and salvation are quite obvious. Nowhere, however, is this so clear as in the insistence of the Mormon scripture on the importance of knowledge. It urges its readers to know the commandments, to know the prophets, and to know the gospel in order to be guided by them. Moreover, the *Book of Mormon* insists upon the necessity of knowledge for culpability. Those who do not know the gospel are saved by the Atonement of Christ (Mosiah 15:24), as are the little children (Mosiah 15:25), and as for the Lamanites, "because of the traditions of their fathers that caused them to remain in their state of ignorance; therefore the Lord will be merciful unto them" (Alma 9:16). But "after a people have been once enlightened by the Spirit of God, and have had great knowledge of things pertaining to righteousness, and then have fallen away into sin and transgression, they become more hardened, and thus their state becomes worse than though they had never known these things" (Alma 24:30).

Knowledge is necessary to choice and therefore to guilt. On this intellectual basis the ethics of the *Book of Mormon* rest.[17] This emphasis and that on free will became cornerstones of the Mormon outlook as it developed in the following years.

That the *Book of Mormon* is not the creation of European sectaries but is rather the product of the new continent is reflected in a number of its subordinate themes. It is obviously an American work growing in the soil of American concerns in terms of its basic plot and its enshrining of America as the promised land, as well as in the unconcealed secular patriotism with which it refers to the United States. "And this land shall be a land of liberty unto the Gentiles, and there shall be no kings upon the land. . . . And I will fortify this land against all other nations" (II Nephi 10:11–12).[18] American sentiments permeate the work. In it are found the democratic, the republican,[19] the antimonarchical,[20] and the egalitarian doctrines that pervaded the climate of opinion in which it was conceived and that enter into the expressions and concerns of its Nephite kings, prophets, and priests as naturally as they later come from the mouths of Mormon leaders preaching to the people in Utah. Monarchy is never really good, and at its best the good kings work with their hands. Taxation is oppressive,[21] and lawyers are not to be trusted.[22]

In the hearts and minds of the pre-Columbian Hebrews live the ideas and sentiments which upland New England carried over into New York. Radical western religion is seen in the emphasis upon the obligation of clergymen to work,[23] a tenet that later finds permanent expression in the structure of the Mormon church. The attitudes of those who lived in the West, their feeling that the government back east neither understood their problems nor showed the proper concern for their interests and that those who lived in the supposed comfort of the settled areas neglected them are seen vividly set forth in the letter of Moroni, the military commander in the field, to Pahoran, his superior, the civil governor in the rear: "We know not but what ye are also traitors to your country. Or is it that ye have neglected us because ye are in the heart of our country and ye are surrounded by security" (Alma 60:18–19). The shadow of the man on the white horse falls across the pages of a piece of early American writing in the threat of Moroni in the same epistle: "I will come unto you and if there be any among you that has a desire for freedom, yea, if there be even a spark of freedom remaining, behold I will stir up insurrections among you, even until those who have desires to usurp power and authority shall become extinct" (Alma 60:27).

There is much more of egalitarianism and democracy than of constitutionality in such sentiments, and the closeness to violence was thoroughly American. Interesting also is the fact that Moroni self-righteously impugns the motives of his opponent in the complete absence of evidence and, although threatening insurrection, does so only in the cause of righteousness. It is the opponent who must be guilty of ambition. Similar attitudes probably exacerbated the antagonisms between Mormon and gentile in the bitter conflicts which marked the later years. The utopianism of the *Book of Mormon* is to be seen again in the fact that Moroni accomplishes his task of rebellion within the structure of established order. Indeed, if those Europeans who today accuse us as a nation of self-righteousness in our relations with them but knew the letter of Moroni to Ammoron, the Lamanite leader—"I will tell you somewhat concerning the justice of God, and the sword of his almighty wrath, which doth hang over you except ye repent and withdraw your armies into your own lands" (Alma 54:6)—they would perhaps attribute our attitudes to less disreputable motives.

The shrewdness with which the cycle from prosperity to sin is delineated in the book seems to be forgotten in these political controversies. The consequent self-satisfaction in public life misrepresents the inner sincerity from which it springs and makes the Nephite leaders lamentable models of statesmanship; yet it is characteristic of a "peculiar-people" mentality. In the *Book of Mormon*, as in the popular opera of both "horse" and "soap" varieties, there are, in effect, "good guys" and "bad guys." The good side always fights in defense of its liberties, its families, its wives, and its children. It is never the aggressor. The good side sends out missionaries to bring the light to those in darkness. The bad side sends out armies of invasion. Moreover, the good side in war does not, like its enemies, break the Geneva Convention—"and there was not a woman nor a child among all the prisoners of Moroni" (Alma 54:3).

In the *Book of Mormon* there is religious freedom and the separation of church and state; yet, despite the fact that consciences are not coerced, religious liberty in practice becomes the legal protection of proselytization by the church of God. Alma becomes high priest and chief judge or supreme governor in the land. The presence of "a great and abominable church which is most abominable above all other churches" (I Nephi 13:26) is given considerable attention at the beginning of the first two books of Nephi.[24] This may have been occasioned by the arrival of the Irish immigrants who worked on the construction of the Erie Canal, or, as is more likely, it may have been merely the usual accompaniment of the left-wing Protestant mentality, the little-understood inheritance of an honored past.[25] At any rate the content was as old as the Reformation; and, when the *Rochester Observer* referred to the Roman Catholic church as "the Beast" and the "mother of abominations" and the *Rochester Album* published (on February 29, 1828) a counterfeit letter from "Pope Leo XII" to the "elect elders of Rochester" which spoke of using "our holy rack, our thumb screws, our Iron Bed, and many other such arguments" in order to convince the unbelievers "of their damnable heresies," no one could have been either surprised or upset.[26] There is no evidence that Catholic-baiting in New York was excessive by national standards, and it is certain that it did not reach the dimensions of the later nativism in many parts of the country or of the anti-Catholicism of England in 1851 when Catholic bishoprics were re-established for the first time since Elizabeth I. If anything, the "very progress of 'the Mother of Harlots' served as one of the prominent prophetic signals of the approaching judgment,"[27] as millennial hopes rose in the late 1830's and 1840's.

The conception of government in the *Book of Mormon* is democratic; among the elect, at least, it is by "voice of the people." "Now it is not common that the voice of the people desireth anything contrary to that which is right; but it is common for the lesser part of the people to desire that which is not right; therefore this shall ye observe and make it your law—to do your business by the voice of the people" (Mosiah 29:26). Yet this confession of democratic faith, so characteristic of the milieu, did not pass without qualification. Not only was the upland Yankee turned Yorker democratic, he was shrewd and realistic. Whether it was the problems of developing his 92 B.C. plot or his reflection upon his experience with his contemporaries that gave him pause, Joseph appended a profound warning: "And if the time comes that the voice of the people doth choose iniquity, then is the time that the judgments of God will come upon you; yea, then is the time he will visit you with great destruction even as he has hitherto visited this land" (Mosiah 29:27).

One does not, however, see any real legislation in the *Book of Mormon*. The definition of law implied throughout the work is not unlike that of ancient Greece. Law is achieved through lawgivers, and it is accepted by and the officers of its administration are chosen by the "voice of the people." Moreover, one carries away the firm impression that, while the *Book of Mormon is* democratic in sentiment, it combines charisma with constitutionality in a manner that would be quite unworkable in real life in a democratic society.

Much has been said of the many references to Masonry in the work. The Gadianton robbers who take secret oaths and are a subversive element in the history of the Nephites are the reflection in the book of the outcry against Masonry of the 1820's, made more strident in New York because of the Morgan case. That anti-Masonry was a democratic movement is confirmed by the picture given in this work of Masonic activities.[28]

The *Book of Mormon* is millennial, but it is calm in its hopes, and neither it nor the movement to which it gave rise ever suggested anything like Millerite enthusiasm. Yet it has held that in the last days the Jews will be gathered, as will their descendants on the new continents, the American Indians. This expectation, which includes in its later interpretation the building of Zion here by the members of the Mormon church, has been a continuous part of Mormon doctrine.[29] An interesting item requiring later reinterpretation is found in the five separate denunciations of polygamy.[30]

There is some ambiguity on the question of baptism in the *Book of Mormon;* an early contention on this point even led to argument between the prophet-translator and his scribe, Oliver Cowdery.[31] In the earlier parts of the book the general import and implication seem to point to a doctrine resembling that of the Baptists, that baptism is a sign witnessing to regeneration but does not remit sins. The second Book of Nephi speaks of witnessing "unto the Father that ye are willing to keep my commandments, by the baptism of water" (II Nephi 31:14), and in the Book of Mosiah the people are urged to be "baptized in the name of the Lord, as a witness before him that ye have entered into a covenant with him, that ye will serve him and keep his commandments" (Mosiah 18:10).

Yet, together with this Baptist doctrine, there is strong emphasis upon free will, upon the intention of the penitent to keep the Commandments. By the end of the book this blend of Baptist definition of the sacrament and Arminian understanding of the choice of the penitent takes on the appearance of a doctrine rather like that of the Catholics, Episcopalians, and others of the more central stream of the Christian tradition. The Book of Moroni, intended to be a manual for the new church, says: "Behold, baptism is unto repentance to the fulfilling the commandments unto the remission of sins" (Moroni 8:11). A little later Moroni declares that, without repentance, baptism is useless and those who do not understand this are "putting trust in dead works" (Moroni 8:23). He stresses the importance of repentance and adds: "The first fruits of repentance is baptism; and baptism cometh by faith unto the fulfilling the commandments; and the fulfilling the commandments bringeth remission of sins" (Moroni 8:25). The result of this teaching has been the doctrine held by the Mormon church that baptism is necessary both as a witness to the covenant and to church membership and for the remission of sins.

Infant baptism is condemned, and Moroni urges that "ye should labor diligently, that this gross error should be removed from among you" (Moroni 8:6). He attributes to Christ the following decisive statement: ". . . wherefore, little children are whole, for they are not capable of committing sin; wherefore the curse of Adam is taken from them in me, that it hath no power over them" (Moroni 8:8). It is typical of the whole direction of Mormon theological development that infant baptism should be rejected not for the conventional reasons advanced by the Baptists but because of renewed emphasis upon the goodness of man. While this is attributed to the merits of Christ, it is nevertheless a part of the developing humanism of the period, which found such striking reflection in all Mormon doctrine.

We must also note that, with all its emphasis upon humility and giving to the needy, all its denunciation of pride and class distinction, the *Book of Mormon* does not advocate communitarian socialism. There are two references to apostolic community of ownership in the book (III Nephi 26:19 and IV Nephi 3). These are conventional repetitions of the New Testament.

The New Testament verses are as follows:

And all that believed were together, and had all things common [Acts 2:44].

And the multitude of them that believed were of one heart and of one soul: neither said any of them that ought of the things which he possessed was his own; but they had all things common [Acts 4:32].

The *Book of Mormon* verses are these:

And they taught, and did minister one to another; and they had all things common among them, every man dealing justly, one with another [III Nephi 26:19].

And they had all things common among them; therefore there were not rich and poor, bond and free, but they were all made free, and partakers of the heavenly gift [IV Nephi 3].

The *Book of Mormon* verses are a description of the disciples of Christ in the New World and are obviously in imitation of the biblical texts. It is curious that the two hundred years of this state are described in two and a third pages and that, before the third page is finished, the Fall has set in.

In no other parts of the text is communitarianism practiced or preached, although it was to play an important role in Mormon history. The *Book of Mormon* is representative of the ideas that went into the formation of the new church previous to its confrontation with communitarian socialism in Sidney Rigdon's Kirtland group.

Other Characteristics

There were many errors and awkward usages in the first edition of the work, but most of them have since been removed.[32] Unfriendly critics have made more than enough of some of its unfortunate mixtures of folk and archaic English, yet there are places where the *Book of Mormon* rises to impressive heights in conveying religious fervor. It was first issued, divided into chapters and verses with references, in 1879 by Orson Pratt; since 1920, the Mormon church has published it in double-column pages, with chapter headings summarizing the contents, revised references, chronological dating at the bottom of each page, an index, and a pronouncing vocabulary. It has been translated into many languages, even Polynesian.

The names used are mostly of biblical origin. Either they are biblical names like Laban (Gen. 24:29), Lemuel (Prov. 31:1), Lehi (Judges 15:9, where it denotes a place), Jacob (Gen. 25:26), Enos (Gen. 4:26), Benjamin (Gen. 35:18), Ammon (Gen. 19:38),

Noah (Gen. 5:29), Gideon (Judges 6:11), Samuel (I Sam. 1:20), Ether (Josh. 15:42), and Jared (Gen. 5:15); or they are close imitations of biblical names, such as Laman, Sam, Nephi, Sariah, Mosiah, Alma, Zeniff, Amaleki, Amalickiah, Chemish, and Helaman. There are some stranger creations, as, for example, in the genealogy of Jared (Ether 1:6–32), which includes Coriantor, Moron, Coriantum, Amnigaddah, and Riplakish, and there are those names that the book has made famous, Mormon and Moroni. The book avoids names beginning with *F, Q, V, W, X,* and *Y,* as does the Old Testament. There are resonances and echoes of the Bible and of a moral and intellectual climate saturated with biblical ideas and phrases throughout the whole work. The crossing of the ocean recalls Noah, while the finding of a promised land recalls Moses and Joshua. The story of Salome is barely hidden in the dance of the daughter of Jared (Ether 8:9–17), and the conversion of St. Paul is found again in the conversion of Alma (Mosiah 27:13).

For quotations and paraphrases of the Scriptures, the *Book of Mormon* relies mostly upon Isaiah, and quite explicitly so. The forty-eighth and forty-ninth chapters of Isaiah are to be found in I Nephi, chapters 20 and 21; and the second to the fourteenth chapters of Isaiah, inclusive, are in II Nephi, chapters 12–24. Also in II Nephi, chapters 7 and 8, are the words of Isaiah, chapters 50 and 51. In all these cases prophecies are being read to the people. To describe the presence of Christ on the American continent, St. Matthew is used, and the Sermon on the Mount is given. In III Nephi, chapters 12–14, are found the fifth, sixth, and seventh chapters of Matthew. Also in this book, Christ, in teaching the people of the New World, quotes from the Old Testament and incorporates the fifty-second and fifty-fourth chapters of Isaiah in chapters 20 and 22 and the third and fourth chapters of Malachi in chapters 24 and 25. In Moroni, chapter 7, where the teachings of Mormon on charity are given, there is a strong resemblance to St. Paul (I Cor., chap. 13), which is most striking in verse 45:

And charity suffereth long, and is kind, and envieth not, and is not puffed up, seeketh not her own, is not easily provoked, thinketh no evil, and rejoiceth not in iniquity but rejoiceth in the truth, beareth all things, believeth all things, hopeth all things, endureth all things [Moroni 7:45].

Every commentator on the *Book of Mormon* has pointed out the many cultural and historical anachronisms, such as the steel sword of Laban in 600 B.C. (I Nephi 4:9) and the use of steel throughout; the finding of horses, cows, oxen, and asses in the New World (I Nephi 18:25) and their possession by the Nephites and Lamanites and also the Jaredites. Some have pointed to the use of swine by the Jaredites despite the Mosaic Law (Ether 9:18).

Most interesting, however, is the attitude of most of the book toward Christ, notwithstanding its presumably pre-Christian character. Throughout the book, prophets and preachers speak of Christ, Jesus Christ, the Son of God, and foretell with striking clarity his death and resurrection. The Christian doctrines of the Resurrection, Baptism, faith in the Atonement, and the like are the common articles of belief of the Nephite prophets and their people. It is as if the author could not imagine Hebraic messianic hopes in any other terms than Christian. Throughout the book there is no usage of the messianic term "Son of Man," although this is the one that Christ usually identified with himself in his own ministry. The expectations of the Nephites are those of nineteenth-century American Protestants rather than of biblical Hebrews. Indeed, in some of the scenes of prophecy and preaching the *Book of Mormon* reaches something like greatness in portraying the tension of hope, the inner soaring of the spirit, of the common man who embraced revival Christianity. It was his hopes, his aspirations, and his exaltation of soul that the author of the *Book of Mormon* projected back into his Nephites. Such, for example, is the case of those who were converted by King Benjamin's exhortation when "the Spirit of the Lord came upon them, and they were filled with joy, having received a remission of their sins, and having peace of conscience, because of the exceeding faith which they had in Jesus Christ who should come, according to the words which King Benjamin had spoken unto them" (Mosiah 4:3), and of those whom Alma describes who "were loosed, and their souls did expand, and they did sing redeeming love," adding, "And I say unto you that they are saved" (Alma 5:9).

Those who are saved are always saved in Christ, and the only difference between what a Nephite prophet and a New York revivalist says is that the former usually adds "who will come" or "who is to come" after the name of Christ. Thus Alma could say in 83 B.C.:

> And now behold, I say unto you, my brethren, if ye have experienced a change of heart, and if ye have felt to sing the song of redeeming love, I would ask, can ye feel so now?
> Have ye walked, keeping yourselves blameless before God? Could ye say, if ye were called to die at this time, within yourselves, that ye have been sufficiently humble? That your garments have been cleansed and made white through the blood of Christ, *who will come* to redeem his people from their sins? [Alma 5 : 26–27; my italics].

There is one instance when one suspects that the tension and excitement of the revivalistic present tense actually got away from the author and that he hurried to regain himself and to keep from exposing himself before his scribe. When Abinadi is preaching in a prophetic passage, he declares: "And now if Christ had not come into the world, speaking of things to come as though they had already come, there could have been no redemption" (Mosiah 16:6).

Yet if this anachronism of feeling and reference is evidence of late origin to the critic, it was not so to the early converts. In fact, in catching and committing to print the hopes and exaltation of the revival meeting and in doing so without the distractions of emotional excess, while at the same time answering many of the most important theological problems which troubled the people of the region, the *Book of Mormon* was admirably suited to become what it did in fact become, the scriptures of an American church.

CHAPTER THREE

The Gathering

The Saints Withdraw from Secular Society

The early months of the new church's existence were prophetic of much that was to come. First of all, it grew from the start. Second, Joseph Smith was arrested twice for disorderly conduct but won acquittal each time, and Oliver Cowdery toyed with revelation on his own and was sent westward to preach the new gospel to the Indians. Cowdery and his companions, among whom was an able former Campbellite, Parley Pratt, stopped at Mentor, Ohio, where they converted the Campbellite preacher, Sidney Rigdon. This conversion had a wide effect in the area: 127 persons, including the members of a socialistic community that Rigdon led at Kirtland, were baptized, and by the following spring there were 1,000 church members.

In New York, Mormon converts were made in those areas that had been settled the longest, and this pattern of drawing converts from the more settled regions continued to characterize Mormon conversions, which were concentrated east of the point of origin long after the Mormons themselves had moved west. The church soon moved to Kirtland, which became a magnet for those seeking novelty in religion. Observers have noted that there were educated men and persons with some training in theology among the converts, who, on the whole, were superior to their fellow citizens in educational background.

Life at Kirtland was marked by enthusiasm in religion and irresponsibility in economics. The former went to extremes among a small number of persons, but Joseph Smith disapproved of extreme religious emotionalism, although he performed "miracles" and encouraged some forms of "primitive gifts." Many seemed to have considered Kirtland the New Jerusalem that Joseph had spoken about in revelation. Land speculation and questionable financial ventures gave an unstable economic base to this early Zion. Rigdon's influence had moved Joseph to a revelation that combined Yorker independence with Rigdonite communism, the so-called Law of Consecration or United Order of Enoch. Properties were to be dedicated to the church and received back to be worked individually, all surpluses going to the bishop, who was the local leader of the church organization. What actually went on in the economic life of Kirtland is difficult to say in any detail. There was no insistence on establishing the entire community on the new plan. Yet the church did play an important part in economic life through land sales and other business enterprises. It is clear that contention was frequent, and the end was financial bankruptcy.

Oliver Cowdery and Parley Pratt had gone to Missouri to missionize the Indians and had informed the Kirtland Saints of its possibilities as the site for the new Zion. When Joseph Smith transformed apostasy into hostility upon his failure in attempting to bring a dead child back to life and when contention grew in Kirtland, the prophet heeded these suggestions. He announced a revelation that sent Rigdon and himself together with twenty-eight other elders off for Missouri immediately. Soon the Kirtland Yorkers who had been dispossessed by apostates followed and were settled outside Independence in what is now part of Kansas City. Independence was a rough frontier boom town, far cruder and of quite different cultural background than eastern Ohio and western New York. Yet Missouri was revealed to be "the land of promise, and the place for the city of Zion."[1] Sidney Rigdon asked the new arrivals: "Do you receive this land for your inheritance with thankful hearts from the Lord?" They answered: "We do." The ground was consecrated, and the next day a temple site was dedicated. Here the new economic plan was tried with a more communal United Order than in Kirtland.

Joseph returned to Kirtland, which remained the scene of squabbles and contention. He soon moved to Mentor, Ohio, and worked on a "translation" of the Bible with Rigdon. Here in March, 1832, he was tarred and feathered by a mob led by a Mormon apostate.

There was resentment in Missouri over Joseph's favoring Ohio, and so in April, 1832, the prophet left again on the 800-mile trip to the frontier. Once there in Jackson County, he had himself sustained as church president, reformed the United Order, and negotiated a substantial loan. The next year was one of tremendous growth of the church in Missouri.

Nevertheless, it appeared that Joseph was making Kirtland the real center of the church, and there in the summer of 1833 a temple was started. There also he laid out a plan for a city of twelve temples, with squared city blocks, intended for a population of fifteen to twenty thousand. In the meantime trouble broke out in Missouri, where the native people feared the increasing numbers of the Saints, which had now reached twelve hundred. Other factors combined to arouse Missourian hostility. The outspoken opinions of the newcomers concerning their divine right to the region, their industriousness and thrift, their purchase of land, their friendly attitude toward the Indians, and their suspected abolitionism (a suspicion that the Mormons repudiated), all produced Missourian antagonism toward the Saints, and that antagonism led to violence. The local people feared that their own properties would be expropriated by the Mormons for the establishment of Zion and regarded the Saints as "fanatics, or knaves, (for one or the other they undoubtedly are)" who "pretended as they did, and now do, to hold personal communication and converse face to face with the Most High God; to receive communications and revelations direct from heaven; to heal the sick by laying on of hands; and in short, to perform all the wonder-working miracles wrought by the inspired Apostles and Prophets of old."[2]

A misunderstanding over free Negroes in the church precipitated violence, and the Mormon printing plant was wrecked and the leaders tarred and feathered. From Kirtland, Joseph advised non-resistance. The Mormons sought redress in the courts and appealed to Governor Dunklin, who responded favorably. Yet the attacks continued, the Saints finally being driven out in a November gale. Joseph Smith did not at first understand the import of all this; he did not recognize the beginning of an irreconcilable conflict that would take his own life in little more than a decade. He tried conciliation and chided the Saints, telling them that their afflictions were "in consequence of their transgressions," their "contentions, and envyings, and strifes, and lustful and covetous desires." Most of the Mormons did not return to Independence but crossed the Missouri River to the north and entered Clay County.

Joseph counseled them to stay near Jackson County and ordered them not to sell their property under these conditions. In the meantime the Saints, who had armed themselves in self-protection and had been disarmed by trickery and force before being driven out, were supported by the arrival of Zion's Camp, which was really a Mormon army sent for defense, although presumably bringing supplies. It was the result of a change in Mormon policy, and its arrival aroused the Missourians to new acts of violence and destruction of Mormon property. Governor Dunklin decided that it was impossible to aid the Saints at this point. Moreover, there had been contention within the Mormon group, and the more well-to-do converts could not be persuaded to join the United Order. No solution was found, and the Mormons, who had been the victims of aggression and were poor and outnumbered, were the sufferers.

After this unsuccessful intervention, Joseph returned to a hostile Kirtland, which, calling him a tyrant and a false prophet, summoned him before a church council on a long list of charges. Weathering this storm, he aroused the Kirtland Saints to undertake construction of a temple, the first of many such Mormon efforts. It was an ambitious project for so poor and divided a group, costing from forty to seventy thousand dollars and made of stone, measuring 60 by 80 feet and rising 125 feet in height. Every male Mormon is said to have given one-seventh of his time to this labor, and the Saints showed great devotion in this effort. The temple was completed in 1836, an event for which Joseph planned ceremonies and rehearsed his elders. For several days, while the temple was dedicated, a height of ecstasy was reached. Some of the Saints spoke of seeing the Lord, others of seeing Moses, while those outside saw a pillar of fire resting on the temple.

During these years Kirtland shared the national craze for land speculation, and much of Kirtland's expansion was undertaken on borrowed money. A bank had been set up in November, 1836, but the Locofocos in the Ohio legislature denied it a charter. The Saints, however, found a simple expedient. They stamped the prefix "anti" before and attached the ending "ing" to the word "bank" which had been printed in large type on the new banknotes, thereby bringing into existence the Kirtland Safety Society anti-Banking Company. This bank turned antibanking company had little but overvalued land behind its issue. Meanwhile, debts piled up. Early in 1837, four months before the national panic began, a run on the Mormon bank started it on its headlong path to ruin. It failed, leaving the Mormon leaders $150,000 in debt to non-Mormon creditors. The High Council broke up in disorder in May, and dissension threatened, while creditors hounded the prophet and antagonism from without increased. Joseph felt that evil forces had taken the field against him. It was at this time that Heber C. Kimball suggested that "there were not twenty persons on earth that would declare that Joseph Smith was a prophet of God."[3]

When the Saints had been driven from Jackson County, Missouri, they went into Clay County, where the local people first welcomed them, gaining for themselves by this the derogative title of "Jack Mormons," a term then applied to non-Mormons who sympathized with the Saints which later shifted to mean an apostate or fallen-away Mormon. The Saints did well in their new location for three years. But here, too, the local people turned against them, antagonized by their success and the machinations of their old enemies. Their continued outspoken talk about building Zion abetted this turn. As a result they were asked to leave and went into a part of Ray County that was largely unpopulated. Here they secured a large amount of land, and in December, 1836, the Missouri legislature granted them the right to organize Caldwell County. They established their county seat at Far West, laid out a town on the basis of Joseph's Kirtland plat, and started over again. Here, too, they soon prospered.

To this new Zion came Smith and Rigdon, where they were welcomed by a flourishing community. Missionary work had begun even in foreign countries, and converts from England were arriving at Far West. Soon six hundred Kirtland Saints followed. Far West was on the edge of the prairie, and here the Mormons expanded into three other counties—Daviess, Carroll, and Ray—an expansion that aroused non-Mormon fears and suspicions.

By this time the years of difficulties were beginning to tell on the Saints. They were in a mood to meet force with force and prove false the common opinion among old settlers that they would not fight. Around June, 1838, a notorious secret body was established by the Mormons, reminiscent of the Gadianton robbers of the *Book of Mormon*. Their leader was Sampson Avard, a tough character who later turned against the Saints in difficulty. They were sworn to secrecy and had secret signs by which strangers who belonged to the organization could come to each other's help in difficulty. They were to defend the Saints against outside aggression and also act as a secret police against internal discord. They were sworn to uphold the Presidency of the church. This group became known as the "Danites," or Sons of Dan, Destroying or Avenging Angels, and Brothers of Gideon, as well as, somewhat inappropriately, Daughters of Zion.

Shortly afterward the Danite bands were extended into the Armies of Israel or Host of Israel, which were organized into groups of tens, fifties, and hundreds, each with its captain. This was, in fact, a defensive army; yet a more truculent spirit was abroad in the church, although many members watched it with apprehension.

This attitude first made itself felt against dissent. Rigdon had pursued Cowdery and the two Whitmers to excommunication and then by Danite threats drove them out of the region. At the same time Smith and Rigdon revived the United Order in modified form; since it was unpopular, it appears that threats of Danite terror were used to secure its acceptance. Smith soon perceived that communitarianism would not work on the basis of coercion and changed the policy to one of establishing large co-operatives.

On July 4, 1838, there was a great celebration in Far West, and here Rigdon, in whom strident truculence had developed as a result of his last years of misfortune and possibly because his position in the church had become insecure, made his now famous speech in which he declared that "we are weary of being smitten, and tired of being trampled upon . . . from this day and this hour, we will suffer it no more." Rigdon rose to a crescendo, threatening "a war of extermination" against any "mob that comes on us to disturb us." The speech aroused the Missourians to a fighting pitch. Whether or not Joseph Smith had seen this oration before its delivery has been disputed, but he permitted it to be published, and the results were disastrous.

August 6 was election day, and non-Mormons attempted to prevent Mormons from voting at Gallatin, Daviess County. The result was a riot, in which the Saints had the better of it. As exaggerated news of this incident spread, both sides prepared for further violence, and a small-scale civil war followed. Carroll County residents first demanded that the Mormons leave Dewitt, and when the Saints refused, they laid siege to the town. Violence followed. Mormon leaders encouraged resistance and aggression, which they unquestionably saw, not without justification, as counteraggression. Danite bands raided and looted, and Mormon troops, numbering 1,200 to 1,500, took up defensive positions at Adam-Ondi-Ahman and Far West. Joseph is said to have compared himself to Mohammed, "whose motto in treating for peace was 'the Alcoran or the Sword.' So shall it eventually be with us— 'Joseph Smith or the Sword!' " On October 29 the terrible massacre of Mormons at Haun's Mill took place, in which 17 Mormons were killed and 15 wounded; immediately thereafter, the militia, outnumbering the defenders 5 to 1, marched on Far West. Boggs, the unfriendly state governor, had declared that the Mormons "must be treated as enemies, and must be exterminated or driven from the state if necessary for the public peace."[4] The militia were on hand to enforce that order.

Smith realized that resistance in such circumstances would be disastrous, and he sent out word that he was willing to surrender, without, however, letting his men know it, for he did not want to damage their morale, if fight they must. A truce was granted on degrading terms, and the Mormon leaders went to jail. Their trial was held under circumstances hardly conducive to taking testimony favorable to the Saints; in fact, very little was given. An attempt to make a treason charge out of the Danite terror fell through, and the Saints, after being ravaged by troops, robbed by neighbors, and insulted by public officials from February to April, crossed over into Illinois. There were some eight thousand of them who turned eastward, away from the frontier toward which they had moved since the beginning of their church and upon which their true destiny still awaited them. Somewhat later the leaders were released by easily bribed officials. Joseph Smith had originally been sentenced by a court martial to be shot, but Doniphan, who was in command of the troops and who was also Joseph's attorney, declined to carry out the order—an act of insubordination for which the officer was never punished. Now, on April 22, riding a chestnut stallion, Joseph Smith joined the last group of refugees from Far West and crossed the Mississippi into Quincy, Illinois.

This first "Mormon War" had been costly to the Saints. Immediately upon his arrival in Illinois, Joseph Smith estimated the losses inflicted upon his people at $1,000,000. Later, in a memorial to the Congress of the United States, to whom he appealed, he estimated the losses in Jackson County at $175,000 and in the whole state of Missouri at $2,000,000. Around forty lives had been lost, compared to one or two among the Missourians. Nor was this all. Prominent men in the church, Marsh, head of the Quorum of the Twelve, a top ruling body that had been established in the church, Corrill, Hyde, and others apostatized. The movement had experienced a serious crisis—one little short of catastrophic. Yet in being short of catastrophe, it became its opposite.

The first phase of Mormon development was over. The acceptance of the *Book of Mormon* and its prophet and adherence to the church he had founded made of the converts a group apart, segregated in spirit by mutual consent from their more orthodox, or at least more ordinary, neighbors. Opposition they met from the start, which they interpreted after the manner of the *Book of Mormon* and their popular Protestant tradition as the persecution of the Saints of God for righteousness' sake. On their peculiarity there was general assent. To themselves they were "chosen in these last days" in "a new and everlasting covenant," while to non-members they appeared a misled, deluded little band.

At Kirtland a common territory and joint effort to build their own earthly city nurtured self-awareness and, together with growth, directed it toward larger goals. In Missouri this consciousness of special identity was intensified by the revelation that it was a "land which I shall consecrate unto my people." The general American feeling of the special character of this continent, which the *Book of Mormon* had made explicit and consecrated as scriptural doctrine, was now identified with a definite piece of ground. In this way did current American hopes and aspirations regarding the promise of America blend with chiliastic convictions concerning the Lord's Second Coming, to make the Saints feel themselves to be the people of God. The selection of a definite location for the New Jerusalem had been promised by the prophet and had been awaited anxiously by his followers. Once it had come, Mormon effort began the transformation of the area into a Zion on the frontier.

But here opposition such as they had met from the start was transformed into active hostility that soon blazed into violence. By arriving as an organized group with its own social institutions, its own internal government, and a firm faith in its own divine calling to build the Kingdom of God in its new location, the Latter-day Saints' church had, with complete innocence of its significance, created a situation that, of necessity, was bound to be characterized by intense rivalry, suspicion, and even animosity between the Mormons and the older settlers. In that rough country in which legal processes were little rooted, it was almost inevitable that such relationships would eventuate in violence.

Missouri was a border state, and the Saints as northerners and non-slaveholders were regarded as possible, if not actual, abolitionists. Moreover, the unusual nature and, from the outsider's point of view, brashness of their doctrines aroused religious prejudice against them. Furthermore, their talk of the Indians inhabiting and inheriting the promised land was considered subversive to national and personal destinies in that frontier region. All these circumstances combined with the strong in-group loyalty, cohesiveness, and even exclusiveness of the Saints and with their intense constructive activity to arouse local enmity. Nothing can ever excuse the ferocity of the anti-Mormon persecutions of the Saints in Missouri, but they were the inevitable product of Mormon activity in this frontier region of a border state.

As part of this interaction between the two groups who made up the unfolding drama of struggle, the Mormons also became truculent. Their leaders acted as the top command of a people at war, which indicated how they perceived their situation, a perception that was not unrealistic. The result was war, and there is nothing like war—the comradeship of arms in defense of homes and ideals and the common suffering and sacrifice—to bring to fruition the consciousness in a group of its unity and peculiarity.

In Illinois the Mormons were to re-enact much of this experience on a larger scale in what was to be both a recapitulation of their past and a prologue to a greater future in the West. Here again they were well received, for the Missouri persecutions had aroused sympathy for them throughout the country. Political motives enhanced the welcome, as Whigs and Democrats competed for their favor. Moreover, Illinois was interested in increasing its population.

There was a moment of hesitation among some of the Mormon leadership, shaken by the experiences of Far West. Up to now it had been assumed that the Mormon restoration would find expression in a separate Mormon community. At their second church conference in Fayette, New York, in September, 1830, their prophet had told them that they were "called to bring to pass the gathering of mine elect . . . unto one place upon the face of this land," for the millennium was at hand. Later he told them that the city they should build, of which the Lord declared, "there shall be gathered unto it out of every nation under heaven," would "be called the New Jerusalem, a land of peace, a city of refuge, a place of safety for the saints of the Most High God." In Far West they had given a demonstration of the determination and heroism that this ideal could call forth in terms of both material accomplishment and courage. Yet their enemies had frustrated their hopes and turned their heavenly city into an earthly hell. Now delivered, some doubted the wisdom of attempting again to build a separate Zion. Perhaps the Saints should scatter and live like the members of other churches.

Upon Joseph's arrival across the river, such temptations to denominationalism were soon to be dispelled. The prophet crossed over to Quincy on April 22, 1839, and on May 1 began the purchase of land in Illinois and also in Iowa, where he was sold land in the Half-Breed Tract by Galland, a slippery speculator, who did not have proper title to it. About a dozen miles north of Quincy, at a place where the Mississippi bends around a great jutting arc of land, the Saints took over a small dying hamlet called Commerce and began to build their city. Joseph named the new Zion "Nauvoo," assuring his followers that the word meant "a beautiful plantation" in Hebrew. The town was laid out, as Far West had been, on the basis of Joseph's plat for the City of Zion, except that here the proportions were revised downward, the blocks from 10 to 5 acres and the streets from 8 to 6 rods in width. On the summit of a hill overlooking the river, a lot was reserved for the construction of a temple, while the city had 3 miles of river frontage.

The first year was a bad one, and many died from the exhaustion of the Missouri experiences or from disease, possibly typhoid or malaria. In 1842, Mormons estimated the population at 14,000–15,000, while, in 1845, *Times and Seasons* (a Mormon church publication) stated that a census showed a "population of 11,057 in the city and one-third more outside the city limits."[5] The gathering had begun again, Mormon spirit proving unquenchable. Moreover, foreign missionaries in England were meeting with great success. In that country a restored gospel that preached worldly as well as spiritual regeneration and that held out a promised land in America appealed to skilled workers in the manufacturing towns.

There were some difficulties. The way that land was sold aroused resentment among the members, and Joseph had to defend himself during a conference of the church against a charge of enriching himself. Yet, on the whole, Mormon enthusiasm and faith were achieving the ideal that had been frustrated in Missouri. A New Jerusalem was rising on the eastern shore of the Mississippi. An English visitor in 1843 spoke of it as a city set on a "gentle incline from the rolling Mississippi," which, although unfinished, was "of great dimensions, laid out in beautiful order." He greatly admired its temple and also the "handsome stores, large mansions, and fine cottages" of the inhabitants, whom he called "a wonderfully enterprising people." He spoke of their attempt to establish manufacturing and remarked that they had "enclosed large farms on the prairie ground, on which they have raised corn, wheat, hemp, etc." What impressed him most, perhaps, was that they had accomplished all this "within the short space of four years." It was his opinion that no other people could have done so much under similar circumstances.[6]

The decade of conflict convinced Joseph Smith that security lay in power. He sensed that a peculiar group like his could not safely rely upon tolerance. He seemed to have grasped the undoubted fact that their beliefs and ideals, as well as their activities and ambitions, were bound inevitably to arouse suspicion and hostility. Power meant politics and armed force, and now the Saints went after both. The situation in Illinois gave them the opportunity to work both sides of the political street. In the presidential election of 1836, that state had given the Democrats 17,275 votes and the Whigs 14,292, while Hancock County, where Nauvoo was located, recorded a vote of 260 for the Democrats as against 340 for the Whigs. Why the Mormons were welcomed by the politicians is quite apparent. Apparent also is the reason for non-Mormon resentment in Hancock County. The older population feared inundation in the Mormon deluge.

The state legislature on December 16, 1840, by an overwhelming vote of both parties granted a charter to the new Mormon city. This Nauvoo Charter, as it has been known since, was an unusual document. It established Nauvoo as an almost independent city-state, and Joseph Smith's interpretation of it would make the Mormon city even more of a separate, self-sufficient unit. It set up a "City Council, to consist of a Mayor, four Aldermen, and nine Councillors." This body was given "Power and authority to make, ordain, establish and execute all such ordinances, not repugnant to the Constitution of the United States or of this State, as they may deem necessary for the peace, benefit, good order, regulation, convenience, and cleanliness of said city; for the protection of property therein from destruction by fire, or otherwise, and for the health and happiness thereof."[7]

The mayor and aldermen were made justices of the peace, and the mayor was made chief justice and aldermen associate justices of the municipal court. The charter further stated that "The City Council may organize the inhabitants of said city, subject to military duty, into a body of independent military men, to be called the 'Nauvoo Legion,' the Court Martial of which shall be composed of the commissioned officers of said Legion." The court martial was the Legion's effective governing body. Joseph Smith was commissioned lieutenant general, a title he both liked and used, and he and Major General Bennett, who was Nauvoo's first mayor, soon appeared resplendent in military uniforms. Since Bennett, a convert who had lobbied for the charter, was also quartermaster general of the state militia, he provided the Legionnaires with 3 pieces of cannon as well with 250 pieces of small arms. Such actions were bound to arouse gentile suspicion and alarm, and soon it was rumored that the Saints had received 30 heavy pieces and several thousand small arms. The charter provided that the Legion should receive its share of the public arms, and Bennett was within his rights in these consignments. By the beginning of 1842, the Legion had 2,000 men. Its martial air and exact discipline amazed and even frightened outsiders who saw it.

The city council was also given the authority to "establish and organize an institution of learning within the limits of the city, for the teaching of the Arts, Sciences, and Learned Professions, to be called the 'University of the City of Nauvoo.' " This university was actually set up. Mathematics, some languages, ancient and modern literature, and church history were among the subjects taught. Its president was a graduate of Trinity College, Dublin, and such Mormon leaders as Orson Pratt, Orson Spencer, and Sidney Rigdon were on its faculty. But a university was beyond the economic and intellectual abilities of the new city at this early stage. It is impossible on the basis of existing data to judge the worth of the instruction offered by the new institution.

Mormon ambitions in seeking the charter were more than fulfilled. Mormon independence was a fact. While remaining within the territorial and constitutional limits of the United States, the Saints had achieved a kind of self-determination or "group liberty" that formalized their actual distinctiveness and cohesiveness and made their exclusive political institutions the law of the land within the limits of their own city.

The Mormons Become a "Peculiar People"

If the original act of conversion for the Latter-day Saint was also an act of withdrawal from gentile society and of joining the gathering of God's chosen people, the task of building the heavenly city in circumstances of conflict and war was one that enhanced new identities and cultivated a new self-consciousness. Conceiving themselves as a special kind of people, the Mormons encountered the very experiences that would strengthen and further develop such convictions. They had chosen for themselves the model of the biblical Hebrews. The circumstances of their lives for the preceding decade had confirmed that model and provided the stage for realistic re-enactment of important aspects of Israel's history.

This experienced separateness provided the context for the further creedal innovations that were introduced as Joseph Smith reported revelations at various junctures when concrete decision and guidance were required. The very separateness of the Mormon group removed them still further from the inhibitions that discourage innovation in the general society. They were not really a part of conventional society. Moreover, hostility set them further apart, increased their separateness, and thereby further weakened the bonds of convention. As separateness encouraged innovation, innovation in return increased separateness by providing a creedal basis for evolving peculiarity. The dynamic decade that lay behind them was one that saw three main kinds of theological development. New definitions of God and new understanding of man developed. In addition, new rituals were invented in terms of the temple and its place in Mormon life. And, most important of all perhaps, new family relations were proposed and made the basis for polygamous family life among certain of the Mormon leaders.

The background of these three developments deserves to be told for the light it sheds on the nature of evolving Mormonism. The new definition of God had an unlikely enough beginning. The Mormon elders had wanted to learn Hebrew, and the School of the Prophets that they set up in 1833 employed Joshua Seixas, a rabbi and teacher from Oberlin and Hudson Academy, to teach them that language for seven weeks. By an odd coincidence, Joseph Smith was at this time approached by Michael Chandler, who had been exhibiting four Egyptian mummies throughout the area. Chandler brought the papyrus rolls from the mummies to the prophet, who declared them to be writings of Abraham and Moses. He eventually "translated" the former, which he did not publish until 1842, and gave a new twist to Mormon thinking about God. Having learned that *Elohim*, the word for God used in some books of the Old Testament, was a plural form, Joseph spoke of "Gods" in his translation of Abraham, which covered much the same ground as Genesis. Moreover, possibly from having read Thomas Dick's *Philosophy of a Future State*, Joseph made Abraham out to be a great astronomer and introduced astronomical doctrine. He spoke of "the Gods" as organizing the earth from matter already existent. Thus was a tendency toward polytheism and anticreationism introduced by way of Hebrew grammar and nineteenth-century scientific thought into Joseph's thinking and Mormon belief.

Joseph Smith reported seven revelations in Nauvoo and two in Ramus, Illinois, from January 19, 1841, to July 12, 1843. A world view is set forth in these that definitely distinguishes the Mormon from older Protestant beliefs. The new outlook proclaimed: "All spirit is matter, but it is more fine or pure, and can only be discerned by purer eyes" (*D & C*, 131:7). God is a material being:

"The Father has a body of flesh and bones as tangible as man's; the Son also; but the Holy Ghost has not a body of flesh and bones, but is a personage of Spirit" (*D & C*, 130:22). Nor is God outside time, for "In answer to the question—Is not the reckoning of God's time, angel's time, prophet's time, and man's time, according to the planet on which they reside? I answer, Yes" (*D & C*, 130:4–5). In April, 1844, Joseph delivered a funeral oration to thousands of Saints who were attending a church conference in Nauvoo. In this discourse he presented his new doctrine in its most forthright form.

"God himself was once as we are now, and is an exalted man, and sits enthroned in yonder heavens! That is the great secret. If the vail were rent today . . . you would see him like a man in form. . . .

"We have imagined and supposed that God was God from all eternity. I will refute that idea. . . . It is the first principle of the Gospel to know for certainty the character of God . . . that he was once a man like us . . . and you have got to be Gods your-selves, and to be kings and priests to God, the same as all Gods have done before you, namely by going from one small degree to another, and from a small capacity to a great one. . . . It is not all to be comprehended in this world; it will be a great work to learn salvation and exaltation even beyond the grave." Genesis, Joseph charged, had been tampered with by "an old Jew without any au-thority"; in the beginning it said: "thus the head God brought forth the Gods in the grand council. . . . God had materials to organize the world out of chaos. . . . The first principles of man are self-existing with God. . . . Intelligence is eternal."[8]

In a revelation on April 2, 1843, the prophet declared: "What-ever principle of intelligence we attain unto in this life, it will rise with us in the resurrection. And if a person gains more knowledge and intelligence in this life through his diligence and obedience than another, he will have so much the advantage in the world to come" (*D & C*, 130:18–19).

A reading of the *Book of Mormon* reveals quite clearly that it is in a fundamental sense a work of the Christian imagination, an imagination that may show a lack of discipline but nevertheless arranges its materials within the general framework of a tradition. These new revelations bespeak a radically new direction. A kind of break with the older tradition has occurred, and a new point of view has emerged, one that affirmed that there was more than one God and that all men, if they obeyed the laws of the new revelation, could advance toward becoming gods themselves.

The subjective guides to truth that revivalistic Christianity had propagated had been transformed into prophecy by Joseph Smith, and, in the church he founded, they took the form of direct revelation through a chosen spokesman. The sectarian idea of the coincidence of the fellowship of believers with the Kingdom of God developed among the Latter-day Saints into the conviction that the Mormons were a peculiar people, a modern Israel. The old concomitance of virtue and worldly prosperity that had characterized so much of Puritan-influenced religion took concrete form among the Mormons in terms of their efforts to build a city that would be a place both of material plenty and of spiritual exaltation. The growing belief in the efficacy of human effort that had become characteristic of American religion was transformed by Mormonism into a theologized liberalism, in terms of which human effort and constructive activity in the world advanced men toward eternal glory and even to "Godhood." The personalized God of revival preaching now became the material being or beings of a new polytheism. Common secular American notions of progress were theologized, while theology itself was secularized. The temporal was equated with the spiritual, the mundane with the holy. These innovations were held not to supplant, but merely to supplement, the more traditional Christianity of the *Book of Mormon*. Mormonism, out of its isolation and separatism, out of its unique experience which confirmed its convictions of election and peculiarity, had brought into existence a new American religion.

Coming from a Protestant background where religious ceremonies were simple and developing new beliefs of its own, Mormonism came to feel the need of new forms of expression. The account of the development of a distinctive Mormon religious ritual during these years is an important element of the Mormon story. When the new temple was dedicated at Kirtland, Joseph introduced new ceremonies which he attributed to revelation. Among these was one that "sealed" blessings upon the heads of members.

At Nauvoo, where the new group achieved a large measure of separation both constitutionally and psychologically from the older community, the prophet announced revelations that again stressed an earlier innovation. First on September 1 and then on September 6, 1842, the prophet explained that it was necessary to build a baptismal font in the temple at Nauvoo to carry out baptism for the dead by having living persons act in proxy for the deceased. Of these baptisms, which have become an important part of Mormon religious activity, records must be kept, and the revelation explains this in detail. It is an "ordinance and preparation that the Lord ordained and prepared before the foundation of the world, for the salvation of the dead who should die without a knowledge of the gospel" (*D & C*, 128:5). This enables the dead to progress in the afterlife, "For we without them cannot be made perfect" (*D & C*, 128:18). In this revelation, which is full of hints of the coming unveiling of plural marriage (already being practiced in secret among the top circles of the church), there is expressed a curious desire to bind the past generations to the present and not to cast aside, as lost, those who came before the miraculous restoration of the Mormon gospel. It seems that at the very time when Mormonism was in fact and in belief immensely widening the chasm that separated the converted from the general run of their fellows, there was needed some countermotion, some symbolic link between the separated and their own past in terms of relatives and ancestors. Joseph provided such a link in baptism for the dead. The new convert could now contribute to the salvation of those who apparently had been left outside the fold.

How much of this need for some kind of symbolization of the new doctrines and the common experiences of the new church was generally felt and how much was confined to Joseph Smith is difficult to say. Joseph's position as an accepted spokesman for God gave any of his convictions strategic importance in the life of his followers. The fact is that the new measures he introduced were taken up and did become part of the worship of the church. To find appropriate materials for ritual development, his own non-liturgical religious background made it necessary to look outside strictly religious practices. Joseph went to Masonry to borrow many elements of ceremony. These he reformed, explaining to his followers that the Masonic ritual was a corrupted form of an ancient priesthood ceremonial that was now being restored.

These rites—baptism for the dead and various sealing ceremonies—are, as far as one can learn about them, practically unchanged today from what they were at Joseph's death. They are considered sacred by the Latter-day Saints, and today a Mormon must get special permission from ward bishop and stake president in order to enter a temple. It is forbidden to tell of these temple rites, and Latter-day Saints do not talk much about them. Yet enough has been written by apostates to give a good idea of what takes place in ceremonies in the temple. These rites were once painted in lurid terms or surrounded by hints and innuendo in the writing of some apostates, but there is actually nothing more to them than a ritualization of the beliefs that Joseph taught at Nauvoo, most of which are part of Mormon belief and published and taught openly in Mormon religious literature today.

The first is baptism for the dead, in which a living person is baptized for a dead person, in order that the latter may receive the restored gospel in the next world if he or she so desires. Without the performance of this "earthly ordinance," the dead person's own will in the world beyond would be insufficient.

Most important are the "endowment" ceremonies, in which men or women come to the temple for a full day. On arrival they are bathed (each separately by one of the same sex) and anointed with oil. All important organs are anointed, including the procreative, with the prayer that they may serve their function well. The anointing begins at the head, "that I might have knowledge of the truths of God," and ends at the feet, "that they might be swift in the paths of righteousness and truth." At this point temple garments, a kind of underwear, originally long but nowadays much abbreviated and supposed to be worn forever after, are given to the member. In these and in robes for the occasion the participants are then witnesses to a kind of drama depicting the organization of the world by Elohim, with Jehovah and Michael aiding.

The members who are receiving the endowment participate in the drama and in the Fall of Adam, which is re-enacted, and put on small Masonic-like aprons covered with figures of nine fig leaves. In the course of the ceremony, grips are given not unlike Masonic grips, and dire threats are uttered concerning those who would break the oaths of secrecy. Even when Mormon in-group feelings were at their greatest height and antagonism toward outsiders and apostates strongest, it seems that such threats were largely ceremonial, for there were many apostates who wrote of the temple secrets and nothing ever happened to them, at least not the disemboweling or throat-cutting said to have been threatened in the oaths.

As part of this ceremony a secret name is given, such as Enoch, or Abraham, or Sarah for women, and a ceremony follows of going through the veil, a curtain which divides the room and is supposed to symbolize the one in Solomon's temple. There are markings on the veil corresponding to the openings in the garments, which suggest a Masonic origin, and other holes through which husband and wife put their arms in the ceremony to be conducted. Going through the veil is symbolic of entering the celestial kingdom, and the man ushers his wife into it.

The tendency toward polytheism, the eternity of matter, the new and restored priesthood with its power to bind and loose on earth and in heaven, the new marriage doctrines (to be discussed later), the eternity of man, and the duty to bring waiting spirits into the world by having children—all these Mormon beliefs are symbolized in the temple ceremony. It has the effect of increasing the loyalty of the church member by initiating him into secrets and thereby making him a privileged sharer in holy mysteries and by his promising in impressive ceremonial circumstances to be loyal to the church and obedient to its priesthood. There has been much discussion as to whether or not an oath against, or at least interpretable as unfriendly to or violating the sovereignty of, the United States of America was ever given at these ceremonies later in Utah. However, even if such charges be true, this is long past and was not really an essential part of the ceremonies themselves. Yet the recognition of the "restored priesthood" as it rests upon the President of the church as the highest authority on earth is a very real and very important element in these temple rites.

These endowment and sealing ceremonies may be performed for the participants themselves or by proxy for the dead. The sealing ceremony seals men and women in marriage for time and eternity. As stated in the revelations of Joseph Smith, without this sealing, the marriages will not be valid after death. As progress to glory in the world beyond the grave will be greatly enhanced by the size of a man's family, for one will become king and eventually a god over his progeny, the importance of sealing is obvious. Children are also sealed to parents to keep the family group together in the afterlife. At times when special circumstances make it advisable, children are sealed to others than their natural parents.

The temple ritual occupies an important place in the thinking of devout Mormons today, although now its relationship to polygamy is of merely historical interest. Temple work, as it is called, is definitely one of the important mechanisms that develop the loyalties of the membership and strengthen the solidarity and solidity of the church. At Nauvoo not all of it was generally known among the rank and file. The polygamous aspects of the doctrine were still confined to a narrow circle. Yet all temple rites, practically in their present form, were performed in the Endowment Room and then in the temple in Nauvoo both before and after the death of Joseph Smith.

The doctrine that was to make Mormonism notorious to so many Americans was the one which commanded the practice of polygamy. Yet this innovation was important to Mormons for other reasons. Not only did it set them apart from gentiles more definitely and more definitively than anything else they had done, but, as a matter of fact, all Mormon doctrinal innovations were to fall into place around this new teaching on marriage. The new Mormon doctrine of marriage made of sexuality a means to celestial glory. The tendency to consider the activities of the world the chief concern of religion had issued in giving sexual relations and procreation the central role in man's progress to divinity. Yet, while confirming the thorough goodness of the flesh, this new teaching set forth a patriarchal form of marriage that gave most of its benefits to the male.

It is an odd fact that the early years of the Mormon church saw repeated charges of polygamy. Just what lay behind them is not clear, possibly a certain moral looseness that had accompanied unrestrained enthusiasm and the exaltation of novelty among some members. Joseph Fielding Smith, an important contemporary Mormon leader, is said to have told Mrs. Brodie that an unpublished revelation foreshadowing polygamy had been given in 1831, but she was not permitted to see it; and Orson Pratt and others said later in their lives that, as early as the 1830's, the prophet had told them about plural marriage and that it was a correct principle. To this, however, must be countered the official denials, which, if they attest to suspicion, suggest that so extreme a novelty was not yet acceptable. It is curious also that in his letters from Liberty Jail in Missouri, when he answered charges that the gentiles had made against his people, Joseph Smith denied polygamy—curious because it was one of the few things that had not been charged against them. There were many rumors of immorality concerning the leadership of the church in Nauvoo, although to the eye of the visitor the town had an almost Puritan look. The fact is that plural marriage was practiced in Nauvoo, although, until 1852 in Salt Lake City, the Church of Jesus Christ of Latter-day Saints denied that it harbored any such doctrine.

Whenever it may have started, there is no doubt that the antinomian tendencies of unrestricted quasi-prophecy expressed themselves in Mormon development despite the Mormon emphasis on law and morals. Yet their expression was characteristically Mormon, for they found expression in terms of a commandment that was to be obeyed. As time went on, the duty of plural marriage in relation to providing fleshly tabernacles for waiting spirits was more and more emphasized. As Brigham Young said later in Utah, making use of a hardly appropriate metaphor, "We must gird up our loins and fulfill this, just as we would any other duty."[9] Mormonism was true to its heritage. It would transgress conventional morality only by claiming the sanction of a higher command. Moral authority must not be questioned in the process.

Joseph had already taken a number of wives in Nauvoo—including women who were already the wives of other men—and so did some other Mormon leaders. He taught them the doctrine of plural marriage and a restoration of those things that had been permitted to the patriarchs and kings of the Old Testament. Some of the women approached about this matter accepted, while others became indignant. Joseph even permitted some trial publicity to be given the idea of polygamy in a pamphlet by a follower in 1842, which, however, he promptly disavowed when the response from the rank and file was unfavorable.

John C. Bennett, major general of the Nauvoo Legion, mayor of Nauvoo for a time, and an urbane and able convert who was also corrupt and potentially dangerous, had risen rapidly in Joseph's estimation and in Mormon leadership. Bennett was delighted with the new doctrine, which seemed to suit his tastes admirably, and he seduced any number of women under its protection. In the spring of 1842 Joseph and Bennett became estranged over this and other matters, and the ill feeling was apparently brought to a head in their rivalry to take young and pretty Nancy Rigdon as a plural wife. As might be suspected, this did not please her father, Sidney, now ailing, who always remained opposed to the new marriage doctrine. Joseph, Brigham, and other elders took plural wives, having them sealed in the new ceremonies that Joseph was introducing in his temple rites. Bennett, however, appears to have seduced a large number of women on a more informal basis. Joseph evidently confronted Bennett with this fact, and the result was an imbroglio that issued in Bennett's excommunication.

In July, 1842, Bennett started his persistent hounding of Joseph. He published his exposé of conditions in Nauvoo, which was republished in papers throughout the country. Danite murderers and Avenging Angels mingled with seduction on an almost glorious scale in these intimations. Organized licentiousness took the form of three levels in a hierarchical structure of "spiritual wives." There were Cyprian Saints, who were, according to Bennett, the mistresses of all the elders; next higher were the Chambered Sisters of Charity, less indiscriminate in disposing of their favors; and highest of all, the Cloistered Saints or Saints of the Black Veil, who were married by a secret ceremony to become the spiritual wives of one husband. Bennett's charges were in all probability greatly exaggerated, and only his last and highest level seems to bear any resemblance to the polygamy that was actually practiced. Such rumors, however, with the kernel of truth that lay behind them, aroused gentile hostility and caused internal discord.

Joseph had taught this doctrine secretly, and on July 12, 1843, it was secretly recorded. In it the Lord commands Joseph to obey the instruction "which I am about to give unto you; for all those who have this law revealed unto them must obey the same" (*D & C,* 132:3). The revelation goes on to present temple marriage for "time and eternity" and declares that only such marriages shall be valid in the Resurrection. Those not married in this new covenant, when they die "neither marry nor are given in marriage; but are appointed angels in heaven; which angels are ministering servants, to minister for those who are worthy of a far more, and an exceeding, and an eternal weight of glory" (*D & C,* 132:16). Such angels cannot "be enlarged, but remain separately and singly, without exaltation, in their saved condition, to all eternity; and from henceforth are not gods" (*D & C*, 132:17).

However, those who marry in the "new and everlasting covenant, and it is sealed unto them by the Holy Spirit of promise . . . shall inherit thrones, kingdoms, principalities, and powers, dominions, all heights and depths . . . and they shall pass by the angels, and the gods, which are set there, to their exaltation and glory in all things, as hath been sealed upon their heads, which glory shall be a fulness and a continuation of the seeds forever and ever. Then shall they be gods, because they have no end . . . [and] all things are subject unto them" (*D & C*, 132:19–20). Indeed, with such marriages men will be saved in the end, if they commit "no murder wherein they shed innocent blood" (*D & C*, 132:26), no matter what else they do except desert the church. Then follows the restoration of the patriarchal order of Abraham, Isaac, Jacob, and David—"Abraham received concubines . . . and he abode in my law" (*D & C*, 132:37). "I am the Lord thy God, and I gave unto thee, my servant Joseph, an appointment, and restore all things" (*D & C*, 132:40). "And again, as pertaining to the law of the priesthood—if any man espouse a virgin, and desire to espouse another, and the first give her consent, and if he espouse the second, and they are virgins, and have vowed to no other man, then is he justified; he cannot commit adultery for they are given unto him. . . . And if he have ten virigins given unto him by this law, he cannot commit adultery, for they belong to him, and they are given unto him; therefore is he justified" (*D & C*, 132:61–62).

Joseph Smith complicated this situation of doctrinal peculiarity and civic independence for the Saints by using their political weight to court friends in state politics. In 1840 and 1841 the Mormons voted for the Whigs, but it was clear that this was no safe and sure political alliance, a fact that became quite obvious in 1842, when the prophet shifted the Mormon vote to the Democrats. Said Joseph, "We care not a fig for Whig or Democrat; they are both alike to us, but we shall go out for our friends, our tried friends."[10] Joseph was exuberant with the power of his new political position, and he was blinded by this exuberance to the realities which his attitude was helping to create. He was, in fact, making both parties the enemies of himself and his people. Moreover, his signature as "Lieutenant-General of the Nauvoo Legion" was not something to allay gentile fears. Non-Mormon attitudes were suggested by the opposition newspaper, which commented that this bloc voting by order was "too bold a stride toward despotism ever to be long countenanced by a free and intelligent people." When in 1844, after unsuccessful attempts to get a statement from Clay and Calhoun on the indemnification of Mormon losses in Missouri, Joseph Smith announced himself a candidate for the Presidency of the United States, non-Mormon suspicions were further strengthened. Exaggerated estimates of church membership by Mormons and non-Mormons alike added to gentile fear of this well-knit group.

In Illinois, despite the fact that they had been well received, the old exclusiveness and peculiarity of the Saints—bound to call forth antagonism in time—were complicated by a new militancy and by an unprecedented success in their efforts to build their own city and aroused opposition once more. The military atmosphere of Nauvoo, its tremendous growth, its virtual political independence, and its bloc voting, playing a strategic part in state politics, evoked the same kind of response from non-Mormons that Mormon activities had aroused in Missouri. Moreover, here there were complaints that the Saints stole gentile property, and the preaching against this sort of activity by the church leaders indeed suggests that the prolonged experience of conflict was creating in some Mormons an outlook that tended to see in the gentile only an enemy to be dispossessed. Mormon peculiarity based on religious doctrine had built up loyalty to the Mormon group and excited antagonism from outsiders. This antagonism, by severing the remaining ties between Mormons and non-Mormons, by creating a threat, fostering a group tradition of persecution and common suffering, and focusing energies on both sides into aggressive and defensive activities, set up a vicious circle that was bound, without outside intervention, to deteriorate quickly into a repetition of Far West. Poor judgment in Mormon leadership would hasten the inevitable. Forced to abandon Kirtland by internal discord, hounded from Independence by force, asked to leave Clay County, and driven from Far West by armed violence after a minor war, the Saints had built a great city in Illinois, where a few years before there had been little more than swamp. But they were now in greater danger than ever before.

Moreover, in addition to gentile antagonism, Mormon dissent

was brewing. William Law and Robert Foster, both contractors and important church leaders, opposed Joseph's policy of economic development and his building the Nauvoo House, a boarding house or hotel requested by the Lord in a special revelation (*D & C*, 124:55–82). Law suspected Joseph of profiteering in land. There were others who were in opposition to the prophet's leadership as well, some objecting to polygamy. The prophet is reported to have attempted in this delicate situation to teach the new marriage doctrine to the wives of both Law and Foster. Law, in a stormy session with Smith, tried to get him to drop polygamy altogether. Joseph collected the stories these men were telling about him to the disaffected in the city and defiantly published them in the *Nauvoo Neighbor*. A trial was set for Foster, but when the prophet was informed that Foster had some forty witnesses and that the trial might turn into an exposé of himself, he anticipated its results by calling a council that met secretly and excommunicated Foster, William Law, his wife Jane, and his brother Wilson.

William Law was a member of the First Presidency of the church, one of the two assistants, called "counselors," to the prophet himself. His brother was a regent of the university and a major general in the Legion. Law sincerely wished to reform the church and apparently considered Joseph a fallen prophet. Joseph felt that he had to defend himself against this charge publicly; he declared in his *King Follett Discourse* in April, 1844, that if he had time to tell them all his new doctrines, he would let them know he was not a fallen prophet. Law now gathered a group around himself, many of whom were convinced that Joseph Smith was an imposter.

These men set up a church of their own, imitating the organization of the larger body. On June 7, 1844, there was published the first and only issue of its newspaper, the *Nauvoo Expositor*, edited by William Law and Sylvester Emmons. The paper was restrained in tone. Its lead editorial exposed polygamy but gave no names. It was followed by affidavits signed by William and Jane Law and Austin Cowles, testifying that they knew of the polygamy revelation. The new church set forth in the paper a series of resolutions accepting the *Book of Mormon* and the *Doctrine and Covenants* but rejecting the "vicious principles of Joseph Smith." The resolutions condemned a number of current practices, including the "doctrine of plural gods, a plurality of wives, sealing, etc."[11]

It seems that some time before this Joseph had organized a Council of Fifty, over which he reigned as king. This apparently is alluded to by the opposition in its resolutions. Said the *Expositor*, "We will not acknowledge any man as king or lawgiver to the church." Joseph's political activity was also condemned.

The publication of the *Nauvoo Expositor* caused a grave crisis within the Mormon group. What of the vast numbers of the Saints who had not yet been told the truth about plural marriage? What of the gentiles outside, whose growing opposition would feed on this latest defection and whose suspicions would find confirmation in these charges made by insiders?

On August 8, 1842, Joseph had been arrested as an accessory to an attempt to assassinate former Governor Boggs of Missouri, with his bodyguard, Orrin Porter Rockwell, charged with the act. This, together with the effort of Missouri to extradite him for the old treason charge, had caused him much difficulty in the preceding year and a half. In the course of this hounding by sheriffs, he had interpreted the Nauvoo Charter in such a way as to expand the power of the city and increase its independence of the state. Now his political opposition, his Missouri enemies, and the fear and hostility that the peculiarity and rapid growth of his movement had evoked were again strengthened by internal dissent. This sort of thing had been weathered once before in the apostasy of John C. Bennett.

But this time Joseph acted with supremely poor judgment. He called the city council without giving the Laws a hearing, and the council, condemning the *Expositor* as a nuisance, ordered the Legion to destroy its press and scatter its type. At eight o'clock in the evening of June 10, 1844, a body of troops of the Nauvoo Legion marched on the printing office and destroyed it. William Law and Dr. Foster fled to Carthage, believing their lives would be in danger in the city. They brought action in a Carthage court, charging Joseph Smith and the council with rioting. Foster wrote an article in the neighboring, fiercely anti-Mormon Warsaw newspaper, calling the prophet a tyrant "dressed in a little brief authority." To the fears of despotism that his monolithic fellowship of faith and community had aroused, Joseph Smith and his colleagues in the leadership of the city had given what appeared to the world to be substance. The conflict was now drawn around the issue of civil rights, with Smith, the leader of a minority that had known persecution and suffering at the hands of its enemies, cast in the role of villain. Such was the result of Joseph's bad judgment in this extremity.

The reaction was not long in coming, as the surrounding country prepared for war against the Mormons. Rumors flew thick and fast, and there were requests upon the governor to call out the militia. Governor Ford came to Carthage to investigate the incident himself and found the militia, which he had not called out, forming under local authorities as a *posse comitatus*. He interviewed the Laws and some of their supporters and then wrote to Smith, telling him that he and others responsible should surrender to arrest and face trial in Carthage. Joseph had already offered to do this on condition that he be permitted an escort from the Legion for his protection. Governor Ford, seeing that the state militia was barely in control, feared that the sight of the Nauvoo legionnaires would cause violence. He promised safety to his person if Joseph came unarmed.

Joseph first toyed with the idea of escaping. During the trying times of the preceding year he had come to realize that his people could not find peace in the settled area of the country and was thinking in terms of a western empire. This would give the necessary isolation and would be an ample stage for his now quite grandiose notions of the New Jerusalem. He sent forth Jonathan Dunham to search out a way to the Missouri River in July, 1843, and is said to have been discussing a westward migration in August of that year. Almost two years before, in 1842, he had suggested that the Saints "would become a mighty people in the midst of the Rocky Mountains,"[12] and in February, 1844, he sent men to "investigate the locations of California and Oregon, and hunt out a good location, where we can remove to after the temple is completed, and where we can build a city in a day, and have a government of our own."[13] The church had even sent a "minister to Texas" to negotiate for land to the west as the place of Mormon settlement. On March 26, 1844, Smith addressed a memorial to Congress, sending a copy to the President, offering "to raise a company of one hundred thousand armed volunteers" to deliver Texas and protect Oregon and to "prevent the crowned nations from encircling us as a nation on our western and southern borders . . . to open the vast regions of the unpeopled west and south to our enlightened and enterprising yeomanry."[14] That he now thought of going west and having his people follow him is hardly surprising.

Yet his better judgment prevailed. He started out across the river but soon came back and surrendered himself to the authorities. He obeyed the order of Governor Ford, disarming the Nauvoo Legion and turning their arms back to the state. However, remembering Far West, he had the Legion keep the arms that were not state property. Once in Carthage, a charge of treason and levying war against the state was added to the charge of riot. The prophet, his brother, and some others were lodged in the Carthage jail. Here they were visited by friends, and here Governor Ford met and discussed the problem with them. Yet Ford, who certainly made great efforts to be fair, made one fatal mistake. He went to Nauvoo to address the Mormons, thinking that the militia companies he had disbanded would go home. Joseph had told him that to go to Nauvoo and leave the Mormon leaders in Carthage would result in their deaths. Smith realized that death was near in these last hours, and when he countersigned the orders disarming the Legion, he is said to have exclaimed: "I am going like a lamb to the slaughter. . . . I shall die innocent, and it shall yet be said of me—he was murdered in cold blood" (*D & C*, 135:4).

On the afternoon of June 27, 1844, death struck, suddenly and brutally. While talking in their upstairs cell, the four Mormon leaders—Joseph Smith, Hyrum Smith, John Taylor, and Willard Richards—saw armed men with blackened faces proceeding around the corner of the jail toward the stairway. A mob of 150 men, many of them members of the Warsaw militia, which had been disbanded by orders of the governor, was attacking the jail with the obvious collusion of the Carthage Greys, the local militia unit that had been assigned to guard the building and its occupants. The men in the prison closed the door to the room they were occupying, but, as it had no bolt, they could not lock it. Hyrum Smith and Richards placed their bodies against it. The attackers fired through the door and hit Hyrum, who leaped back. He was immediately hit again, once in the nose by a ball through the door and a second time in the back by a bullet fired through the window from below. He fell, exclaiming, "I am a dead man."

Joseph, who had a six shooter that one of his friends had

brought him after his arrest, opened the door and fired into the attackers. Although two or three of the chambers did not discharge, his attack was not without effect, for three of the assailants were wounded. As soon as they recovered from Joseph's counterattack, the assailants stuck their guns into the partly opened doorway and fired into the room. Taylor and Richards parried with their canes, their only weapons. John Taylor tried to leap out of the window but was wounded in the thigh, and soon afterward three more balls entered his body.

Joseph, after Taylor fell, attempted to jump from the window some twenty-five feet to the courtyard below. As he started through the window, he was hit by two shots from behind and one from the courtyard below him. He fell outward, crying, "My Lord, my God." According to some accounts, the assailants who crowded around him below propped his body against a well curb and riddled it.

Fourteen years after he had founded his church and before his thirty-ninth birthday, the Mormon prophet gave his life in the struggle that his religious innovations had caused between his followers and their neighbors. To his adherents, his brutal murder and his exemplary bravery in the face of it only proved his genuineness. He had kept his appointment and, having restored all things, now sealed his testimony with his blood. To the heroism and suffering, the effort and accomplishments, of the Mormon group was added a new and more precious sacrifice. The immediate practical effect would be disorganization, but the long-range effect of martyr's blood would be to strengthen the people whose cause he led.

The news of the deaths of Joseph and Hyrum Smith stunned Nauvoo, while it raised great fears among the non-Mormons, especially in ferociously anti-Mormon Warsaw, that the Saints with their Legion and their superior numbers would take vengeance. The reaction of the Saints, however, was one of sorrow and patience, and, after they had buried their dead with moving tributes, they voted unanimously to rely upon legal action for retribution. The movement was now leaderless, and those tendencies that leadership had restrained or inhibited soon made themselves apparent.

Sidney Rigdon came forward to claim the succession, not in a formal sense, for that seemed beyond reach, but as "guardian" of the church to build it "up to Joseph." He reported revelations he had had earlier and pointed at divine selection to back his claim. In this effort he was unsuccessful and soon afterward was excommunicated. He went to Pennsylvania, whither he had advocated that the church retreat, and with a small body of adherents established a church that at first used the same name, but soon took simply the title "Church of Christ," which had been the official name of the Mormon church when he joined it and for the first three years of its existence. Moreover, the Smith family claimed that Joseph's eldest son should succeed him when he came of age and quoted statements of the martyred leader to show he intended this course to be followed.

Brigham Young was president of the Twelve, and he claimed that this body should now rule the church with the Presidency vacant. In a meeting of the Saints on August 8, 1844, at which Rigdon pressed his claims, Young replied in a speech that won him the leadership and was so moving that many of his followers said he took on the appearance of Joseph Smith as he spoke, and others felt sure they saw the mantle of Joseph fall upon his shoulders. The affairs of the church were for the time placed in the hands of the Twelve, and Brigham as their president now became its effective leader.

As was to be expected, there was a certain amount of splintering. Some people followed Rigdon east, while others went to Texas with Lyman Wight, where they set up a small polygamous and communistic colony that fell apart at the leader's death just before the Civil War. One contender came forward who attracted considerable attention by his romantic and picturesque appearance. James J. (formerly Jesse James) Strang was a Wisconsin lawyer of ability and ambition, who has been described, not inaccurately, as an infidel. He had been attracted to Mormonism when a small colony of the Saints was established in Wisconsin to procure timber for the Nauvoo Temple. Visiting Nauvoo in February, 1844, he had himself baptized and made an elder, and, when Joseph was killed, four months later, he offered himself, with a forged letter from the prophet bearing a forged Nauvoo post-office mark, ostensibly appointing him to the succession.

He received considerable attention especially among Mormons outside Nauvoo. He made an attempt to win those Saints who were conducting missionary activities in England. This English mission was to be of great importance in the church, but Strang did not succeed in his effort to bring it over to his cause. He was joined by John C. Bennett, and also for a time by William Smith and Martin Harris. In 1847 he took his followers from Wisconsin, where they had first taken up their residence, to Beaver Island (or Mackinac Island) in Lake Superior. Here at one time he ruled over three thousand subjects, having been crowned "King in Zion" in accordance with a revelation he had announced. There were internal conflicts in his group as well as apostasy—Aaron Smith, who had converted him to Mormonism, leaving and setting up an opposition church—and economic difficulties. Yet Strang became a factor in Michigan politics and had ambitions in national politics. His group was polygamous and indulged in secret orders, such as that of the Illuminati. On June 15, 1856, he was shot to death by two of his followers, who were immediately regarded as heroes by non-Mormons on the mainland. Soon afterward, despite efforts to keep it going, the church died out.

Alpheus Cutler, Austin Cowles, James Emmet, and Gladden Bishop each led groups out of the church. William Bickerton, who joined Rigdon's church, left it and slowly developed a group of his own, incorporating in Pittsburgh in 1865, while Granville Hedrick established a sect during the Civil War which in the following years returned to Independence. In 1842 George M. Hinkle and W. E. M'Lellin had started a faction of their own. M'Lellin later joined Strang and still later, with Martin Harris, set up a "Church of Christ" at Kirtland, making David Whitmer prophet. Another "Whitmerite" church was later established by John C. Whitmer and others, and David supported it. Martin Harris eventually went to Utah to join those who had followed Brigham Young.

The only group among these dissidents destined to become large and important was that which met as the "New Organization of the Church" in 1852. This group, which later became the Reorganized Church of Jesus Christ of Latter-day Saints, won the adherence of the prophet's immediate family, and his son Joseph Smith III became its president in 1860. Most of the Saints who had remained in Illinois and southern Iowa after the main body had left joined this group, which soon established the United Order of Enoch in Decatur County in southern Iowa. In the decade of the 1870's Saints migrated there, and over three thousand acres were purchased by the order. Lamoni was founded and was for years the headquarters of the church; later Graceland College was established. Under Frederick M. Smith, the prophet's grandson, who studied sociology under Charles A. Ellwood, the church stressed its social ideal. It rejected polygamy and the plurality of gods from the start, and, although it first spoke of Joseph as having fallen from prophetic status, such talk soon ceased in its ranks. It has been recognized by the courts as the legal successor of the original church founded by Joseph Smith and was awarded title to the Kirtland temple, which it still owns and in which it conducts religious services. It also owns several important sites in Nauvoo, including Mansion House and the graves of Joseph and Hyrum Smith. In 1921 it moved its headquarters to Independence, thus returning to Zion. At the beginning of the present century it had around forty-five thousand members and today has well over a hundred thousand.

It had so far proved impossible for Mormonism to live in peaceful neighborliness with its fellows. Mormon peculiarity and Zionist ambitions, complicated by local prejudices and incidents, had resulted in driving the Mormons from three places in Missouri. Now, having achieved a greater success than ever before, they again found themselves in a state of war with their neighbors. Mormon-gentile relations seemed inevitably to develop toward hostility and from hostility to war. As Mormon efforts enlarged Nauvoo, they simultaneously increased fear and enmity among the gentiles. As Joseph Smith made Nauvoo more independent, to fulfil his ever more grandiose dream of the New Jerusalem, gentile opposition perceived an ever greater threat of despotism. As Mormon beliefs and practices became increasingly further removed from those of their gentile neighbors, the latter charged the Saints with immorality and held them to be public nuisances. As the Saints used politics to improve their position in relation to the community at large, the community at large saw in their efforts a threat to dominate it. "There is a time when forbearance ceases and when suffering longer without resistance is a sin," cried Joseph Smith. "Resolved that the time . . . has arrived when the adherents of Smith, as a body, should be driven from the surrounding settlements into Nauvoo; that the prophet and his miscreant adherents should then be demanded at their hands, and if not surrendered, a war of extermination should be waged . . ." said the gentiles.[15]

The struggle reached a climax in Smith's arrest and murder, and the temporary satisfaction of the blood lust of the opposition and the sorrow and mourning of the Saints lowered tension for a brief time. But before the Mormons were permitted to recover, more trouble was in store, and peace was not to be. The original causes of conflict—the radical incompatibility of the Mormon group and their ambitions with the expectations and standards of their neighbors—remained untouched. The old charges of stealing that the gentiles had made before were heard again in the winter of 1844–45. These were vigorously denied by the Saints, who, moreover, accused outsiders of planting stolen goods in Nauvoo to "frame" them. In January, 1845, the legislature repealed the Nauvoo Charter. This was a blow to the Saints, who had returned to their labors and were continuing the construction of their temple. Their paper, the *Nauvoo Neighbor*, declared this beyond the legitimate power of the state and asked why a law that had given no protection to the Saints should have any call on their loyalty or obedience. There were accusations of a revival of Danite activity, especially across the river in Iowa, which were also denied by the Mormon authorities. Participation in state and national politics continued to make enemies instead of friends, and in 1845 the Democrats, whom the Saints had supported in 1844, deserted them.

Again aggression came from the anti-Mormons, who, using an incident they seem to have staged for the purpose of blaming it on the Saints, started the infamous "burnings," in which a band of one or two hundred men burned Mormon houses, outbuildings, and grain all over the southwestern region of the county. The pro-Mormon sheriff attempted to aid the Saints, but to no avail. Group conflict was again the order of the day, and those who had been burned out by the anti-Mormons gathered in Nauvoo and "sallied forth and ravaged the country," according to Governor Ford's account. It was war once more.

There now took place a movement of mass indignation against the Saints, one that soon became a mob uprising and involved open armed conflict in which both sides used artillery pieces. Citizens of neighboring counties, egged on by the provocative *Warsaw Signal*, called mass meetings and demanded that the

Saints leave, a movement that culminated in a citizens' committee from Quincy that came to Nauvoo to present the demand. The Mormon leadership had long recognized that they must go, and they now agreed, trying to get conditions that would permit them to make preparations and to dispose of their property. It was agreed that the Mormons would leave in the spring. Meanwhile, commissioners appointed by the governor made a similar request and were given a similar answer. The Mormons prepared to leave the city where they had expended so much effort and where they had completed and dedicated their temple in May, 1845. Work on the temple had proceeded despite their intention of moving, its completion being regarded as a religious duty.

Rabid anti-Mormons, however, were not satisfied, and after the winter of 1845–46 had passed without a serious outbreak, they began to reassemble and demand action. This was, in fact, little more than troublemaking of the sort that had plagued Mormon-gentile relations in the region for a long time. Early in February the first group of Mormons departed, and in May the population was leaving the city at a rapid rate.

Yet the anti-Mormons gathered at Carthage and declared the time had come for armed action. They were led by Sharp, the editor of the *Warsaw Signal*, among others. Soon thereafter the *Signal*, whose editor seems to have hoped that the Mormons would not leave, in order that there might be trouble, announced in a headline, "War declared in Hancock." What was called at the time the "last Mormon war" had begun.

Properties in Nauvoo had already been advertised for sale, and the Saints, forced into a poor bargaining position, had to take what they could get. Newcomers had come into the town, and soon they found themselves suspected by rabid anti-Mormons and were forced by circumstances to band themselves with the remaining Mormons to protect the city from the aggression of the angry mob. Open fighting followed, and the city successfully defended itself against the first day's attack. A citizens' committee intervened, and the Saints surrendered, again agreeing to leave at once, which they had been doing in any case until interrupted by mob aggression. The anti-Mormons, when they took possession of the city, drove out many of the new citizens who had sided with the Mormons, according to an official report, "with many circumstances of the utmost cruelty and injustice."[16] Eventually a group of French utopian socialists called "Icarians" took over the town. The temple, which an incendiary from the mob had fired, was further destroyed by a cyclone in 1850. The Nauvoo interlude had closed.

The impossibility of finding an equilibrium in relations with the gentiles had been amply demonstrated to the Mormon leadership. Their Zion within the borders of Babylon was bound to lead to conflict, suffering, and the consequent loss of all that had been built up by hard labor and willing sacrifice. The West, unknown but unoccupied, now lay before them. To it they were bringing vast spiritual resources. The experience of group conflict had confirmed their loyalties and solidarities, and the isolation that violent antagonisms had brought had enhanced their religious conception of their own separateness and peculiar character. They had a tradition—a legend preserving past heroism and nurturing future hopes—that had been inscribed upon their hearts in letters of fire. Religious peculiarity had been confirmed, and what had at first been a scriptural idea and a convert's wish was now transformed into a fundamental world view permeating their consciousness and making them not just a church but a people. The religious core of this tradition had seen continual modification and had progressively differentiated itself from the Christianity of ordinary Protestantism. A highly optimistic humanism, promising worldly prosperity in a promised land here below, where the City of God would be built by a chosen people, and an endless development toward divinity in the world to come, was added to the more orthodox notions of the Redemption and the Resurrection of the dead still held and taught in the *Book of Mormon* and the New Testament. The inner circles of the leadership knew that to these blessings was added the restoration of patriarchal marriage, permitting more than one wife, to advance man on his way to Godhead.

It is small wonder that it has been said that the Mormons left Nauvoo with "their creed singular and their wives plural." For these beliefs they had suffered; in these hopes they had persevered. Their common beliefs and their common mentality, formed in common effort and struggle, gave them a unity that nothing hereafter would destroy. The Mormon people turned now from their bitter conflict with men to an equally harsh struggle with elemental nature, one that would add new and celebrated pages to their tradition.

CHAPTER FOUR

Zion in the Mountains

The Mormons began their exodus on the morning of February 4, 1846. Before dawn, ferries started taking the shivering evacuees across the ice-choked Mississippi. The temperature was twenty below zero and the wind bitter. In the freezing camp of their first night on the road nine babies were born. At eleven o'clock on the morning of February 15, Brigham Young crossed the river with a party and followed the first two thousand pilgrims to Sugar Creek, nine miles beyond, where a temporary rude shelter was set up. The great Mormon trek had begun under the most inauspicious circumstances.

For the first month on the road they never made more than six miles a day. Soon the cold of March gave way to April wet, and in that April in Iowa it rained every day. Deep mud was added to the difficulties. At one time the pioneers were forced to remain in camp for two weeks, during which time they were unable to build fires. While the spring sun thawed the roads by day, the nights were so cold that grass would not grow, and, because animals were weakened by lack of fodder, the pace was further slowed. It took four and a half months to reach Council Bluffs, some four hundred miles away, beside the brown waters of the Missouri River, where they established a temporary settlement (now Omaha, Nebraska) that they called "Winter Quarters." Here they built log cabins and dugouts and planted crops.

Across Iowa, they constructed roads and bridges to facilitate the passage of those who were to follow. They even planted crops at strategic places along the course, to be harvested by those who came after them. The ingenuity of the Mormons was proving equal to the tremendous task before them.

Moreover, Mormon morale was standing up under the awful strain. This does not, of course, imply that there were no internal troubles. There were grumbling and the usual clashes and difficulties among personalities. But Mormon beliefs supported them, and they even reported miracles, such as the curing of a sick horse by the laying on of hands. Nor did all the hardship and effort of the trip cause them to abandon lighter entertainment. Captain Pitt's brass band, which had been converted in England and had followed the Saints to Nauvoo, came along, and when the weather did not make it impossible, dances were held to cheer the travelers.

By the time the first group of emigrants had reached Council Bluffs, the main body of Nauvoo Saints was ready to go. All during the summer months their parties marched across Iowa. By the fall of 1846, Father De Smet estimated the number of persons at Council Bluffs at ten thousand, while other writers place the figure as high as fifteen thousand. The first leg of the trek was accomplished, and the problem now was to prepare for the great effort ahead. Brigham Young, who had kept firm control over the group, and other Mormon leaders recognized that in its present condition the Mormon party would require years to reach the Rocky Mountains, if, indeed, it ever did reach them. Reorganization was necessary, and anything less than the establishment of a tight organization would invite disaster.

Once before, when their leaders were in jail and their enemies upon them, it was Brigham Young who organized their exodus from Far West. Now once again it was fortunate for the people and perhaps decisive for the movement that this superb organizer was in command. Born on June 1, 1801, at Whitingham, Windham County, Vermont, he was the ninth child of John Young, a veteran of the Revolutionary War, and his wife Nabby Howe, a girl of Hopkinton, Massachusetts (John's own birthplace), whom he married after his demobilization. They are said to have been the poorest family in Whitingham and did not own a cow or a horse or any land when Brigham appeared in the world. Earning an inadequate living as a basket-maker, John Young soon moved his family to New York State. Death took the mother when Brigham was fourteen years old and left the youth under the firm discipline of his father, of whom he said, "It used to be a word and blow with him, but the blows came first."[1] Brigham said later that he had worked hard instead of going to school and that the "proper and necessary gambols of youth" were denied him. Much of Brigham's thrift, ability for hard work, and dislike of luxury can be traced to his early background.

Brigham Young did not show any great interest in religion in youth and adolescence but rather displayed great independence of mind. His family had become fervent Methodists and took him to hear Lorenzo Dow, the noted evangelist whose antipredestinationist preaching is said to have been particularly welcomed by the folk of the New England back country. In fact, so impressed was John Young that he named one of Brigham's brothers Lorenzo Dow Young. Later, Brigham told a congregation of Saints that he had learned from Dow "nothing but morals . . . but when he came to teaching the things of God he was as dark as midnight."[2] Yet at the age of twenty-two Brigham Young became a Methodist.

Brigham's sister and her husband, a minister of Livonia, New York, were converted to Mormonism by Samuel Smith, Joseph's brother, soon after the publication of the *Book of Mormon*, and his sister quickly converted Brigham's brother Phineas. Brigham was aware of these conversions and had seen the new scripture within two or three weeks of its publication. Yet he did not join the movement for two years. Before he became a member, his sister, two brothers, his father, and his best friend, Heber C. Kimball, had all joined. In March, 1832, after returning from Canada, where he had gone to ask the advice of his brother Joseph, a Methodist lay preacher, Brigham finally became a Mormon. His brother, whose advice he had sought, preceded him into the church by a few days.

After the death of his first wife in September, 1832, Brigham Young, together with Heber C. Kimball and his family, went to Kirtland to join the first stake of Zion. From the day of his conversion, Brigham was steadfast in his loyalty to Joseph Smith. In the final exodus from Missouri he was the only important leader to escape arrest, and it was he who organized and led the evacuation. Furthermore, he had been head of the Quorum of the Twelve for some time and in that office was in charge of missionary work for the church. In March, 1840, he went to England to take charge of the mission there. Thus Brigham brought varied organizational experience to the task that now faced him. During the last years of Joseph's life he became an important adviser to the prophet, and from his former relative unimportance he is mentioned more frequently than any other leader in the latter part of Joseph Smith's journal.

Brigham Young was one of the great American organizers, practical, efficient, and with a strong sense of order. His conversion had rescued him from oblivion as an itinerant painter, carpenter, and glazier. His leadership showed itself not only in the prodigious tasks in which he brought his people to success but also in the clever and quiet manner in which he consolidated his position as *de facto* head of the church and ousted Rigdon, whose claim was by far the oldest and in some ways the most honorable in Mormondom. Although Brigham never won over Joseph's immediate family, the great majority followed him, often with devotion. He was a man who could both demand and receive unquestioning obedience and one whose performance inspired confidence. He had led his people to Council Bluffs, and now he paused to re-form the ranks for the next fateful step.

Brigham had hoped to get employment of some kind from the federal government on construction projects in the West to aid the Saints as they sought a new home "within the Basin of the Great Salt Lake, or the Bear River Valley."[3] After the declaration of war against Mexico in 1846, President Polk's original unwillingness to make use of the Mormons vanished, and Mormon participation in the new Army of the West became of immediate concern, with plans made to establish a Mormon unit to go to California. At first, the enlistment of 2,000 men was contemplated, but the President cut this figure to 500. General Stephen W. Kearny was ordered to "use all proper means to make a good understanding with" the Mormon emigrants "to the end that the United States may have their cooperation in taking possession of, and holding, that country."[4] By July 18 there were five companies, totaling 526 men. The Mormon Battalion began its long march in October, 1846, and on January 29, 1847, arrived at the mission of San Diego in California. In July, except for 81 officers and men who had re-enlisted for six months, the Battalion personnel were mustered out of service. They left for the Valley of the Great Salt Lake. Some had suffered illness on the long march, and a few had died, but they had done no fighting. Financially, the

Battalion was a godsend to the new church. The government clothing allowance amounted to some $21,000 for the unit, most of which went either to the families of the men or to the church itself. In addition, the men were paid salaries, which they sent back to the main body.

By the end of 1846, besides the main body at Winter Quarters, there were 500 Mormons marching westward in the Battalion and a small group of 19 wagons wintering at Pueblo, Colorado. These had set out from Independence, Missouri, in the spring, hoping to meet the main body along the trail. Their number was enlarged by 12 or 15 families of the men in the Battalion, who had gone along on part of the journey with the troops, and by sick soldiers whom General St. George Cooke, the commanding officer, had sent to Pueblo and who were known as the "Sick Detachment." A few Saints who had set out under George Miller were wintering in northern Nebraska. On February 4, 1846, the ship "Brooklyn" left New York to round Cape Horn for California, with 238 Mormons aboard under Elder Samuel Brannan. There were some 600 dead in the cemetery at Winter Quarters, and there were those who had dropped out or stayed behind in Iowa, many of whom later went into the Reorganized Church.

On April 7, 1847, after much collecting of information about the West and considerable revision of plans and reorganization of the group, Brigham Young and the pioneer party set out on the westward trip. There were 148 persons—143 men, 3 women, 2 children—and 72 wagons, 93 horses, 52 mules, 66 oxen, 19 cows, 17 dogs, and numerous chickens.

William Clayton recorded the daily routine and the events of the trip in his journal. The bugle was blown at five in the morning, and the party was on the way at seven. The party halted around four in the afternoon, and everyone went to bed at 8:30 after prayers. Dice and cards were played, but Brigham objected to such vices. One woman discovered that the motion of the wagons would churn butter, and Clayton invented a meter to record the distance traveled.

The party had crossed the desolate prairies and had come to the foothills of the mountains by June. Their speed increased, and they soon averaged 15 miles a day instead of 10. They met emigrants to Oregon and California, a welcome sight in the lonely expanses of the unsettled continent, although the party was careful to avoid Missourians. North of the Platte River in Wyoming the pioneer party left the regular route they had been following—one that had been used by many travelers and emigrants, by the wagons of the fur traders and others, since 1824. Brigham Young thought it wiser to leave the trail at this point, probably to avoid competition for fodder and possible conflict with Missourians. He and Heber C. Kimball blazed the "old Mormon Road" that was followed by the later comers and in part by the Union Pacific Railroad.

On July 7 they arrived at Fort Bridger, and on the twelfth Brigham Young was stricken by "mountain fever." This disease struck many of the company, who suffered from its violent headache, burning temperature, and delirium. Possibly it was a tick fever, although in many cases it may have been a less serious adjustment to high altitudes. It took no lives but caused much suffering. In addition, mosquitoes plagued men and cattle. Brannan came to meet Brigham and joined the party, as did some members of the Battalion. Others were sent to bring to the main party the message that "our destination is the Great Basin." Brigham had decided, on the basis of the information he had been collecting and sifting in his mind, that the Salt Lake Valley, if livable at all, would be the best location. It would give the needed isolation and, with hard work and discipline, could be made a base for a successful Mormon society.

The advance party and the others that were to follow were characterized by their almost military discipline. Although, like all discipline, it sometimes wore thin on the long trail, it saved much waste of effort and needless suffering. It was based upon the authority of the priesthood and of Brigham Young, now head of the church's ruling council, the Quorum of the Twelve. A contemporary account said: "Discipline everywhere prevailed. Every ten wagons were under the command of a captain, who obeyed a captain of fifty; and the latter in turn obeyed a centurion or captain of a hundred, or else a member of the High Council of the Church."[5]

Brigham Young became so ill that he had to remain behind while an advance party under Orson Pratt set out to find the best way into the Valley. This group was soon joined by others under Heber C. Kimball, and all except Brigham and a small group who remained with him reached the floor of the Great Salt Lake Valley on July 22. At 11:30 the next day the advance party planted potatoes, and Orson Pratt recorded in his journal that City Creek was dammed and water diverted to the new garden.

By the morning of July 24, 1847, Brigham, though still weak and lying in a bed in Wilford Woodruff's carriage, came to a high benchland overlooking the Valley. Some thirty-three years later, Woodruff described the scene. He said that Brigham had seen the Valley in a vision before this. That day he saw in another vision "the future glory of Zion." When this vision of Zion's future had passed, Brigham said: "It is enough. This is the right place, drive on."[6] By mid-afternoon Brigham's party had entered the Valley itself and rejoined the main body. Ever since, July 24 has been celebrated as Pioneer Day in Utah and throughout Mormondom and is the greatest Mormon holiday. After a journey of 102 days from the Missouri River the Mormons had arrived in their new home.

Brigham formulated plans for a city, the survey of which was started on August 2, that followed Joseph Smith's plat for the City of Zion. Exploring parties were sent off in several directions to learn more of the surroundings. A "bowery" for Sunday services was erected almost immediately, and Brigham selected the site of the new temple. Adobe houses were begun. Five days after the pioneers, some 200 Saints arrived from Pueblo, Colorado, where they had wintered, about 150 of them being from the Sick Detachment while the rest were of the Mississippi group. On August 26, Brigham and several other leaders and a party of 107 started back to Winter Quarters, Nebraska. After covering about half of the 1,031 miles from Winter Quarters to the Salt Lake Valley, as recorded on another road meter which Clayton had made at the command of Brigham, they met a large body of Mormon emigrants on their way to the new home. The first party of this group arrived in the Valley on September 19, the last on October 8. They were in good condition except for seven deaths on the way, three of them infants. They were 1,540 in number and "possessed 540 wagons, 124 horses, 9 mules, 2,213 oxen, 887 cows, 358 sheep, 35 hogs, and 716 chickens."[7]

Brigham was back at Winter Quarters on October 31, 1847. Before leaving the "Great Salt Lake City of the Great Basin, North America," Brigham had organized an August conference which set up a government to serve in his absence. Now in Nebraska he called the Apostles, the members of the Quorum of the

Twelve, into his small turf-covered log cabin and had himself made President of the church with the titles "Prophet, Seer, and Revelator." His position was now completely established, and a new era in the history of his people had begun.

At the end of May, 1848, Brigham Young led out a new group of 2,417 men, women, and children, which arrived at the Great Salt Lake on September 20. The new arrivals found a city of some 423 houses of adobe and logs. The winter had been mild, although provisions were short and many had suffered hardship. Besides Salt Lake City, with a population of over 1,500, ten other settlements had been established in the Valley. There were two grist mills and four sawmills. The Mormon Empire was started.

Having failed to build Zion within the confines of American society, the Latter-day Saints found in the Great Basin the isolation that would enable them to establish a distinctive community based upon their own beliefs and values. This was, as the Mormon hymn declared, the place where "none would come to hurt or make afraid," not at least until sufficiently strong foundations had been laid. Brigham Young resisted the blandishments of California, presented to him in glowing terms by Brannan and the veterans of the Battalion, and refused to follow the major streams of emigration from the east to that territory or to Oregon, realizing that such attractive areas would soon draw large gentile populations and merely prepare the stage for the re-enactment of the tragedies of Far West and Nauvoo. Here in their isolation the Mormons would attempt to work out their destiny and to construct a society upon their peculiar ideals of the kingdom.

Up to now, the Mormons had withstood both the ferocity of men who had fought them with violence and the cruelties of elemental nature, upon whose inhospitable bosom they had so often been cast. Now, however, with their enemies behind them for the time being, the struggle against men was supplanted by the contest with nature. The co-operative ethic commanded by Mormon revelation and enforced by the conditions of life experienced in the last decade and a half would now become the most valuable spiritual resource of the Saints in the face of their new tasks. Disciplined co-operation, backed by a close-knit but flexible organization, was to be required. These were specifications that the Mormon church was prepared to meet.

The tendency toward authoritarian leadership implicit in the rule of a prophet-president and formally embodied in the priest-hood of the church had been increased by the successes of Nauvoo, the repeated crises of Missouri and Illinois, and the discipline required by the westward migration. Brigham Young had emerged as unquestioned leader, and the higher leadership generally had complete dominance over the body of the church. Yet the initiative of the rank and file was hardly impaired, and the new country, with its challenge to individual hardihood and ingenuity, offered an outlet to talents that counterbalanced the restriction often associated with such authoritarian rule. Moreover, the common faith, for which so much had by now been paid in blood and tears, consecrated every effort. Under the leadership of Brigham Young, the Saints set about in what has been called "one of the most interesting and instructive experiments in the world."[8]

From 1847 to 1857 there were established ninety-five Mormon communities, most of them clustering around Salt Lake City, which became the center of a growing empire. Although the first villages settled in the Salt Lake Valley itself grew up by unplanned and undirected individual initiative, as was the case generally with American settlement, the Basin was settled mainly by centrally directed colonization. Men and their families were often "called" by the President of the church and sent into irrigable valleys and to other strategically important sites to set up agricultural villages or, as in the case of Parowan, where iron had been discovered, to establish industry. While Brigham supervised the whole colonization process and was guided by the strategic considerations of building a Mormon Empire and getting first hold of the valuable sites, the early period of settlement could not be minutely directed by one man. Consequently, he divided the selected areas into large territorial units and put members of the Twelve in charge, assigning an Apostle to each area.

In the decade 1847–57, settlements were planted around an axis a thousand miles long, running from north by northeast to southwest; the width of the scatter was 800 miles from east to west. Three hundred miles to the north of Salt Lake City was the outpost of Fort Lemhi, its nearest Mormon neighbor being 225 miles south. To the southwest, 750 miles away, was San Bernardino, California, to which Brigham had sent men in 1851 and which he intended to be an important Mormon center, a second Salt Lake City for Saints who would do better in southern California than in the Basin. He felt that San Diego would become the port of entry for Mormon immigration, and he established settlements from Provo to Las Vegas, to claim, settle, and make a highway along what he conceived to be a Mormon corridor to the sea. To bring this ecclesiastical commonwealth to reality, he concomitantly speeded up missionary activities and expanded the mission field during 1849 and 1850. Great efforts were made to develop and improve transportation to the sea, and the federal government was petitioned many times for aid. Later, Brigham explored the possibilities of using the Colorado River as a route from the Mormon settlements to the sea.

In 1861, after he had called 309 families at the October conference of the church to establish the city of St. George at the confluence of the Santa Clara and the Virgin rivers, Brigham planned to initiate the new Mormon route and to test the new transportation program he had in mind. He wanted to have European immigration of Saints, as well as the shipping of goods from Europe and New York, move through the Caribbean to the Isthmus of Panama. There passengers and freight were to proceed overland, and, once again by water, to sail by way of the Pacific and the Gulf of California and up the Colorado river as far as possible. In the troubles involved in the so-called Mormon War of 1857, San Bernardino had to be given up, and this new plan was a substitute for what had originally been envisaged as the San Diego outlet. Almost immediately, however, before any shipping worthy of note took place, the railroad arrived in the north. Mormon empire-building, which had been directed mainly to the south for two decades, found itself connected with the outside world in a new direction and was soon to feel tied to Babylon by cords of steel.

Not since the original Puritan settlement in Massachusetts had American colonization seen such a centrally directed group effort marked by such wholehearted co-operation. On the first Sunday in the Valley, July 25, Brigham announced the fundamentals of Mormon policy with regard to land and water. The Mormon leaders looked upon land as a gift of God and as belonging to the community, and it was promulgated by the President that land, water, and timber would be the property of the people. Believing with most of their contemporary Americans that agriculture was the basis of wealth and the proper foundation for community life and sharing the general frontier notions about free land, the Mormons made a religious version of widely held American ideas the basis of economic life in their new commonwealth. Land in the new settlements was often distributed by lot, a policy that had been generally followed in early Massachusetts as well. Often land was farmed in a large area inclosed by a common fence. The military formation used in crossing the plains, which emulated the Israelites in the wilderness (with whom the Saints felt closely identified), was readapted to agricultural co-operation in the first period of settlement. Under this system, about 10 acres were allotted to each man—small farms remaining characteristically a Mormon adaptation in the arid region of their co-operative village pattern—and the combination of communal effort with individual ownership and supervision under an authoritarian, church-sponsored organization gave a new expression to the ideals of the United Order that had been abandoned in Missouri.

Colonizing efforts and all the related tasks were looked upon as religious duties and called "missions." The farm-village system, with its homes grouped around the ward meeting house, its small farms, and its diversified agriculture, gave a firm foundation to the growing Mormon commonwealth. Led by God's representatives and intensively organized in a structure of church and lay participation, these villages were at first governed under the leadership of the Mormon bishops, local lay and religious leaders of the ward group. Brigham's great abilities were matched by the loyalty and the considerable capacities of his colleagues at the top and his followers below. Capitalizing upon the firm group attachments and the concomitant separation from the outside world that persecution and emigration had brought about, supporting a communal religious doctrine, Brigham developed a firmly united co-operative community. A theocracy was growing up, but one in which the individual found considerable room for expression as well as satisfying participation in the great struggle to build God's kingdom in the unfriendly desert.

In 1857 the first period of Mormon settlement closed, and the struggle with nature took second place in relation to the older struggle with unfriendly fellow men. The arrival of federal troops and the conflict with the government in Utah's Mormon War (see pp. 101–4) caused Brigham in alarm to call back the Saints from the outskirts of the Mormon area, from Fort Bridger, Fort

Supply, Lemhi, Carson Valley, Las Vegas, and San Bernardino; after the conflict was settled, the colonists were never sent back to these posts. The next decade, to 1867, saw a second burst of colonizing activity, and 135 new settlements were established. From 1861 to 1868 some twenty thousand European converts arrived and were settled in the new villages by Brigham Young. Expansion in this decade was more gradual, and, whereas the previous decade had seen mostly southward movement, many of the new towns established this time were in northern Utah and southern Idaho.

The approach of the railroad in 1867 ended the second decade, and from then to the death of Brigham Young ten years later, 127 new settlements were established. Mormon expansion continued; colonies were founded along the Little Colorado, and settlers were sent to the Gila River area. The death of the greatest colonizer closed a full generation of Mormon enterprise. Salt Lake City was the capital of the Territory of Utah and the regional center of a larger area, whose total Mormon population was approximately 140,000. Favored as it was by its location within the Wasatch Oasis, the basic factor that was making and would make Salt Lake City the regional center of all the neighboring hinterland was its peculiar position as center of the Mormon church and headquarters for its planned development and settlement of the intermountain west. In three decades of intensive occupation, the foundations of Mormon primacy had been securely laid.

After Brigham Young's death, new Mormon settlements continued to appear, especially in Mexico and Canada, whither Mormons went to avoid prosecution for polygamy. In Sonora they established Colonia Morelos and Colonia Oaxacao, while in Chihuahua they founded Colonia Díaz, Colonia Dublan, Colonia Juárez, Oacheco, García, and Chauichupa. At one time President Porfirio Díaz publicly expressed the wish that he had more industrious citizens of this caliber. In Canada, Cardston was established in the Province of Alberta.

The region where all this intense and well-planned exploration and settlement took place was one of abundant land but all of it lay under low rainfall. The control of water would obviously be vital to the success of Mormon efforts, a problem to be solved by irrigation, a mode of water distribution with which the Saints had had no direct experience before their emigration. Indeed, before the Mormon efforts in Utah, extensive irrigation was unknown among the Anglo-Saxon peoples. Mormons first saw irrigation in New Mexico, whither some of them had gone as teamsters before the migration and through which as members of the Mormon Battalion many of them had marched on their way to California. There had been aboriginal irrigation among some Indian tribes, not only the Pueblo peoples but the Utah Indians as well. Moreover, when the Saints arrived in the Basin, Miles Goodyear, who had come to the area in the employ of the Hudson's Bay Company and who had received a grant of land from the Mexican government in 1835 embracing most of what is now Weber County, Utah, had for some years been farming near what is now Ogden. Catholic missions in the west had made use of the technique on a small scale. But the founding of large-scale settlement on irrigation farming had not before been accomplished by Americans.

The Saints were not the first farmers in the Basin, nor, indeed, were they the first white men. Since 1824 trappers and hunters had mined it of its fur crop, depleting the fur-bearing animals almost to the point of extinction by the time the Mormons arrived. At one time Ogden, which was the trappers' rendezvous, had a population of around six hundred, including the Indian wives and half-breed children of the trappers. The fur traders' frontier was passing when the Saints entered the Basin. Jim Bridger, who was among the most famous of the trappers in the region, is said to have wagered Brigham Young in the form of a promise to pay him a thousand dollars for the first bushel of wheat grown in the area, a wager which, of course, Brigham won. Pre-Mormon efforts among both trappers and Indians would have suggested that Bridger's was the losing side, and, indeed, it has been suggested that he was deliberately trying to discourage the Saints.

Permanent white settlement and permanent irrigation farming, on which alone it could be based, began with the Mormons. From the time of the ancient empires of Egypt and Mesopotamia, communal water control had always been accompanied by and presumably always demanded authoritarian leadership and co-ordination in a tightly knit social organization. The Mormons had both of these, and they had the religious conviction and the experience of common effort and shared sufferings and hardships to give them intense group consciousness. Richard T. Ely, a pioneer in the study of the economic aspects of Mormonism, commented in

1903: "Individualism was out of the question, and in Mormonism we find, precisely, the cohesive strength of religion needed at that juncture to secure economic success." Moreover, before migration the Mormons had suspected that irrigation might be necessary in their new location and had discussed the problem in Nauvoo and at Winter Quarters. Though experienced only with rainfall or humid farming, they were not unaware of the problems that were awaiting them. Orson Pratt's diversion of City Creek on July 23, 1847, bears testimony to that. An irrigation ditch and a diversion dam were the first works of Mormon construction in the Valley, started one day before Brigham Young arrived to make the entry official. The Mormons soon became expert in building canals and ditches, dams and reservoirs. They had to learn by the difficult method of trial and error the techniques of irrigation farming.

A co-operative system of water control was devised both for construction and for ownership and was established in Salt Lake City, setting the pattern for the other settlements. Under the bishops of the wards, the spiritual heads of the colonies who worked under a high council, construction, yearly repair, and maintenance were apportioned according to the amount of water used. If Mormon co-operation made this possible, the irrigation experience would suggest a workable co-operative form for much later Mormon experimentation. Out of the water associations that grew up informally in the early days of settlement came the incorporated mutual irrigation companies.

The Mormons were interested in an opportunity to pursue their own ideals. They had come to stay and wanted to build permanent habitations. Mining, cattle-raising, and other more adventurous activities attracted men to other parts of the West, but in Utah men came to build homes and to establish communities upon the basis of agriculture. The Saints obeyed Brigham's counsel, although it seemed difficult to some and even perverse to a few, to eschew mining and the more comfortable humid valleys of California. Only farming, operated on a family basis within the larger context of church co-operation, could, Brigham believed, develop an adequate basis to support a Mormon civilization. Only isolation could bring the chance of success. The chosen people with a special covenant and a divinely appointed mission, gathered out of sinful Babylon, were to root the Kingdom of God in the irrigated soil of their new homeland. The accomplishment of the divine purpose was adventure enough, and, despite all the difficulties of territorial days, Utah grew and became more and more livable. Mormon efforts conquered hostile nature.

From Mormon colonizing grew the Mormon culture region of today, spreading out in the Great Basin and centering on Salt Lake City. In the 1930's, a careful study found Salt Lake City, with a population of 150,000, "the capital of a state, the seat of a religious denomination, a nucleus of commercial and financial enterprises, a focus of transportation, a leading center in educational activities, and the largest city in a vast section of Western United States." It was a center that served and dominated a region of 790,000 people and that derived its integration from "the binding qualities of Salt Lake City, rather than from inherent physical qualities."[9] The economic base of this region was agriculture, although the gentiles came and developed mining and World War II brought large-scale manufacturing. Agriculture in the 1950's, as a century before, was based fundamentally upon irrigation. If Mormon organization and centralized leadership have left a lasting imprint upon the West, as recorded in the central position of Salt Lake City in the Great Basin, the rank-and-file ability to co-operate, which backed up that organization and leadership, has left a permanent monument in irrigation and the peaceful farming communities it has made possible. Small wonder that devout Latter-day Saints still consider the opening words of the thirty-fifth chapter of Isaiah to have been prophetic of the Mormon experience: "The wilderness and the solitary place shall be glad for them; and the desert shall rejoice, and blossom as the rose." If their faith was not quite enough to move mountains, it was, combined with their labor and intelligence, sufficient to turn the desert into a garden.

Mormon millennialism demanded that the scattered seed of Israel should "stand in chosen places, that they may watch the coming of the Holy One."[10] "To bring to pass the gathering of mine elect" (D & C, 29:7) was "Mormonism's oldest and most influential" doctrine.[11] When in June, 1837, the Mormon church established the English mission, a new continent was brought within reach of the Mormon call, and after April, 1840, the emigration of converts from Europe became part of Mormon policy.

Mormon immigration, while part of the general movement of

population from Europe to the New World, had its own special characteristics. These ranged from its mixture of sacred and secular utopian motivation to the organized and supervised character of the crossings themselves. To the British mission founded in 1837 was added in 1849 a mission to Scandinavia; this proved to be second only to England in importance. Scandinavia provided Mormonism with strong and sturdy colonists, loyal and dependable, to aid in the settlement of the western Zion. Also in 1849, men were sent to the Society Islands, where subsequently thousands of converts were made, and to Switzerland and Italy, the former offering a field of some fertility while the latter was largely barren. In 1851 missions were established in France, Germany, Hawaii, Australia, and Latin America, while in 1852 work was started in India, New Zealand, and Malta and, in 1853, in South Africa. Mormon missionaries were ejected from, or refused entrance to, China, Burma, Thailand, Spain, Gibraltar, the West Indies, and British Guiana. But England and Scandinavia and, to a lesser extent, Germany remained the main fields of the Mormon harvest.

Immigration had begun soon after the founding of the English mission, and some immigrants had come to Far West. Between 1840 and 1846, 4,750 emigrants sailed through the Mormon agency at Liverpool, most of them coming to Nauvoo and its immediate environs. The ship "North America" apparently carried the first regularly organized company of Mormon emigrants, numbering about 200 persons, when it left Liverpool on August 7, 1840, although some families had gone earlier the same year on other vessels. Of this company, it is estimated that about 100 got to Nauvoo. As was to be expected, the difficulties of the Saints in Illinois caused confusion in the missions and led to a suspension of the emigration policy by the church. However, near the end of 1847 the emigration policy was re-established and soon put into operation.

Probably close to 90,000 immigrants were attracted to American shores by the Mormon message between 1840, when the first groups left, and the end of the century. Many came under church supervision, even with their passage paid in advance by church funds. It has been estimated that 85,220 came between 1840 and 1887,[12] of whom over 70,000 came during Brigham Young's presidency (1847–77). The largest portion of these were from England, whence 5,074 Mormon converts had migrated by 1846 and 15,642 by 1854. Second in numbers were the Scandinavians, of whom 297 left Liverpool on the "Forest Monarch" in 1852, with a total of 1,003 by 1854. By 1855 about 2,000 Scandinavians had left Europe, and by 1900 the figure had risen to approximately 30,000. In fact, in the three-year period from 1878 to 1880, Great Britain as a supplier of Mormon colonizers accounted for only 48 per cent, while Scandinavia increased to 39 per cent; this, together with the 8 per cent supplied by the Swiss-German mission, almost equaled the number from the British Isles. By 1899, Scandinavia led even the English, sending 5,438 souls to 4,588 from Great Britain. At the same time the Swiss-German mission sent 2,276 and the Netherlands 1,556, thus bringing the total Nordic immigration to double that from the United Kingdom. Most of the Scandinavians—about half the total—came from Denmark, where the constitution of 1859 granted religious freedom.

Today Utah is of Anglo-Scandinavian stock, and, if English-speaking leadership has eclipsed the contribution of these Nordic immigrants to the eye of the casual observer, it is in part because of the quick assimilation that in one generation made them native Mormons. In Utah the old languages died out more rapidly than elsewhere. Once arrived, the immigrants came largely under the leadership of native Americans, although John Taylor, the third President of the church, was English-born and had been converted in Canada. Moreover, language auxiliaries to the usual church organizations hastened assimilation. Seven Scandinavian publications were issued by the immigrants, mostly newspapers and periodicals; the Germans issued four, one of which lasted until 1935, and the Netherlanders three, one also lasting until 1935. There have also been three Japanese papers, one Greek, one Slavonian, and a short-lived Italian *Gazetta*.

It was charged by an American Secretary of State in 1879 that the Mormon immigrants from Europe were "drawn mainly from the ignorant classes, who are easily influenced by the double appeal to their passions and their poverty."[13] He apparently referred to the fact that the converts were from the working population, chiefly farmers and mechanics, whose restrictions of life in the Old World rendered them susceptible to the appeal of the New. Linforth's data on the Mormon immigration through the British agency from 1850 to 1854 show many skilled craftsmen; a similar picture is seen in the data on immigration from England for the years 1849–52 compiled by Larson from the records of the church historian's office. The fact is that the Mormon immigrants do not appear to have been of a type differing in any major respect from the non-Mormon arrivals.

Mormon immigration was, like other Mormon activities, efficiently organized. Charles Dickens has left us a vivid description of a Mormon immigrant ship he visited, on which he was struck by the order, discipline, and thorough organization.[14] Ships were contracted for in advance, and experienced elders were sent "to superintend the voyage, in connexion with the masters." Passengers went on board the day of their arrival in Liverpool or the day after, saving them "the ruinous expense of lodging ashore" and preserving "many an inexperienced person from being robbed by sharpers, who make extensive experiments in this port upon the unwary." Liverpool was the most important port of embarkation for the entire European mission. The elders appointed to supervise the voyage were accepted by the immigrants by vote, and a daily routine under their direction was followed.

Church organization into wards and branches took place aboard ship, and under the direction of the elected officers of these smaller groups "passengers rise about 5 or 6 o'clock in the morning, cleanse their respective portions of the ship, and throw the rubbish overboard. This attended to, prayers are offered in every ward, and then the passengers prepare their breakfasts, and during the remainder of the day occupy themselves with various duties. At 8 or 9 o'clock at night, prayers are again offered, and all retire to their berths. Such regularity and cleanliness, with constant exercise on deck, are an excellent conservative of the general health of the passengers, a thing already proverbial of the Latter-day Saints' emigration." Linforth reported in 1855 that, as a result of the exemplary behavior of Mormon immigrants on the voyages, "few ships now reach New Orleans without some conversions taking place."[15]

An English ex-Mormon has commented: "The ships conveying the Mormon immigrants have been so free from accident, that it is not strange that the Saints should believe that the peculiar favour of 'the Lord' is extended to them." He declared that the captain "who could get the Mormon immigrants was considered fortunate for that voyage."[16] Dickens in 1861 found the ship he visited "as orderly and quiet as a man of war."[17] Lord Houghton writing in the *Edinburgh Review* in 1862 said: "The Select Committee of the House of Commons on emigrant ships for 1854 summoned the Mormon agent and passenger broker before it, and came to the conclusion that no ships under the provisions of the 'Passenger Act' could be depended upon for comfort and security in the same degree as those under his administration. The Mormon ship is a family under strong and acceptable discipline, with every provision for comfort, decorum, and internal peace."[18]

The route of immigration led to New Orleans and from there up the Mississippi, first to St. Louis and thence to the camping grounds; these were located at Keokuk, Iowa, and later at what was known as "Kanzas in Jackson County, Missouri." At this latter destination, the Saints built a camp known as "Mormon Grove." Here the immigrants were organized for transportation to Salt Lake City.

Various plans were tried to accomplish this journey. Crossing the plains was not inexpensive. In 1853 Erastus Snow, a frontier agent of the church, declared: "One wagon, two yoke oxen, and two cows will be sufficient (if that is the extent of their means) for a family of eight or ten persons, with the addition of a tent for every two or three families." The same notice gave the following prices: "Choice wagons, made to order and delivered at the point of outfit with bows, projectors, etc., will be about $78, without projectors, $75. Oxen with yokes and chains from $70 to $85 per yoke; cows from $16 to $25 cash."[19] Linforth in the same year estimated the cost of one team made up of one wagon, two pair of oxen, and two cows at £40 sterling. The church also tried that year to send immigrants at a flat rate of £10, but, because of the increased costs resulting from the demand from the great California and Oregon migrations, had to increase the sum to £13 the next year. However, the number to go on this plan fell while Perpetual Emigrating Fund immigrants increased in number.

The Perpetual Emigrating Fund was a co-operative financial venture set up by the church to aid emigration from Europe to the Valley. Established as a revolving fund in the fall of 1849 on the initiative of Brigham Young and incorporated by the territorial legislature in September of the following year, it began by aiding the Nauvoo Saints left in Iowa to get to the Great Basin. The last of these arrived in Salt Lake City with fund company aid almost exactly at the same time that the first European converts assisted by the fund, a group of 250 who left Liverpool in January, 1852, got there.

The Perpetual Emigrating Fund Company paid in advance for those Saints selected for emigration by the missions abroad, when these emigrants could not pay their way. Still others were brought by relatives in the Valley who paid the fare into the fund. Section 16 of the fund's incorporating ordinance stated: "All persons receiving assistance from the Perpetual Emigrating Fund for the Poor, shall reimburse the same in labor or otherwise, as soon as circumstances will admit."[20] It has been said that many immigrants were in no hurry to repay what they owed after they were established on farms in the Valley. It is a fact that Brigham in his sermons did exhort the people to pay their debts to the fund. Enemies of the Mormon leadership have accused them of keeping such immigrants in "bondage." One critic claimed that interest of 10 per cent per annum was charged.[21]

The costs of sending immigrants continued to increase in the 1850's. In 1854 teams rose in cost from £40 to £45, and in 1855 the sum of £13 per person was raised to £15. Moreover, in 1855 the Mormon colony in Utah experienced a serious crop failure. In 1856 Brigham Young conceived a plan to cut costs drastically, an idea that had been on his mind for some time but was not proposed until this difficult juncture. He designed a handcart that immigrants could pull and that could carry their belongings across the plains. The cost of the trip from Liverpool to Salt Lake City by this method was said to have been $45 in the 1856 season.

In the summer of that year five parties left Iowa City, proceeded to Florence, Nebraska, and from there went across the plains to Salt Lake City. The first three groups left Florence on July 20, 24, and 30. Apparently they fared well and arrived without trouble at their destination. The last two groups, however, left Florence on August 14 and 26 and were the victims of a great disaster. Winter overcame them on the way, which added to many other problems, such as the breakdown of handcarts apparently made of green wood. The mortality rate was heavy in both groups, 75 out of 400 in one, 150 out of 576 in the other. Brigham Young rushed teams out to aid the sufferers, and upon their arrival the Saints rallied to their support. Brigham's new method was continued for several years but evidently not on a large scale.

From 1861 on, still another method was used to bring immigrants to Salt Lake. Teams were sent to meet the railroad that was under construction, and from its farthest terminus the newcomers were taken to the Valley. In the years from 1861 to 1868, 1,913 wagons went east to meet the trains. On June 25, 1869, the railroad was completed, and the first party to come the whole way by rail arrived. From then on, immigrants came by train, although, interestingly enough, in the first years after the completion fewer came than in the years just before.

While colonization with the use of irrigation was making the desert bloom, "all nations" were flowing into the mountain Zion.

CHAPTER FIVE

The Return of Secular Life

It was church organization and discipline under the rule of the prophet-president, Brigham Young, and the priesthood that had shepherded the Saints from Nauvoo, from the eastern states, and even from Europe to the Great Basin. Moreover, the first government established in the West was of similar nature, set up by Brigham in the summer of 1847 before he left to return to the main body of the Saints at Winter Quarters.

From 1847 to 1849 there was a complete absence of regular civil government, the ecclesiastical organization serving also in the civil capacity and appointing what additional officials were found necessary. In recognition of the need for civil government and also of the sovereignty of the United States, which had become fact in the region according to the terms of the Treaty of Guadalupe Hidalgo (signed on February 2, 1848), Brigham Young in February, 1849, sent out a call to "all the citizens of that portion of upper California lying east of the Sierra Nevada" for a political convention to meet in Salt Lake City. In March, 1849, a group assembled there as a constitutional convention.

At first, the convention apparently decided to petition Congress for territorial status but then changed its mind and decided to adopt a constitution for the "Provisional Government of the State of Deseret." The name is from the *Book of Mormon*, where it means "honey bee." The new state claimed a large region comprising all of present-day Utah and Nevada; small sections of Oregon, Idaho, and Wyoming in the north and of Colorado and New Mexico in the east; over two-thirds of what is now Arizona; and a large section of California, including the San Bernardino Valley and the port of San Diego, thereby including the Mormon corridor to the sea.

With the adoption of this constitution and the election of temporary officers under it in March, 1849, the openly theocratic period came to an end. Unquestionably, theocracy in the manner in which it existed in this transition period was seen as temporary. The church had remained the stable context of Mormon life at a time when violence and migration had uprooted all other political institutions. The church filled the vacuum and handled all important problems. While church government itself was, in theory and in structure, theocratic, the need for a non-ecclesiastical civil government was recognized, although, once the millennium arrived, that civil government would be replaced by a theocratic government of which the church was the precursor. Yet the church persisted as the most significant human organization after the establishment of the civil government and in fact remained, though no longer undisguised, the effective governing agency in the region.

The constitution, which, like most state constitutions, provided for the usual tripartite division of powers, set the first Monday of May—May 7, 1849—as the date of the election in which public acceptance or rejection of the new instrument and selection of state officials should take place. However, the election actually took place on March 12, and the officers elected did not coincide exactly with those named by the constitution. This somewhat irregular procedure seems to have stemmed out of earlier plans of Brigham Young. Evidently, Brigham did not hesitate to override the plans of the constitution-makers or their instrument when it suited his own designs for Zion. The strength of his will and the nature of his determination are revealed in his action.

The period of open theocratic rule from 1847 to 1849 now gave way to its masked expression, first in the provisional state of Deseret and soon thereafter in the Territory of Utah. The republican prejudices of the Saints and, perhaps more important, the presence of a growing number of non-Mormons made civil rule necessary. For the Saints themselves, theocratic church government supported by the devotion of a large majority of the rank and file— what some have called Mormon "theo-democracy"—could have sufficed, and a Mormon leadership unhampered by outside pressures would possibly have let it suffice. It is quite true that the Saints never did repudiate the legitimacy of the civil state and tended naturally to think in terms of civil government as it was understood in America. Yet, as Stansbury so well observed: "While, however, there are all the exterior evidences of a government strictly temporal, it cannot be concealed that it is so intimately blended with spiritual administration of the church, that it would be impossible to separate one from the other."[1] He was describing the operation of the state of Deseret. And Brigham declared, when later removed from the governorship of the Territory: "Though I may not be Governor here my power will not be diminished. No man they can send here will have much influence with this community, unless he be the man of their choice."[2]

The fact is that the Mormon group had set up a civil government in all its attempts to build the kingdom. It had always been subordinate to church organization, which was the basic mechanism of social direction and control. And this latter instrument placed large responsibility for decision and initiative in the hands of the leader, upon whose acceptance as a divinely appointed prophet all the rest of Mormonism hung. The experiences since the expulsion from Nauvoo had only strengthened authoritarian tendencies and made Brigham Young in a certain sense the embodiment of both church and state. Actually, the Mormons had not thought out the implications of their basic position with regard to relations between church and state. They had, from the start, accepted the republican convictions and prejudices of their milieu, while at the same time they acted in terms of the solidarity of the new, total, religious-secular community they had created. If, as Franklin D. Richards, a Mormon commentator writing in territorial days, stated: "Theoretically church and state are one. If there were no gentiles and no other government there would be no civil law,"[3] the facts were that the gentiles and the other government were very much there and Mormon doctrine developed under the pressure of these two alien influences.

Mormonism created the most orderly American community to be established on any sizable scale in the great West, but it established it upon the basis of religious and moral innovations supported by particularist group allegiances, all of which had led time and again to bitter conflicts in the East. When Congress began its discussion of the Deseret petition for statehood in the spring of

1850, the Mormon request was met with a torrent of abuse, ominous of much that was to come. Territorial ambitions and the immorality of polygamy, as well as an insufficency of population, were raised as objections.

In September, 1850, Congress passed an omnibus bill which President Millard Fillmore signed immediately. Among other provisions, the law established the Territory of Utah, much shorn but still including what is now Utah and Nevada, one-third of Colorado, and a corner of Wyoming. Although Brigham Young took the oath as territorial governor on February 3, 1851, it was some time before other appointees arrived, and the new territorial government was not really under way for about a year. Half the important positions went to Utah Mormons, the other half to nonresident non-Mormons. The gentile officials came with their own prejudices against the Mormon experiment and without the confidence of the Mormon people. Dissension within the officialdom, reflecting this division, began immediately.

Conflict between Mormons and gentiles had not been left behind but developed both within and without the Territory, as anti-Mormon sentiment continued to grow throughout the country. To these difficulties the years 1854 and 1855 added hard times, almost to the point of famine. This period saw a marked religious reaction, inspired by the leadership of the church, against a certain laxness that the experiences of the previous decade had introduced into Mormon behavior. Some Saints were lured by gold to California, there were quarrels about property, some had been ignoring the Sabbath, stealing was not unknown, and what Brigham H. Roberts, the Mormon historian, called "sex sins" had become common, or at least temptation had become continuous in the circumstances of unsettlement and mobility. The result was the "Mormon Reformation" preached by Jedediah M. Grant, Brigham Young, and others. Mormon missionaries went to every settlement and questioned each person individually about his sins, ranging from murder, treachery, adultery, failure to pay tithes, and infidelity to non-payment of debts, lying, stealing, and even personal cleanliness. It was a kind of Mormon revivalism and was accompanied by inner anxiety and high emotion. People were then rebaptized for the renewal of their covenants and for the remission of sins.

The result and in part the aim of the movement were to increase group loyalty as well as religious enthusiasm and to strengthen the authority of the church leaders. Pressure was put on the lukewarm, and it appears that there was terrorism by such mysterious figures as Bill Hickman, "Brigham's Avenging Angel," who seems to have committed some of the crimes to which he later confessed with unabashed straightforwardness with at least the tacit approval of Brigham. Apostates had caused the church much trouble, and there was in the Reformation an attempt to forestall that kind of difficulty as far as possible. Brigham Young preached the doctrine of "blood atonement," declaring: "There are sins that men commit for which they cannot receive forgiveness in this world, or in that which is to come, and if they had their eyes open to see their true condition, they would be perfectly willing to have their blood spilt upon the ground, that the smoke thereof might ascend to heaven as an offering for their sins."[4] Such talk, in the mounting tension between the federal officials and the Mormon people, was symptomatic of the closeness to violence.

In Missouri and again in Illinois the Mormon-gentile conflict had been violent, with both sides resorting to aggression. John D. Lee stated in a book published after his death (which may bear too much of the retouching hand of his lawyer, W. W. Bishop): "It has always been a well understood doctrine of the Church that it was right and praiseworthy to kill every person who spoke evil of the Prophet. This doctrine had been strictly lived up to in Utah, until the Gentiles arrived in such great numbers that it became unsafe to follow the practice, but the doctrine is still believed, and no year passes without one or more of those who have spoken evil of Brigham Young being killed, in a secret manner."[5] Blood atonement certainly enkindled this sort of spirit, and, although it seems that it was rarely practiced, the atmosphere was one of inordinate group loyalty to the point of fanaticism. Obedience to authority became a most important mark of religious fervor.

It was in these distraught conditions that President Buchanan decided to replace Brigham with a gentile governor and to send along 2,500 troops under General Albert Sidney Johnston to keep order. The result was Utah's "Mormon War." Mormon ambivalence about Babylon seemed to dissolve. The Saints interpreted these moves as open aggression against them. Once again they recalled Missouri and Illinois, and many made up their minds not to let those tragic events repeat themselves here in the mountains.

The Saints' fighting spirit was thoroughly aroused. Brigham Young declared that the time had come not only to fight for freedom from "mobocracy and oppression" but to separate from the federal Union. He stated that the "time must come when there will be a separation between this kingdom and the kingdoms of this world," and he concluded: "We will wait a little while to see; but I shall take a hostile move by our enemies as an evidence that it is time for the thread to be cut."[6]

Brigham prepared a scorched-earth policy as the troops drew near, and the militia was mustered into service. The outlying settlements were given up and their people called back, and the Saints in Salt Lake prepared to burn their homes and move south, ready to make "a Moscow of Utah, and a Potter's Field of every canyon." Mormon militia units burned grass in advance of the federal army, stampeded its cattle, and set fire to its trains but avoided the shedding of blood, if possible. Brigham explained the burnings as preparing better grass for next year, as "is customary in prairie regions." Although many of the rank and file were fearful, the Mormon leaders were determined, and the willingness of their followers to burn the fruits of a decade's labor both testified to and strengthened group solidarity.

It has been estimated that thirty thousand Mormons packed their movable possessions into wagons and set out for the southern part of the Territory. War hysteria swept Mormondom. Meanwhile, Johnston and his troops, who slowly made their way westward, arrived in November, 1857, at Fort Bridger, Wyoming, and found the old post burned to the ground and Fort Supply, twelve miles farther west, in the same condition. They made winter quarters there with much discomfort while an advance party camped not far from Salt Lake City, now greatly depleted in population.

The most unfortunate event of the Utah War was the Mountain Meadows Massacre, which took place in southern Utah, where feeling ran highest. An emigrant party headed for California was openly anti-Mormon in its attitude as it passed through the Territory, making reckless boasts, and all its adult members were murdered in cold blood by Mormons and Indian allies who had united with them against the United States. The Mormons, because of religious scruples, organized the affair so that the Indians would kill the women while the Saints devoted their attention to the men.

Mormon treachery prepared the event, and Mormon indignation inspired it. It was certainly not planned by Brigham Young and the top leaders, though they set the general atmosphere that made it possible and it was planned and carried through by their lieutenants in the south. In this frightful and treacherous assault, the Mormons, who were presumably leading the party to safety, turned upon their wards and, together with Indians from whom they were supposed to protect them, killed over 120 persons, sparing only 17 small children.

For this grave crime, which horrified Mormons as much as it did gentiles and which fanned the flames of anti-Mormon sentiment, giving it a solid basis in fact almost as lurid as some of its inventions, only one man paid the penalty of losing his life, and he was by no means the most responsible. Yet the church leaders decided to sacrifice John D. Lee when they saw that there was no other way to avoid making the whole complicated story public, a course which they felt would have done them inestimable harm in the eyes of the nation. Despite suppression of information and obstruction of prosecution for over a decade, the church was forced by public opinion at large to take some action in 1870. During these years the massacre remained a secret concern of the Mormons themselves and a cause of guilt for many who knew the story. So in that year two of the leaders of the Mormons in the massacre, Isaac Haight and John D. Lee, were excommunicated from the church. This action did not assuage the feelings of either gentiles or Mormons, for the prying of the former and the revulsion of the latter continued. Yet the church leadership was afraid to reveal openly before the nation that such a dastardly action had been planned and carried out by local church leaders in an atmosphere condoned by the leadership. The top leadership did not condone the massacre, nor would they have, had they known of it, but they had set the tone of antagonism and alarm that made it possible. And they remained to the end afraid to speak frankly about it, hoping to smother gentile interest and Mormon concern with silence. Their importance in territorial government made it possible for them to obstruct investigation and prosecution for years.

Yet the pressure of the gentiles and the federal government finally required that someone be punished. John D. Lee, who was unquestionably important in the massacre itself, was made to bear the whole guilt, although it is hard to see why he was any more guilty than a number of others. He was sentenced by a federal court and shot to death on the scene of the original butchery on March 25, 1877, after a moving final address in which he confessed his faith "in the gospel that was taught in its purity by Joseph Smith, in former days," and declared: "I have been sacrificed in a cowardly, dastardly manner."[7] Lee's resentment of Brigham Young and the church leadership, who evidently felt he must be abandoned to protect the community at large, is quite understandable. He had in many other respects rendered great service to the Mormon movement and had shown himself a man of ability.

The Utah War itself ended in anticlimax. President Buchanan had sent peace commissioners to the Territory as well as troops, and Brigham Young accepted from them the President's pardon for his "rebellion" and in effect concluded peace. The Saints returned to their homes and their peaceful activities, and the war was over.

Most important, however, was the struggle within the Territory and between the Mormons and aroused gentiles throughout the nation on the issue of polygamy, with which Utah's admission to statehood soon became inextricably involved. From the beginning, plural marriage was an open secret in Utah. It was announced to the general membership for the first time at a conference held in Salt Lake City on August 28, 1852, which was publicized in a special edition of the *Deseret News* on September 14. Up to that time, Mormon missionaries abroad had denied the fact, although practicing the new marriage form themselves. This special edition of the Mormon journal printed the official public announcement of the secret revelation of Joseph Smith in 1843 and addresses by Brigham Young, Heber C. Kimball, and John Taylor. For many, the new doctrine was hard to take, but it caused no major rift, as it had in Nauvoo, where it was basic to the destruction of Mormon accomplishments in that area.

Tales of immoral practices and rumors of Mormon separatism prompted the federal government to keep troops in Utah. In 1856 the Republican party platform had coupled polygamy with slavery as the "twin relics of barbarism." While the blunder of Buchanan in sending federal troops actually won sympathy for the Mormons in the States, the news of Mountain Meadows increased suspicion. Moreover, the gentile population began to increase in the Territory, especially with the discovery of minerals in the autumn of 1863 and the completion of the railroad in 1869, and, as the decade came to a close, a conscious gentile group was emerging. This situation found legislative expression in the passage by Congress of the Morrill "anti-bigamy law" in 1862 "to punish the practice of polygamy in the territories." The importance of this law lay in the fact that legislative measures were finally accepted by Congress as the proper way to deal with the "peculiar institution." In Utah the law remained inoperative, for no grand jury in Utah would indict men for this offense. The decade also saw further anti-Mormon legislation under congressional discussion.

In Utah, local conflict continued to grow. The Mormons kept up the pretense of the state of Deseret and held annual elections to a state legislature which had the same members as the legal territorial legislature and which met with Brigham Young after listening to the federal appointee. Moreover, Mormondom suffered internal dissent as well. A new prophet who had joined the church in England, Joseph Morris, claimed to be setting up a true church. He gathered some five hundred members and produced a scripture, *The Spirit Prevails*, which is the longest piece of latter-day revelation (664 pp.) and is reminiscent of early Christian heresies. After inner and outer contention, the Morrisites refused to submit to the demands of the Mormon militia acting on a writ of the governor, and the militia in a posse of about five hundred attacked the heretical settlement in Weber Canyon, where Morris was shot. The sect broke into dissenting groups, going first to Idaho, then to Nevada and California. Several later prohets came forward, the most important of which was one George Williams, who was called "Cainan."

More serious, perhaps, was the defection, in 1868 and 1869, of several men of importance in the church, among them William S. Godbe, E. L. T. Harrison, E. W. Tullidge, Eli B. Kelsey, Henry W. Lawrence, and T. B. H. Stenhouse. These educated elders, many of whom were polygamists, objected to the totalitarian claims of the priesthood resting upon Brigham's claim as ruler of the kingdom. They themselves claimed communication with the spirit world and took a position which for Godbe and some of the others developed into spiritualism. As businessmen, they objected to the economic policies of the church and advocated Mormon interest in mining, which Brigham Young had sought to restrain within the limits useful to an agricultural society, as he had earlier opposed Mormon gold-seeking in California. Godbe and Harrison later said that the spirits had advocated mining. Most of all, they were opposed to the strict control of Brigham over all aspects of life, and they found the doctrines of Mormonism crude and sought to reinterpret them in a more spiritual (actually, spiritualistic) direction. They founded the *Utah Magazine* in 1868, and somewhat later the *Tribune*, which soon, however, passed into gentile hands. The group also opposed the boycott of gentile and apostate merchants carried on by the church leadership.

This last movement—the boycott—marked a sharpening of the Mormon-gentile conflict and its spread to the economic field. It was based upon a policy of non-intercourse with gentiles and was intended to drive their businesses to failure. It was not successful, however, since, by the mid-sixties, the Mormon church was not able to enforce this sort of discipline upon its members. Though "counseled" to boycott, many Saints did not obey. The Mormon leadership then launched a co-operative movement to keep trade under church control. Zion's Cooperative Mercantile Institution was founded in 1868 and, if started earlier, might have strengthened Mormon exclusiveness and the position of the leadership. The movement placed co-operative stores even in outlying regions and was at first received with considerable enthusiasm as an expression of the Mormon co-operative tradition. After the coming of the railroad, however, the semimonopoly of merchants was destroyed, and the need for such action more or less disappeared.

The leaders of the "New Movement," as the Godbeite schism was called, were finally excommunicated. They continued to hold meetings for some time and attracted much Mormon interest, but some of them eventually returned to the church while others joined the Utah gentiles against their former friends. While the movement lasted, gentiles, including Schuyler Colfax, Vice-President of the United States, were in open sympathy with it, while apostate Mormon merchants contributed financial aid.

One other event temporarily shook official Mormondom in the 1860's. Two sons of Joseph Smith, Alexander H. and David H., the "child of prediction," were sent to Utah by the Reorganized Church. Would Brigham stand aside, now that Joseph's sons had come to Zion? Not unless they came into the true gospel on the path recognized by the priesthood of the Utah church. The two men interviewed Brigham, who informed them that their mother was "the damnedest liar that lives," and preached in the city, but their effect appears in the long run to have been superficial.

The next decade, the 1870's, which saw such a sizable increase in the gentile population with the steady development of mining in gentile hands, began with the founding of the Liberal party at the all-gentile town of Corinne, Utah. The party put forward some Mormon candidates in the Salt Lake City biennial election but managed to get only about three hundred of some twenty-three hundred votes cast. Throughout this period the conflict found ample journalistic expression in the *Tribune* (first a Mormon opposition and then a gentile paper) and the Mormon *Deseret News*, as well as in such earlier gentile and anti-Mormon papers as the *Vedette*.

While the conflict continued within Utah between the anti-Mormon, antistatehood Liberal party and the Mormon People's party, on the one hand, and between federal officials and local people, on the other, the gentiles throughout the nation became ever more interested and involved. Protestant churchmen and aroused gentile ladies launched a nation-wide campaign against the "Asiatic Church" and the "degrading bondage" of women. Local evangelical efforts to convert Mormons back to Protestant Christianity, while not generally successful, raised the pitch of conflict to unprecedented heights. Congregationalists, Methodists, and Presbyterians considered Mormonism a threat to American morals and saw in the doctrine and practice of polygamy an institution especially to be combated. Mormonism was a challenge to the missionary zeal of these groups. Catholics were the largest gentile religious group in Utah, but they lived their own lives and took little part in the conflict between the other gentiles and the Saints. While Protestant schools tried to evangelize the children of the Saints, the gentile ladies through their organizations built a home for polygamous wives who cared to escape from their bondage. Few Mormon women availed themselves of this philanthropy, and the Industrial Home of Utah remained a touching monument to the "Christian but undenominational" energy of American women. While these developments kept Utah in turmoil, they were perhaps more important in arousing a righteous—a self-righteous—public opinion in the States against the Mormon experiment.

There were really two sets of courts in Utah, the probate

courts controlled locally (that is, by Mormons) and the district courts where the three members of the supreme court, federally appointed, sat as judges of lower courts in their own districts. Under these difficulties and with the added problems of getting an indictment from a grand jury, the federal officials, many of whom were extremely hostile to Mormonism and its institutions, continued to try to prosecute polygamy. In fact, polygamy became for Mormon and non-Mormon alike the mark of peculiarity around which the energies of both contending forces converged. In 1874 George Reynolds was convicted of bigamy after a trial that may have grown out of collusion between church and federal authorities to produce a test case. Whether or not this is the fact is not easy to determine. Although Reynolds was found guilty in April, 1875, the territorial supreme court set aside the conviction for technical reasons. He was tried again and again found guilty in December and was sentenced to two years' imprisonment at hard labor and a five-hundred-dollar fine, a heavier sentence and fine than had been imposed at the first trial. The case was appealed to the Supreme Court of the United States, which heard the arguments in 1878, rendering its decision in January, 1879.

This important case set the precedent for the convictions that were soon to follow. The Supreme Court, in view of the defense which Reynolds made, using religious belief to justify his marriage behavior, asked itself "whether religious belief can be accepted as a justification of an overt act made criminal by the law of the land." Pointing out that Congress cannot prohibit the free exercise of religion in territories, the court further asked: "What is the religious freedom which has been guaranteed?" After a review of English and American common and civil law with regard to religion and marriage, it concluded with regard to the latter: "In the face of all this evidence, it is impossible to believe that the constitutional guaranty of religious freedom was intended to prohibit legislation in respect to this most important feature of social life." Of marriage, the court further declared: "Upon it society may be said to be built." Precedent combined with public policy to justify congressional action. Concluded the court: "In our opinion, the statute immediately under consideration is within the legislative power of Congress." The "anti-bigamy act" of 1862 was constitutional.

But, asked the court, are "those who make polygamy a part of their religion . . . excepted from the operation of the statute?" To this the court replied in the negative: "This would be introducing a new element into criminal law. Laws are made for the government of actions, and while they cannot interfere with mere religious belief and opinions, they may with practices. Suppose one believed that human sacrifices were a necessary part of religious worship, would it be seriously contended that the civil government under which he lived could not interfere to prevent a sacrifice? Or if a wife religiously believed it was her duty to burn herself upon the funeral pile of her dead husband, would it be beyond the power of the civil government to prevent her carrying her belief into practice?"

The reply of the court is unambiguous: "So here, as a law of the organization of society under the exclusive dominion of the United States, it is provided that plural marriages shall not be allowed. Can a man excuse his practices to the contrary because of his religious belief? To permit this would be to make the professed doctrines of religious belief superior to the law of the land, and in effect to permit every citizen to become a law unto himself. Government could exist only in name under such circumstances."[8]

By the end of the 1870's the whole country was aroused against polygamy, and the hour of showdown was approaching. Despite the conviction of Reynolds, Utah gentiles felt that more stringent legislation would be necessary. Yet in the last years of the decade Congress debated but passed no new laws. In 1882, however, Senator George Edmunds of Vermont sponsored a bill that not only disfranchised polygamists and made plural marriage a crime but also established an electoral commission to supervise Utah's voting. The more extreme gentiles considered the bill too mild, although it actually provided for action against "unlawful cohabitation" in cases where marriage could not be proved. The gentile extremists wanted outright federal rule of Utah, preferably by a commission of Utah gentiles. Nonetheless, the anti-Mormon forces in the Territory genuinely rejoiced when the bill was finally passed in 1882.

The federal net was slowly closing. In 1874 the Poland Bill had reduced the power of the Mormon-controlled courts, and in the same year John D. Lee was brought to trial, and the church leadership was sufficiently on the defensive to desert him. Now, with animosities aroused on both sides, the battle raged around polygamy and admission to statehood. In 1882 the Mormons held another constitutional convention and, as at the previous conventions in 1850, 1856, 1862, and 1872, asked for statehood. It was, of course, to no avail, and in 1884 Rudger Clawson was sentenced to four years in the penitentiary under the Edmunds law of 1882, which the Supreme Court upheld in 1885. The final conflict had begun.

President Hayes declared in 1880 that it was a duty "to suppress polygamy," and in 1881 President Arthur called plural marriage an "odious crime."[9] James G. Blaine compared the peculiar institution to "the claim of certain heathen tribes, if they should come among us, to continue the rite of human sacrifice."[10] There were some Mormon apostates who succumbed to the pressure—what Kimball Young has called a "constant trickle"—and the rank and file, perhaps often less than completely convinced about the new marriage system that went against so much in the background of Mormonism, were uneasy. Yet the leadership stood firm. Polygamy was a revelation, it was a divine commandment, and by it the church would stand or fall. Raids and arrests were met by the "Mormon Underground," which was nothing less than a hidden set of institutions designed by the Mormons to conceal persons and facilitate their escape from pursuing federal officials. Some families were dispersed to different areas, wives were sometimes sent back to their parents, some polygamists left the Territory to settle in Mexico and Canada or to do mission work abroad, while the leadership went into hiding, often under elaborately organized protection, as in the case of President John Taylor, who died in hiding in 1887. The underground resorted to false names, made use of disguises and other tricks, and developed spying and signaling and other methods of meeting the federal drive.

To make matters worse, Congress passed the Edmunds-Tucker Act, which became law in March, 1887, when President Cleveland neglected to sign or to veto the measure. It was a bill, in short, to make more stringent the earlier Edmunds law. The Corporation of the Church of Jesus Christ of Latter-day Saints was dissolved, woman suffrage was abolished, and a more inclusive voters' registration oath demanded. The church was shaken to its foundation, and, with the death of President Taylor, compromise sentiment began to make itself felt. In June, 1887, a year when almost two hundred Mormons were in jail and many more in hiding, another constitutional convention met in Salt Lake City. At this convention Mormons who still had the vote took the initiative in introducing and passing Article XV, Section 12, which made polygamy a misdemeanor punishable by fine and imprisonment. This constitution was subsequently approved by the electorate by an overwhelming vote. The Republican members of a federal commission appointed to study the situation felt that the Mormons should be made to "manifest by their future acts that they have abandoned polygamy in good faith."[11] The Democratic minority felt that the Saints were sincere. Mormon sentiment itself was anxious to give up the struggle and settle into a more normal way of life.

In September, 1890, the new president of the Mormon church, Wilford Woodruff, issued his "manifesto" declaring: "Inasmuch as laws have been enacted by Congress forbidding plural marriages, which laws have been pronounced constitutional by the court of last resort, I hereby declare my intention to submit to those laws, and to use my influence with the members of the Church over which I preside to have them do likewise."[12] Mormon separatism had been defeated, and when in 1896 Utah was admitted to the Union, a Mormon political ambition of forty-six years' standing was achieved amid the defeat of the peculiar Mormon dream of their own Zion in the mountains. There had been 573 convictions for plural marriage (most of them—557—under the unlawful cohabitation provision, Sec. 3, of the Edmunds Act), and perhaps over $1,000,000 worth of property, including $400,000 in cash, had been taken away from the disincorporated church. Israel without a Cyrus had succumbed to Babylon. Its only recourse was to adhere to its new master. This it soon did, for, although there was at first a last stand of the polygamists in the closed councils of church leadership, they soon gave way before the new trend, and Mormonism accommodated itself and became reincorporated within the American community from which it had gradually and half-consciously seceded.

The Mormon Experience: Its Social and Historical Structure

In the decades that intervened between its withdrawal from the secular society at its birth and its reincorporation into that society with President Woodruff's manifesto, Mormonism displayed several important social and historical processes. These wrought within it a great transformation and became the distinctive ingredients of a unique Mormon experience. There remains here but to indicate summarily the structure of these processes, whose content and interrelations have been treated previously.

The first and most obvious was that of withdrawal itself, a process that began when the first followers exposed themselves to disapproval and ridicule by their acceptance of the new prophet and his golden bible. Withdrawal was more than a single act; it was a continuing and developing affair, with respect to both the relationship to the larger society and the content of Mormon internal relations themselves. With the removal of the Saints to Kirtland, withdrawal took on two positive characteristics that it continued to display throughout Mormon history. The "gathered" identified their fellowship with a definite and separate piece of land; the attachment to a Mormon homeland was established. At the same time, the promulgation of the co-operative ideal in the Law of Consecration supplied positive ethical and social content to the inner group life that was to be associated with such a separate homeland. Thus in Kirtland in the first years—even in the very first year—a distinctive social ethic, a separate geographical location, and a separated community were established as fundamental characteristics of Mormon life. "The Gathering" as Mormonism's basic doctrine took on concrete form.

The "gathered" condition provided the base for a further development of Mormon distinctness in three important spheres: in that of values, in the internal structure of the Mormon fellowship, and in the relations between Mormonism and the larger community. The idea of a separated Mormon group with its own territorial integrity developed into the notion of a promised land in Missouri, with the construction there of a divinely appointed, holy city. Frustrated by the ensuing conflict, the Saints next attempted to realize this ideal in Nauvoo, where success, if brief, was brilliant. Defeat in Illinois was followed by success in Utah, where the conception of Zion expanded beyond that of a single city to what might be called imperial dimensions and where distance from the older settled areas and unity of effort and social relations over a wide expanse combined to make a genuine homeland out of the intermountain region. Moreover, the tasks of settling this vast area gave ample opportunity for a redevelopment of the distinctive Mormon social ethic as the content of the separated way of life.

Within this developing separation, Mormonism elaborated its own ideas and values, its own theological innovations, and its own socioeconomic and familial ethic. This development not only provided the distinctive content of the fellowship of the gathered but also served to distinguish the Saints from their gentile fellows both in their own minds and in those of the gentiles. A separate Mormon community with its own peculiar culture was evolving out of the original situation of separation, that very separation providing the occasions for the increasing development of separateness.

Yet, from the very start, Mormons attempted both to be gathered out of Babylon unto the New Jerusalem which their efforts were creating and to remain within the political structure of the larger community. All America was in some sense Zion. The New World, the North American continent, the territory of the United States, the political institutions of the Republic—all these participated to some degree in the chosen and divinely designated quality of the new Zion, although that quality was present in its undiminished plenitude only in the Mormon community itself. Yet the Mormon Zion, peculiar and gathered, would remain a part of the United States and of the particular state in which it was located. The Mormons tried to combine secession from the secular community with citizenship in the American commonwealth. This aspiration reached its legal formulation in the Nauvoo Charter, which made the Mormon city a state within the state.

The simultaneity of withdrawal from and participation in the larger secular community did not, as we have seen, prove workable. The presence of an exclusive body convinced of its own unique role in relation to the region—to wit, to make it a holy city for itself—with its own distinctive beliefs and ethic, resulted inevitably in intergroup conflict. The result was the Saints' expulsion from Jackson County, the Mormon War at Far West, and the second war at Nauvoo.

If this situation proved unworkable in the long run, it did, nevertheless, offer ample opportunity for the consolidation of the peculiar Mormon community, distinctive in all three spheres—values, internal structure, and relations with outsiders. It was not surprising that failure to make a *modus vivendi* of the coexistence of secession and inclusion was followed by the attempt to build a genuinely separated Mormon community in the arid lands of Utah. Even there, as we have seen, isolation was never complete, and, as we shall see presently, a conscious program of political secession never became genuine Mormon policy. Yet an attempt was made in effect to build a separated Mormon commonwealth, and its real, if incomplete, isolation changed its relationships with hostile gentiles, who gradually encircled and infiltrated the Mormon Empire itself.

In the Middle West the Mormons were always newcomers—always spiritually squatters upon lands interstitial to older gentile settlements. In the West, they were first settlers, always a majority, possessing the sense of first identification with the new Territory, its history and its institutions. They may have developed a minority mentality in relation to the rest of the country where public opinion was aroused against them, but in Utah they were first settlers, the pioneers. Utah was Zion. The nation might reincorporate Mormondom into itself, but it could not break the primary association of the intermountain region with Mormon self-consciousness. It could not dislodge the Saints or make them feel strangers. In 1857, when Mormons started to scorch the earth and evacuate northern Utah, this identification may not yet have been complete; but Mormon success in that "defeat" testified to the basic strength of the Mormon identification.

This combination of distinctive values, separated and peculiar social institutions, and geographical segregation, strengthened by three "Mormon wars" and constant Mormon-gentile conflict, was always reinforced by the total nature of the Mormon cultural environment. Church, civic community, family, education—in short, those institutional forms generally decisive for the formation of outlook and the shaping of character—were all dominated by Mormon values and a world view becoming progressively more distinct. Isolation and the orientation to building a sacred community here and now guaranteed that this would be the case. Moreover, the intermittent purging of dissent, whether Cowdery, Rigdon, the splinter groups after the murder of Joseph, the withdrawal of those who refused to follow Brigham to Utah, the Morrisites in the West, or the New Movement of the Godbeites, strengthened internal unity among those who remained. While wars and intergroup hostility generally strengthened group allegiance, splintering and excommunication removed possible sources of division.

During this time the sufferings of persecution and war, the hardships incident to constructive effort, the western exodus itself—all these, together with the development of a peculiar religious system of belief, gave birth to a Mormon tradition. To the peculiar institutions and values of Mormonism was added the poignant self-perception of a chosen people, enshrined in common experiences which provided the stuff of a sacred history and in an image of themselves evoking dedicated identification.

The Mormons had acted upon the biblical model of Israel—had chosen to emulate the example of a holy nation—and in so doing had found themselves in circumstances that rendered such emulation more than mere symbolic commemoration. Indeed, they found themselves cut off, embattled, defeated and victorious, wandering; they had plunged into a historic maelstrom that was making of them a people apart, separated by the ever widening chasm of divergent values and history from their fellow Americans. The Saints had withdrawn from Babylon to build the modern Zion. Owing to circumstances over which they had but little control but which in part their own character and action created, history provided them the concrete setting for a re-enactment of the Israelitish parallel. For sixteen years they were driven about, attempting four times to build their holy city. Their number, the extent and duration of their suffering, and the way in which defeat several times crowned the most palpable successes combined to transform the bread and water of sectarian affliction into the real presence of potential nationality.

What had begun as a sectarian religious group, through its emulation of the Old Testament Hebrews in the unsettled conditions of the Middle and Far West, had been transformed into the Mormon people. The Saints had not achieved territorial monopoly of power and influence; but they more than compensated for this lack by the nature of their common experience, which developed in them strong group solidarity. Mormonism had indeed gone from "near-sect" to "near-nation." The Mormons had not merely avoided becoming a small isolated sect; they had developed so far away from that possibility that they almost became a separate nationality.

The reality of such quasi-nationality becomes clear when we make the "thought experiment," to use Galileo's term, of imagining what might have happened if two major historical events had occurred otherwise than as they did. Suppose the Mexican War had not taken place and that upper California had remained Mexican territory. How long would it have taken a growing and expanding Mormondom, with its own seaport, its economic autarchy, its theocratic political autonomy, to repeat the Texan experience and set itself up as an independent government? Whether such an independent Mormon entity would have proved immune to American infiltration, after the discovery of gold in California, is another question. Suppose in a second instance that the Confederacy had achieved its aims in the Civil War. Would not this precedent have elicited from Mormonism a similar attempt to assert independence, at first probably inside the loose federal structure and later perhaps outside it? It is not hard to imagine the large-scale repetition of "bloody Kansas," if Yankees, bitter over the recent defeat, attempted to assert sovereignty over the intermountain region.

But there is, in fact, no necessity to engage in such futile attempts to manipulate historical factors. The long-drawn-out, last-ditch policy of President Taylor in the 1880's, following upon the earlier struggle of the School of the Prophets to resist economic integration, bears ample testimony to the potentialities for separation that slumbered within Mormonism. A common homeland, a common culture, a common religion, common social institutions, a deeply felt common tradition, and the self-image of a separate and divinely chosen group with its own peculiar destiny —of such stuff is nationality born. In the Mormon case these possibilities stopped short of full national entity. Yet they sought political expression in the attempt to gain the limited sovereignty of a state in the federal Union, a state that embraced a tremendous area.

Despite the marked and genuine peculiarity of Mormonism, however, its typical American quality is no less real; for here is one of the great paradoxes of the Mormon experience. The Mormon group came closer to evolving an ethnic identity on this continent than did any other comparable group. Moreover, it was a genuine, locally and independently conceived, ethnicity, born and nurtured on this side of the water and not imported from abroad. Yet it also has been "an America in miniature."

The chief processes of American history have been repeated within the smaller context of the peculiar Mormon experience. The original colonization and breaking of the wilderness was re-experienced not once but several times. The development of political self-government and the conflict with the mother political institutions were also experienced in Mormonism. The development of group self-consciousness associated with the new continent, its problems and characteristics, was a general American experience which Mormons repeated within their own idiosyncratic setting. The attraction of immigrants from Europe and the utopianism associated with it found theological expression and organized implementation in Mormon history. The process of assimilation to a native English-speaking culture was carried out even more rapidly in Utah than in the country generally. The experience of westward movement that Turner saw as strategically influential in the formation of the United States was certainly of tremendous significance in the formation of Mormon character, culture, and institutions.

When we add to these historical processes the fact that in its values Mormonism offers an analogous spectacle of distinction and similarity, the strange combination of peculiarity and typicality stands out as the most striking Mormon characteristic. Mormonism, in many respects the most American of religions, is also the only one to carry out a prolonged conflict with American institutions and to have displayed potentialities for separate national development.

The manifesto of Wilford Woodruff reincorporated Mormonism into the United States. In the first years of the present century, Mormonism pursued a policy that has been best described as "accommodation." The Mormon church tried to show itself genuinely patriotic and strove to meet the expectations of the now dominant gentile milieu. Older peculiarities were played down. Polygamy and distinctive economic ethics were given up. Yet even at this time the church tried to preserve its separate identity and to remain unobtrusively "gathered" while still a part of the larger nation. When the depression came to Utah in the 1930's, the Mormons met it with their own economic experimentation (which we shall discuss presently). But let us note here that this Mormon Welfare Plan gave separate and distinct expression to Mormon efforts to aid their own people and organized separate Mormon projects for that end.

In the last three decades a Mormon migration eastward has become noticeable. This interesting reversal of a long-term trend of Mormon movement saw the establishment of Mormon groups in many eastern cities. In 1950 there were some thirty-five thousand Mormons in New York City. In the depression years, Chicago Mormons operated a huge Welfare Plan farm. In 1953, the Saints in Cambridge, Massachusetts, started the construction of a chapel for Mormon students at Harvard and other colleges and universities in the area. Moreover, westward movement did not stop, Mormons were and are prominent in the great continuing migration to California, and in 1956 they dedicated the most expensive of Mormon religious structures, the Los Angeles temple.

At the same time there has arisen a large Mormon middle class in business, education, and government. In 1956 there were some two thousand Latter-day Saints in college and university education and in school administration. Mormonism today faces the problem of prosperity and of assimilation in a new form. Yet, so far, Mormonism in winning a new respectability has managed to preserve its genuine peculiarity.

One development of note has been the building of temples outside the United States and its territories. The recent dedication of a Swiss temple testifies to the first stage in the separation of the Mormon notion of Zion and the gathering from a definite piece of land and from the New World. A more abstract, more spiritualized, conception of the gathering, in which a Mormon way of life is seen as possible without physical removal to and residence in a Mormon community in America, is developing. A unique concatenation of circumstances and aspects of its own values and structure enabled Mormonism to escape the common sectarian fate of reaching early stabilization and stagnating in isolation, a fate that overcame many similar utopian groupings. Instead, there evolved the Mormon people and the Mormon culture area of today.

CHAPTER SIX

The Values of Mormonism

Mormonism is the product of a time when common men were beginning to conceive great expectations for self-improvement based upon individual effort and of a place where such expectations were infused with millennial aspirations and made more poignant by the emotionalism of enthusiastic religion. It developed and grew in the context of its own self-consciousness, its strong group loyalty reinforced by its belief in its own peculiarity and its special covenant. This covenant involved a commitment to build a separate commonwealth for the gathering of the elect. Mormon expectations were projected upon the task of building Zion, which channeled Mormon energies into mundane constructive effort.

This effort, carried on with an attitude of exclusiveness, evoked strong resentment among non-Mormon neighbors, resentment that resulted in violent conflict. The resulting exerience of conflict and persecution strengthened the very convictions of peculiarity and exclusiveness that had contributed so much to their cause. Constructive effort, conflict, victory, and defeat marked the two decades of activity from Kirtland to Nauvoo, decades during which Mormonism was part of the general movement of settling the Middle West but still quite separate and distinct, with its own conscious objectives and separate loyalties.

With failure in Nauvoo, Mormonism moved west to final victory, moving together with and yet separate from the rest of the nation, sharing the challenges and lessons of pioneers, but perceiving them from the angle of its own peculiarity. In fact, this very peculiarity and separateness gave the Mormons a sharper sense of historic mission. Manifest destiny became the fulfilment of Old Testament prophecy of Zion in the mountains. Moreover, the close personal integration into the church community lent a heightened intensity to the Mormon experience and gave it added personal relevance. Religious fellowship and religious sanctions came to be the supporting bulwarks of earthly empire-building. The belief in the perfectibility of man through human effort on the new continent and the infectious current belief in progress took on religious expression in theological and creedal innovation. The importance of the secular was enhanced while, simultaneously, secular concerns were integrated into an over-all theological context from which they derived special significance.

Starting from the position of the *Book of Mormon,* a position that added to accepted doctrine the revolutionary notion of restored revelation while supplementing the older canon of Holy Writ with a new scripture, Mormonism continued to evolve. The intense experiences of construction and conflict, which increased the consciousness of separateness, led Mormon innovation further and further away from the positions of traditional Protestant Christianity, while the common American experience, in which the Mormons participated in their own way, introduced Mormon religious thinking to ideas and sentiments current in the secular milieu. The result was a new religious doctrine, a new world view, compounding traditional Christian and current secular themes in a religious creed that found expression in and reinforcement from the separated society and peculiar experience of the "gathered." It is this world view, its definition of existence and of the meaning of human effort, that is set forth here.

The Origin and Nature of the Universe

The theology of the Church of Jesus Christ of Latter-day Saints denies the tenet of orthodox Christianity that God created the world *ex nihilo.* It considers that "the elements are eternal" (*D & C*, 93:33) and uncreated. It holds: "There is no such thing as immaterial matter. All spirit is matter, but it is more fine or pure, and can only be discerned by purer eyes" (*D & C*, 131:7). An *"immaterial being* is a contradiction in terms. Immateriality is only another name for nothing. It is the negative of all existence. A *spirit* is as much *matter* as oxygen or hydrogen."

Of these eternal elements, some "are tangible or visible, and others invisible. Those which are tangible to our senses, we call physical: those which are more subtle and refined, we call spiritual." The eternity of matter and spirit means not only that the elements are uncreated but also that they are indestructible. "Of one thing the Gospel, as well as science, is perfectly certain, that the energy in the universe is indestructible. . . . Like matter, energy had no beginning and can have no end."[1] Intelligence as well as energy is uncreated and indestructible. "Intelligence, or the light of truth, was not created or made, neither indeed can be" (*D & C*, 93:29).

In one particular, however, the Gospel goes beyond the teachings of modern science. The Gospel teaches that associated with the universal energy that vivifies universal matter, and possibly identified with it, is universal intelligence, a force which is felt wherever matter and energy are found, which is everywhere. The forces of the universe do not act blindly, but are expressions of a universal intelligence.[2]

It has been suggested that the Holy Spirit supplies this intelligence to matter: "It [the Holy Spirit] is the most active matter in the universe, producing all its operations according to fixed definite laws enacted by itself, in conjunction with the Father and Son."

"That a degree of intelligence is possessed by every particle of energized matter cannot be said; nor is it important. The great consideration is that, since intelligence is everywhere present, all the operations of nature, from the simplest to the most complex, are the products of intelligence."[3]

This uncreated world of intelligence and matter is not a static but a dynamic one. "And as one earth shall pass away, and the heavens thereof, even so shall another come; and there is no end to my works, neither to my words."[4] And it is a place of order and not of chaos. "And again, verily I say unto you, he hath given a law unto all things, by which they move in their times and their seasons" (*D & C*, 88:42). In such a universe: "The innumerable interactions of the matter, energy and intelligences of the universe must be held together by some great law." What is this great law, the basic principle of a universe so conceived?

Constant action or movement characterizes the universe. The multiplicity of actions upon each other, of the various forms of matter, energy and intelligence, composing the universe, must cause an equal multiplicity of effects. Moreover, increasing intelligent wills, acting upon matter and energy, must and do produce an increasing series of reactions among the forces of the universe.

Moreover, each new set of effects becomes the cause of still other effects. Thus, in our universe, as we conceive it to be constituted, increasing complexity would seem to be the resultant law of the operation of universal forces. This is the great law of nature, to which every living thing must conform, if it is to be in harmony with all other living things.[5]

Thus, through a radical repudiation of creationism, Mormonism arrives at the conception of an eternal universe, of which intelligence and energy are the two chief characteristics. Moreover, this conception of the universe is one of an ongoing process characterized by increasing complexity.

God: His Nature and Place in the Universe

In such a universe God is seen as a part of the world of time and space. "The true God exists both in time and in space, and has as much relation to them as man or any other being."[6] Furthermore, "God's time, angel's time, prophet's time, and man's time" are declared to be "according to the planet on which they reside" (*D & C*, 130:4). Joseph Smith asked: "What sort of a being was God in the beginning?" And he answered: "God himself was once as we are now, and is an exalted man and sits enthroned in yonder heavens."[7]

In the *Book of Mormon* itself there is already a concrete conception of God somewhat anthropomorphic in implication. Yet this was little more than the literalness of evangelical Protestantism. But in the new conception of a God who has developed in power and stature, there is a complete break with older Christian notions of Godhead. Earlier Joseph had declared of God "that he was God before the world was created . . . that he changes not, neither is there variableness with him; but he is the same yesterday, today and forever; and that his course is one eternal round without variation."[8]

This doctrine was made even more concrete by Brigham Young: "When our father Adam came into the Garden of Eden, He came into it with a celestial body, and brought Eve one of his wives with him. He helped to make and organize this world. He is Michael the Archangel, the Ancient of Days! about whom holy men have written and spoken. He is our Father and our God, and the only God with whom we have to do. Every man upon the earth, professing Christians or non-professing, must hear it, and will know it sooner or later."[9] Said Brigham at a later date: "I have learned by experience that there is but one God that pertains to this people, and he is the God that pertains to this earth, the first man." This innovation went too far for Mormon taste, for many disbelieved it.

Of Brigham's power there was no doubt, but of his inspiration there was some question, at least in matters that went against the teachings of Joseph Smith. In the prophet's writings there was already an identification of Michael and Adam (*D & C*, 27:11; 78:15–16, 107:54; 128:21), and in one place Adam is also called "ancient of days." Yet, for Joseph, Adam was clearly made by God and was not himself God. Orson Pratt openly disagreed with this new doctrine, and after some argument it was given up by Brigham, who thought it best to "lay it aside and not to teach it till the Saints were more fully prepared."[10] It was taken up again, but it never became firmly established; it is not taught today as official doctrine but is still believed by some Saints. Brigham Roberts declared that Adam "will eventually attain to the dignity of the governorship of this earth" and "be thus the God of this world."[11]

Mormon religious writers often speak of God in the same terms as those used in older, more traditional theologies, referring to omniscience, omnipotence, creation, etc. Yet obviously the meaning of these terms is to be understood in the context of Mormon developments. The creative function of God is conceived differently from that in orthodox Christian belief. For Mormonism, God's relation to the universe is not unlike that of man; God, like man, is subject to the law of progression:

As already said, God is the supreme intelligent Being in the universe, who has the greatest knowledge and the most perfected will, and who, therefore, possesses infinite power over the forces of the universe. However, if the great law of progression is accepted, God must have been engaged from the beginning, and must now be engaged in progressive development, and infinite as God is, he must have been less powerful in the past than he is today. . . . It is clear also that, as with every other being, the progress of God began with exercise of his will . . . until he attained at last a conquest over the universe which to our finite understanding seems absolutely complete. We may be certain that, through self-effort, the inherent and innate powers of God have been developed to a God-like degree. Thus he has become God.[12]

In the midst of this eternal, dynamic, self-complicating universe, God has developed to his present status through his own effort. In the place of the God of Christianity, Mormonism has developed the notion of a self-made deity, who through activism and effort has achieved a relative mastery over the world. In the place of the transcendent God of more orthodox faiths, Mormonism proclaims a God whose transcendence is merely relative to human perception and whose relatively transcendent position with regard to man and other uncreated elements of the universe is the result of a conquest. God is God because he has risen to "Godhood" by his own labor. God's relation to the world is that of a powerful artificer, a projection of the relation of American man to the American continent.

Yet intelligence is not a monopoly of God in this energized and intelligent universe. This doctrine must be understood in relation to Joseph's polytheistic innovations. The prophet's brief study of Hebrew was sufficient to acquaint him with the fact that Genesis uses a plural form in speaking of the Creator (though that plural is modified by singular adjectives and takes singular verbs). In his "translation" of what he called the Book of Abraham "from some papyri," Joseph spoke of "the Gods."

Although the papyri were discovered in 1835, the Book of Abraham did not appear until 1842. Yet Mormon doctrine had prepared for this innovation. In 1839, in Liberty jail, Joseph spoke of the "Eternal God of all other gods" (*D & C*, 121:32). The prophet suggested that Genesis had been badly translated, and he proposed that the first verse should read: "In the beginning the head of the Gods brought forth the Gods," or "The head of the Gods called the Gods together." The doctrine of the plurality of gods introduced other developing beings into the Mormon universe. Moreover, Mormon insistence on the materiality of God had reduced the Trinitarian doctrine of the three persons in one God to a conception of three separate gods (*D & C*, 130:22).

The *Book of Mormon*, in its one gesture toward Christology, identified the Son with the Father. We have seen that Mormonism arose in a situation in which Universalism—which denied the doctrine of the Trinity—was of some influence. Moreover, western New York had been affected by rationalism and unbelief. Mormonism had been directly influenced by the Campbellites, or Disciples of Christ. Alexander Campbell, probably influenced by Unitarian ideas, had declared that the word "Trinity" was unscriptural, an important statement to his listeners, but he insisted that Jesus was the Son of God.

Arbaugh in his study of Mormon revelation, which exaggerated Campbellite influence, also asserted that the effect of the sensate psychology of John Locke is an important factor in explaining the materialism of Mormon conceptions.[13] He sees related to that source the concrete nature of the visions of Joseph Smith in which God the Father, Christ, and various angels appear as men, and also the later development of tritheism and polytheism. Yet such an interpretation sounds excessively bookish. How else would common men visualize God? How else are visions reported in a great diversity of cultures? This is not to deny that the culture of New York may have imparted an extreme literalness and materiality to Joseph's reports of his visions. Yet anthropomorphism in the conception of God and especially in imagining what God might be like was certainly widespread and hardly seems to have been restricted to one sect or group. The same may be said with regard to a literal understanding of the Bible, which tended to support such human representations of God. Certainly the kind of ideas found in Locke's psychology were too widespread in America to be attributed to any one source in New York or Ohio. Yorker mentality, which exhibited worldly practicality together with religious enthusiasm and emotionality, possessed tendencies preparing the ground both for materialism and unbelief and for fervent faith and visionary experiences.

Mormonism developed both sides of these Yorker tendencies. It combined Trinitarianism and anti-Trinitarian confusions, and the result was tritheism. It combined materialism and visions, and the result was the conception of a God of flesh and bones, which later led to the doctrine of polytheism. It combined this-worldly hopes for a reformed society with the doctrine of the Second Coming of the Lord and produced the Mormon idea of building the kingdom on earth in preparation for the millennium. It combined secular progress and evangelical enthusiasm, and the result was eternal progression. It combined anthropomorphism and the universe of nineteenth-century science as common men were beginning to understand it, and the result was a finite God. These developments reconciled the contrarieties of the time and place in a creative eclecticism which, although it failed to achieve logical consistency, nevertheless possessed a cohesiveness of tendency and congruity of fundamental principle that rendered it a unified point of view. As the creed of a close-knit group who were experiencing common effort and suffering, it became a firmly believed religious faith.

While the discourses of Brigham Young never achieved canonical status among the "Standard Works" of the Mormon church and hence the Michael-Adam-God doctrine remains unofficial but often believed, Joseph Smith's Book of Abraham is accepted by the church and is an official source of doctrine. Polytheism was often played down in Mormon missionary work and is generally subordinated to a more traditional emphasis in Mormon religious teaching. Yet it remains a part of the Mormon conception.

In 1855 Parley P. Pratt declared:

Gods, angels and men, are all of the same species, one race, one great family widely diffused among the planetary systems, as colonies, kingdoms, nations, etc.

The great distinguishing difference between one portion of this race and another, consists in the varied grades of intelligence and purity, and also in the variety of spheres occupied by each, in a series of progressive being. . . .

It may then consistently enough be said, that there are in a subordinate sense, a plurality of Gods, or rather of sons of God; although there is one Supreme Head, who is over all, and through all, and in all His sons, by the power of His Spirit.[14]

Apostle John A. Widtsoe, writing some sixty years later, stated:

During the onward march of the Supreme Being, other intelligent beings were likewise engaged, though less vigorously, in acquiring power over the forces of the universe. . . . Next to God, there may be, therefore, other intelligent beings so nearly approaching his power as to be coequal with him in all things so far as our finite understanding can perceive. These beings may be immeasurably far from God in power, nevertheless immeasurably above us mortal men of the earth. Such intelligent beings are as Gods to us. Under this definition there may be a great number of intelligent beings who possess to a greater or lesser degree the quality of Godhood.[15]

Man and His Place in the Universe

"Man was also in the beginning with God" (*D & C*, 93:29). "Men and God are eternal intelligences, members of a vast society of eternal beings." "Eternal man lived a personal life before the earth-life began, and he continues a personal existence hereafter."[16]

Yet, while speaking of the eternity of man and the uncreatedness of intelligence, Mormonism also refers to man as an offspring of God, of man's "creation before the world was made" (*D & C*, 49:17). "Sometime in man's pre-earth existence, the Creator took the intelligence of man and gave it spiritual form. Man became a spirit, and God, the Father of our spirits."[17] There has even been speculation about a divine mother in connection with God's fatherhood. Eliza R. Snow, a Mormon poetess and plural wife of the prophet Joseph, has given expression to this idea in a poem that remains a sacred Mormon song and is retained in the Deseret Sunday School songbook.

> In the heav'ns are parents single?
> No! The tho't makes reason stare!
> Truth is reason; truth eternal
> Tells me I've a mother there.[18]

James E. Talmage, an authoritative spokesman for Mormon religious tenets, in an address before the San Francisco Congress of Religious Philosophies in 1915, called mankind "literally the sons and daughters of Divine Parents, the spiritual progeny of God, our Eternal Father, and of our God Mother." This doctrine did not achieve official status in the teachings of the Mormon church, although it is held by some members.

The Book of Abraham states that "if there be two spirits, and one shall be more intelligent than the other, yet these two spirits, notwithstanding one is more intelligent than the other, have no beginning; they existed before, they shall have no end, they shall exist after, for they are gnolaum, or eternal" (Abraham 3:18). Talmage, in a book that is recognized as an authoritative statement of Mormon doctrine, says:

While existence is eternal, and therefore to being there never was a beginning, never shall be an end, in a relative sense each stage of organization must have had a beginning, and to every phase of existence as manifested in each of the countless orders and classes of created things, there was a first as there will be a last; though every ending or consummation in nature is but the beginning of another stage of advancement.[19]

Widtsoe said of the primeval condition:

All that is really clear to the understanding is that man has existed "from the beginning" and that, from the beginning, he has possessed distinct individuality impossible of confusion with any other individuality among the hosts of intelligent beings. Through endless ages, man has risen by slow degrees to his present state.[20]

Not only is man eternal, but he is also the possessor of "Godlike attributes," which "need only cultivating, improving, developing, and advancing by means of a series of progressive changes, in order to arrive at the fountain 'Head,' the standard, the climax of Divine Humanity."[21] Man is of the same race as God and the gods. This was the meaning of the statement that early became proverbial among Latter-day Saints: "As man is now, God once was; as God is now, man may become."

Mormonism preserved its early emphasis upon human freedom and its repudiation of doctrines that defined man as sinful or corrupted by the Fall of Adam. The *Book of Mormon* declared: "Therefore, cheer up your hearts, and remember that ye are free to act for yourselves—to choose the way of everlasting death or the way of eternal life" (II Nephi 10:23). In 1830 Joseph reported that the Lord declared of man: "Behold, I gave unto him that he should be an agent unto himself" (*D & C*, 29:35). Talmage comments: "The Church holds and teaches as a strictly scriptural doctrine, that man has inherited among the inalienable rights conferred upon him by his divine Father, absolute freedom to choose the good or the evil in life as he may elect."[22]

Free and uncreated, the human individual, according to Parley Pratt, "in its heavenly home," where it resided before coming to this earth, "lived and moved as a free and rational intelligence, acting upon its own agency, and like all intelligence, independent in its own sphere. It was placed under certain laws, and was responsible to its great Patriarchal Head."[23]

Man came to earth by free choice in order to develop his knowledge further through experience with "gross matter" (Abraham 3:24–26). Mormonism speaks of a great council in heaven at which God proposed to man that he take mortality upon himself in order to advance in power and knowledge. "As the Supreme Being, God had in mind a plan, the Great Plan, whereby each spirit could enter upon his second estate and become acquainted with the properties of gross matter."[24] The plan was submitted to the spirits for their decision:

When the plans for creating and peopling the earth were under discussion in heaven, Satan sought to destroy the free agency of man, by obtaining power to force the human family to do his will, promising the Father that by such means he would redeem all mankind, and that not one of them would be lost. This proposition was rejected.[25]

It was on the rejection of this proposition of Lucifer that the prince of the morning rebelled and that he and his followers were driven out. From that time on, they have sought to make war against the accomplishment of the Great Plan. The original plan "to use persuasive influences of wholesome precept and sacrificing example with the inhabitants of the earth, then to leave them free to choose for themselves, was agreed upon, and the Only Begotten Son was chosen as the chief instrument in carrying that purpose into effect."[26] Thus man came to the earth to continue his development in this developing universe. Man,

as he gathers experience, becomes more powerful in using the forces of nature in the accomplishment of his purposes. With this thought in mind the great law [of increasing complexity] becomes a law of increasing power, of progressive mastery over the universe. For that reason, the law expressing the resultant of the activities of universal forces is often called the law of progression.

Widtsoe commented:

The law of progression is then a law of endless development of all the powers of man in the midst of a universe becoming increasingly complex. No more hopeful principle can be incorporated into a philosophy of life.[27]

Mormonism had early embraced an extreme Arminianism, placing great emphasis upon the freedom of the human will. This view became integrated with the belief in the goodness of human nature, accepting the rejection of Calvinist pessimism that came to characterize so much of American Protestantism. In its fully developed doctrine of man, it departed from even the most liberal of Protestant interpretations and came to accept an extra-Christian evolutionism of man's eternal development. Mormonism conceived the accomplishment of the plan of salvation as involving the Fall of Man, which appears as the inevitable concomitant of the earthly experience. Adam's sin, far from vitiating the human race, is seen as a necessary and foreordained part of the plan proposed at the great council.

It is evident that the Fall was foreordained, as a means whereby man could be brought face to face with both good and evil; that of his own agency he might elect the one or the other, and thus be prepared by the experiences of a mortal probation for the exaltation provided in a glorious plan of his creation.[28]

Rejecting the vitiating effects of original sin upon the human race, Joseph declared: "We believe that men will be punished for their own sins, and not for Adam's transgression."[29] Coming to earth as a free agent, man, as was foreseen by God, would sin, and from the beginning the Great Plan involved the coming of Christ who would atone for human sins. "Jesus actually came on earth . . . and . . . suffered death so that the act of Adam might be atoned for."[30] Moreover, "individual salvation or rescue from the effects of personal sins is to be acquired by each for himself, by faith and good works through the redemption wrought by Jesus Christ." In this way Mormonism preserves and reinterprets the doctrine of the Fall of Man and the Redemption by Christ.

Progression will not stop with death, but human progress will continue in the afterlife. There, too, it will depend upon intelligence and will. But, as progress in a lawful universe depends upon a proper knowledge of and use of laws, obedience to Mormon doctrine plays an important part in advancing man in his progress in this life. Joseph has the Lord declare in an early revelation: "For if you will that I give unto you a place in the celestial world, you must prepare yourselves by doing the things which I have commanded you and required of you" (D & C, 78:7). Knowledge, too, is necessary, for "without knowledge we cannot be saved." "A man is saved no faster than he gets knowledge, for if he does not get knowledge, he will be brought into captivity by some evil power in the other world, as evil spirits will have more knowledge, and consequently more power than many men who are on the earth. Hence it needs revelation to assist us, and give us knowledge of the things of God."[31] Knowledge gained here will be carried beyond the grave.

About the afterlife three degrees of glory have been revealed— celestial, terrestrial, and telestial. Latter-day Saints, to whom is given the knowledge of the full gospel, possess an obvious advantage in gaining greater glory in the world to come. But "through the Atonement of Christ, all mankind may be saved, by obedience to the laws and ordinances of the Gospel." Consistent with its emphasis on free will, Mormonism continued its earlier insistence upon works, as seen in the Book of Mormon. "All men share in the redemption of the human race by Christ. Thus all may partake in the plan of general salvation. This opens the way for the salvation of the individual which will depend upon his own efforts here below." "Through Adam man was brought on earth, subject to death; through Jesus, the Christ, he was lifted out of death to continue an eternal life in association with an earth-acquired body." Thus is the Atonement given a central place in Mormon doctrine, despite the greatly altered context in which it is understood. Moreover, the traditional doctrine of the resurrection of the body is preserved. "The purpose of the earth career was, however, twofold, to learn to understand gross matter, and to acquire a body made of the essence of such matter. The bodies laid in the grave must, therefore, be raised again."

This is a doctrine of man's essential goodness. "There is judgment ordained for all, and all will be judged 'according to their works.' "[32] Yet sectarian advantage is preserved in the greater knowledge of the Saints and their special task in building the kingdom. Moreover, in an earlier day this doctrine of progression was closely integrated with polygamy. Progress to "Godhood" was understood to be related to numerous progeny. Sealing ceremonies in the temple bound people together, husbands and wives and parents and children, for eternity. The command to multiply and fill the earth was understood to mean a filling and subduing of the universe in an unending progression. Those with a plurality of wives would gain highest exaltation, and "they shall pass by the angels, and the gods, which are set there, to their exaltation and glory in all things," whereas those without temple marriages become "angels in heaven, which angels are ministering servants, to minister for those who are worthy of a far more, and an exceeding, and an eternal weight of glory. For these angels did not abide my law; therefore, they cannot be enlarged, but remain separately and singly, without exaltation in their saved condition, to all eternity; and from henceforth are not gods, but are angels of God forever and ever" (*D & C*, 132:19, 16–17).

Yet sectarian advantage has its price, for those who know and reject the gospel are the only men who are sentenced to eternal perdition. For Christ came "That through him all might be saved whom the Father had put into his power and made by him; Who glorifies the Father, and saves all the works of his hands, except those sons of perdition who deny the Son after the Father has revealed him" (*D & C*, 76:42–43). Mormon apostates and fallen, and conscious persecutors of the Saints, seem to be those who belong in this category. And they "shall go away into everlasting punishment, which is endless punishment, which is eternal punishment, to reign with the devil and his angels in eternity, where . . . the fire is not quenched" (*D & C*, 76:44). Talmage commented:

> Some degree of salvation will come to all those who have not forfeited their right to it (by conscious disobedience); exaltation is given to those only who by active labors have won a claim to God's merciful liberality by which it is bestowed.[33]

The relationship between God and man is one of co-operation, but not a co-operation between equals. God aids man, but he is also aided by man. Yet for man this entails obedience to God's laws. Such obedience involves revelation and the Mormon church as its earthly channel. Moreover, the church is more than a teacher: it is also a preserver of ordinances which must be obeyed if exaltation is to be gained:

> God, standing alone, cannot conceivably possess the power that may come to him if the hosts of other advancing and increasing workers labor in harmony with him. Therefore, because of his love for his children and his desire to continue in the way of even greater growth, he proceeded to aid others in their onward progress.[34]

God's relation to man is essentially one of patriarchal activism—the relation of a father and his children engaged in an eternal task.

Such is the world view that Mormonism developed in the 1830's and early 1840's and has taught without major change ever since. It is a dynamic conception enjoining a high degree of activism upon its adherents. It is also an outlook that stresses the materiality of the universe and the importance of the human will in advancing man in his mastery of matter.

Nothing exists which is not material.

> "Mormonism" claims that all nature, both on earth and in heaven, operates on a plan of advancement; that the very Eternal Father is a progressive Being; that his perfection, while so complete as to be incomprehensible to man, possesses this essential quality of true perfection—the capacity of eternal increase. That therefore, in the far future, beyond the horizon of eternities perchance, man may attain the status of a God. Yet this does not mean that he shall overtake those intelligences that are already beyond him in advancement; for to assert such would be to argue that there is no progression beyond a certain stage of attainment, and that advancement is a characteristic of low organization and inferior purpose alone. We believe that there was more than the sounding of brass or the tinkling of wordy cymbals in the fervent admonition of the Christ to his followers—"Be ye therefore perfect, as your Father which is in heaven is perfect."[35]

Thus has restored revelation led to the abandonment of traditional Christian positions. The emphasis upon man's goodness, the recognition of the efficacy of human effort, the acceptance of activity in the world, the belief in progress—all these take on new meaning in the context of an extra-Christian evolutionism. The divinization of man becomes a literal progression to Godhood. Active effort and obedience to the law, combined with knowledge, will lead man to such perfection. "In short, man is a god in embryo. He comes of a race of gods, and as his eternal growth is continued, he will approach more nearly the point which to us is Godhood, and which is everlasting in its power over the elements of the Universe."[36] Mastery and power are prizes to be gained in continuous increments through vigorous expenditure of effort.

Within the context of space and time, God and men raise themselves to greater degrees of control over the other elements. Eternity has disappeared, and in its place is infinitely prolonged time. God's transcendence is but the height of self-improvement along a path upon which we are also traveling. Thus has Mormonism given theological expression to the opportunity for betterment, the challenge to active mastery, and the evocation of effort that America came to mean in the nineteenth century. Yet at the same time the Mormon church preserved the older doctrines and insisted upon the importance of its own elaborate ecclesiastical organization.

The Restoration Aspects of Mormonism

Arising in the "burned-over district" of western New York, Mormonism developed the current notions of interpreting Scripture by the inner promptings of the spirit into a belief in present-day revelation. It was contemporary revelation that was to become the particular mark of the new dispensation in the eyes of both its adherents and its adversaries. To the followers of the new prophet, it appeared that the channels of communication between God and man had been reopened and that this offered a way out of current religious confusion.

The Mormons hold that the early Christians "did not retain the kingdom of God after the second century of the Christian era; that from that time to the present, they have had no more authority to administer Christian ordinances than the Apostate Jews;

and that all their forms and ordinances, and ministrations, are an abomination in the sight of God." This is "the great Apostasy of the Christian Church," which "commenced in the first century. . . ." For seventeen centuries these falsehoods continued. Such is the religion "of the Papal, Greek, and Protestant Churches of the nineteenth century. . . . Instead of having apostles, prophets, and other inspired men in the church now, receiving visions, dreams, revelations, ministrations of angels, and prophecies for the calling of officers, and for the government of the Church—they have a wicked, corrupt, uninspired pope, or uninspired archbishops, bishops, clergymen, etc., who have a great variety of corrupt forms of Godliness, but utterly deny the gift of revelation, and every other miraculous power which always characterized Christ's Church."[37]

The Mormon church claimed to be the restoration of communication between God and man and the re-establishment of Christ's church. Congruent with its emphasis upon the construction of a sacred commonwealth in the present world, Mormonism placed a not inconsiderable emphasis upon the restoration of Hebrew ideals. Mormon co-operativism, finding expression in those forms of social experimentation to which reference has been made above and which will be discussed in detail below—the United Order of Enoch, or Law of Consecration—was greatly influenced by the Christian and secular socialism of the period, which was directly introduced into the new religious outlook by Sidney Rigdon. This aspect of Mormon aspirations was also affected by the strong emphasis placed by the new church upon this-worldly conceptions of ancient Israel and the postdiluvian patriarchs. As Abraham, Isaac, Jacob, and Joseph prospered in this world as part of their covenant with God, so would the new chosen people, who soon thought of themselves as spiritual and even literal descendants of the old, prosper under the new covenant. "Mormonism, in its attempt to introduce Israelitish ideals, was setting up a material kingdom, a Zion on Earth."[38]

In the Book of Moses, which Joseph Smith claimed to have translated from papyri and held to be an older and more complete version of the Genesis story, there appears the "Prophecy of Enoch," in which Enoch preaches repentance and those who repent build a City of God, "the City of Holiness, even Zion." In a vision Enoch sees all the important events of later sacred history, including the discovery of the *Book of Mormon*. There is a promise that Enoch's city, which has been mysteriously translated into heaven with Enoch himself (see Gen. 5:24), will return to dwell amid the holy city to be built by the Mormons (Moses 7:19, 62–63). This part of the Book of Moses was written early, and its doctrine of a holy city to be built by the Saints was related to the problem of the new church's move to Kirtland. Soon the Saints were told that it would be revealed unto them "when the city of the New Jerusalem shall be prepared, that ye may be gathered in one, that ye may be my people and I will be your God" (*D & C*, 42:9). It was at first indicated that this city would be built in the "regions westward," but in the same year of 1831 the Saints were told through Joseph that "if ye are faithful ye shall assemble yourselves together to rejoice upon the land of Missouri, which is the land of your inheritance" (*D & C*, 52:42).

Thus, from the very first, a doctrine of the "gathering" became a central theme in the Mormon outlook.[39] This idea, so influential in missionary work and the emigration of converts, was integrally tied up with the notion of building the holy city, the "New Jerusalem" (*D & C*, 28:9; 42:9, 35, 62; 45:66, 67; 84:2, 3, 31). This in turn was closely related to the peculiar Mormon form of semisocialism, the Law of Consecration (*D & C*, 42:30–35, 42, 55). In the prophecy of Enoch, the Lord promises to "gather out mine elect from the four quarters of the earth, unto a place which I shall prepare, an Holy City, that my people may gird up their loins, and be looking forth for the time of my coming; for there shall be my tabernacle, and it shall be called Zion, a New Jerusalem"(Moses 7:62). This whole complex of holy city, gathering, and co-operative effort is to be seen as part of "a new and everlasting covenant" (*D & C*, 22:1), a covenant involving a "land of your inheritance, and for the inheritance of your children forever" (*D & C*, 38:20).

Not only has Mormonism restored an emphasis upon the this-worldly ideals of the Old Testament, but it took the materials of chiliastic revivalism and molded a doctrine of peculiarity. It came to see itself as a new Israel, of "the children of Israel, and of the seed of Abraham" (*D & C*, 103:17). These developments could proceed upon the *Book of Mormon* with a naturalness that made their acceptance easy for new converts. Both they and the new scripture continued to emphasize aspects of current thinking in that enthusiastic region of the country. Mormonism, however, focused these hopes and beliefs upon the concrete, mundane task of earthly construction.

The importance of the Indians in American thought had been one of the factors conditioning the reception of the *Book of Mormon*. The new church had been directed to their conversion, holding that they were apostate Hebrews and that upon their reconversion they would become a "white and delightsome people." The Mormons were not the first to see the Indians involved in millennial expectations. Yet, by locating their own city of Zion on "the borders by the Lamanites" (*D & C*, 28:9) and seeing the reconversion of the Indians as part of their divinely appointed task, they not only naturalized the covenant and the gathering; they created a peculiar, American, this-worldly vocation to build on this continent a place for Christ's Second Coming in which they and the Indians and those whom they should gather from the ends of the earth would play the central role.

Such this-worldly notions were not simply Hebraic, they were also millennial. For it was Christ who would dwell in the city of the Saints, presiding over an American Zion from Missouri. Mormonism attempted not only to restore Hebrew ideals but also to restore the apostolic church. Moreover, the Mormon idea of the eternity of covenants destroyed any conception of the supersession of the old covenant by the new and any notion of one as preparatory and the other as consummatory. It has been pointed out that in the *Book of Mormon* there is no sense of pre-Christian messianic expectations. Nephite prophets speak of Christ as though he had already come, although they indicate that he has not by the addition of a phrase such as "who is to come." In the vision of Enoch in the Book of Moses, Enoch is shown the events of the New Testament. In all revivalistic movements there was a strong tendency to fuse Old and New Testament notions, and in Mormonism the identification of the new church with Israel was but one aspect of the expectation of the "gathering" and of the Second Coming of Christ.

Mormon millennialism remained a strong motive in Mormon constructive efforts. Mormonism today still largely adheres to such a notion, although the time remains indefinite. The church periodically issues warnings to the world, and advice from leading churchmen to store a year or two's supply of food arouses considerable support among the membership. However real such beliefs may be, they have never taken the Adventist form, as in Millerism. In fact, they have been integrated into the general framework of Mormonism in such a way that they always arouse enthusiasm for preparation, and in Mormon terms preparation always involved constructive work here and now. In 1843 Joseph did ask the Lord when the coming would be and was told: "Joseph, my son, if thou livest until thou art eighty-five years old, thou shalt see the face of the Son of Man; therefore let this suffice, and trouble me no more on this matter" (*D & C*, 130:15). Since Joseph would have been eighty-five years old in 1890, there was some tendency to identify millennial hopes with that year, but such identifications were never of major importance in Mormonism. At the time of its publication in 1843, this revelation had the effect of postponing both immediate hopes and disappointment (*D & C*, 130:17).

Moreover, so-called "primitive gifts" were believed to have been restored. "We believe in the gift of tongues, prophecy, revelation, visions, healing, interpretation of tongues, etc."[40] People spoke with tongues in Mormon meetings, and in Kirtland, Ohio, where enthusiasm was intense, even Brigham Young did so. In the new church people believed that they saw visions. They prophesied and performed such works as casting out devils and curing the sick by the laying on of hands. While Joseph disapproved of certain excesses, he did cast out devils[41] and engage in faith healing. In fact, these practices were considered to be irrefutable signs of the genuineness of the new dispensation. In 1832 Joseph reported:

And these signs shall follow them that believe—
In my name they shall do many wonderful works;
In my name they shall cast out devils;
In my name they shall heal the sick;
In my name they shall open the eyes of the blind, and unstop the ears of the deaf;
And the tongue of the dumb shall speak;
And if any man shall administer poison unto them it shall not hurt them;
And the poison of a serpent shall not have power to harm them.
But a commandment I give unto them, that they shall not boast themselves of these things [*D & C*, 84:65-73].

This restorationist emphasis was to some extent common to the spirit of sectarian groups and was especially marked in the Campbellites, whose influence was brought to bear upon the new church through some of the early converts, especially Sidney Rigdon and Parley Pratt. What was characteristic of Mormon chiliasm was the focusing of such hopes upon tasks requiring group effort. This was new, however, only in the dimensions of its successes and failures. Nor was the this-worldly Old Testament emphasis an innovation, for this also is to be seen in Puritanism in New England. In one respect, however, the Mormon emphasis upon this-worldly ideas and their Old Testament expression led to genuine innovation so far as American religion is concerned. Holding to the eternity of covenants, Mormonism revived polygamous marriage and, indeed, made the plurality of wives a central tenet of its belief, a peculiar mark of its dispensation, and the symbol of its separation—its condition of being gathered—in the eyes of both its adherents and its enemies.

Plural marriage, so central to the world view of Mormonism and so meaningful as a symbol of Mormon separateness and innovation, was justified by Mormon apologists by Old Testament precedent. Just as Joseph found the plural form of the Hebrew *Elohim* necessary, at least as an occasion for and later as a justification of his ventures into polytheism, so did he find the Old Testament precedent of polygamy a necessary precondition for his own doctrine, and it proved a most important weapon in the days that followed.

Just when polygamy was first practiced is still a mystery, but it was certainly announced and very probably practiced before the recording of the revelation in July, 1843. That revelation openly cited the Old Testament precedents:

Abraham received concubines, and they bore him children; and it was accounted unto him for righteousness, because they were given unto him, and he abode in my law; as Isaac also and Jacob did none other things than that which they were commanded; and because they did none other things than that which they were commanded, they have entered into their exaltation, according to the promises, and sit upon thrones, and are not angels but are gods.

David also received many wives and concubines, and also Solomon and Moses my servants, as also many others of my servants, from the beginning of creation until this time; and in nothing did they sin save in those things which they received not of me. . . .

I am the Lord thy God, and I gave unto thee, my servant Joseph, an appointment, and restore all things [*D & C*, 132 : 37, 38, 40].

This interpretation reverses the usual and, indeed, the obvious interpretation of Genesis, where marriage is first presented as two in one flesh (Gen. 2:24) and where polygamy first appears among the Cainites, who are eliminated from the covenant lineage (Gen. 4:19). Moreover, Isaac was a monogamist. Since the Mormons held a belief in the eternity of covenants and did not recognize the new covenant as a supersession and fulfilment of the old, they have accepted this new revelation without being concerned with its obvious conflict with the teaching of Christ in the Gospels (Matt. 19:5-8; Mark 10:5-8). In the new doctrine, restoration and innovation meet, and the patriarchal practices of postdiluvian nomads are revived as part of an extra-Christian evolutionism, which holds a doctrine of a finite head God, the existence of many gods, and the development of men to Godhood. Old Testament polygamy is joined to polytheism. Yet the importance of the ancient prototype was considerable in Mormon eyes. Writing in 1855, Parley P. Pratt said:

> It was a law of the ancient Priesthood, and is again restored, that a man who is faithful in all things, may, by the word of the Lord, through the administration of one holding the keys to bind on earth and heaven, receive and secure to himself, for time and all eternity, MORE THAN ONE WIFE.
>
> Thus did Abraham, Isaac, Jacob, Moses, the Patriarchs and Prophets of old.[42]

Mormon interpretation even suggested that there was polygamy in the New Testament and suggested the marriage of the Lord to Mary and Martha. Orson Hyde declared: "If at the marriage at Cana of Galilee, Jesus was the bridegroom and took unto him Mary, Martha, and the other Mary whom Jesus loved, it shocks not our nerves."[43]

Since the defeat of the church in the severe conflict with the United States government and an aroused public opinion in the 1880's, Mormonism has accommodated its teachings to the dominant monogamous mores. Although there was some inner conflict before the church wholeheartedly accepted the new situation and although some polygamous marriages were performed after the manifesto of 1890 and some polygamous husbands had children by plural wives after that date, the Mormon surrender of plural marriage was sincere. In fact, so important has conformity to the laws of the state and nation on this score become that the Mormon church today is merciless in proceeding against recusants who from time to time may in such out-of-the-way places as Short Creek, Arizona, not far from old John D. Lee country, revert to celestial marriage and the plurality of wives, and in aiding the civil law in protecting society from the threat of marriage irregularity.

Yet the official doctrine of the Mormon church still holds that in some sense polygamy is the divinely preferred form of matrimony. However, this has become associated with conditions not likely to exist in the real world very soon. Even more than the millennium, polygamy has retreated to the limbo of theological relics. What has remained, however, is an emphasis upon family and the desirability of children.

The need to provide earthly bodies for waiting spirits was one of the Mormon justifications of plural marriage, although actually the birth rate per wife was lower for plural than for monogamous wives. The result has been a strong preference for large families among these farming people. Moreover, the patriarchal position of men in the family has been preserved in official teaching, although, since Mormonism also placed great emphasis upon the equality of women in other respects and since the general trends in the country affected Mormonism both before and especially after accommodation, patriarchalism seems to be largely ceremonial, at least within the family. This is especially true among the urban Saints, but it is also true to a great extent in rural areas.

Yet the importance of family is genuine. Officially the church teaches, as President David O. McKay has declared: "The family is the unit of society. Mormonism teaches . . . that parenthood is next to Godhood, and that the marriage bond and family relationships are as eternal as life itself." The church holds that "sex is an eternal principle. The equivalent of sex has always existed and will continue forever." Marriage is considered "a solemn agreement which is to extend beyond the grave," and the marriage ceremony performed in the temple—the preferred and encouraged form—seals the contract "for time and eternity." Providing bodies for spirits who "must be born as children into the world" is "a high purpose, if not the main one, of the earth work."[44] Although the church, in accordance with its emphasis upon family, rejects sexual promiscuity, it is not ascetic in its attitude toward sex. Joseph Smith taught: "And again, verily I say unto you, that whoso forbiddeth to marry is not ordained of God, for marriage is ordained of God unto man" (*D & C*, 49:15). This revelation, which is part of Section LII of the original *Book of Commandments* published in 1833, also contains the statement that a man "should have one wife" (*D & C*, 49:16), and, although Mormon teaching changed on this point, this verse remains unaltered in the modern versions. Talmage comments that to teach "that celibacy is a mark of a higher state, more acceptable in the pure sight of God" is to teach "pernicious doctrine."[45]

Extra-marital sexual relations are forbidden by Mormon ethics, although illicit unions occur among the Mormons, as in all other cultures. Divorce is disapproved and discouraged; it "is not a part of the Gospel plan and has been introduced because of the hardness of heart and unbelief of the people." "The Church recognizes the validity of divorces obtained according to the law of the land and the subsequent marriages if any, but looks with disfavor upon the growing frequency of divorce as an indication of an unhealthy state of society and as contrary to the condition which must prevail in the kingdom of God." "The sanctity of the home and the values of parenthood can only be preserved where marriage laws are upheld and enforced by society and the improper relationships of the sexes aside from the marriage vow censured and punished."[46]

The family is a very important institution to Mormons. This refers to both the nuclear family of husband, wife, and children, which is, of course, the basic social unit, and larger kinship groups. In fact, such loyalty to and identification with family and extended relations assumes a form which, to an outsider, often seems to approach ancestor worship in homage to the pioneers of settlement and the progenitors of family. Despite familial attitudes and their explicit cultivation by the church, however, the rate of divorce is high in Utah and among Latter-day Saints. Temple divorces are granted, and bishop's courts have not been successful as marriage counselors. Birth control is also forbidden and disapproved, although it, too, is practiced. The church shuns open campaigns on the issue of birth control and seems to have taken the position of largely ignoring the question. Yet, despite this tendency not to disturb things, the basic position of the church is actually quite clear:

The doctrine that wedded man and woman should not beget children or should limit the number of children born to them, is contrary to the spirit of the Great Plan, and is a most erroneous one. Let the waiting spirits come! Let children be born into the earth! Let fatherhood and motherhood be the most honored of all the professions on earth.[47]

This familism articulates with church teaching in another direction. In the first place, there is great emphasis upon extended kinship relationships, and large family reunions, which may have as many as a thousand persons in attendance, are common to Mormondom during the warmer part of the year. The Mormon consciousness of group accomplishment fits in with an awareness of family contribution to the larger tasks of the Mormon people throughout their history. The formal structure of the church is penetrated and supported by strong ties of extended kinship, both of blood and of marriage. The official church emphasis upon temple work, with its vicarious rites for the dead, increases family awareness and reinforces family loyalties. In receiving baptism for the deceased and other such rites, the church keeps careful records. This has resulted in a great interest in searching out genealogies and "going through the temple" for dead ancestors. This temple work is done by the most devout Mormons and has become an important task for the older people. There is a church genealogical society which maintains at Salt Lake City what is probably the best genealogical library in the world and publishes a monthly magazine. The importance of this work is stressed in church publications and is of genuine interest to members.[48]

Perhaps what Mormons consider most important in their restoration is what they call the "restoration of the ancient priesthoods." The church claims to have restored all ordinances and priestly orders of both Old and New Testaments. The result is a church that holds itself to be headed by a prophet from whose authority is derived a complex, hierarchical priesthood structure, divided into two orders, the Aaronic or lesser and the Melchizedek or higher. All males who live up to the church's teaching are members, proceeding by rites of passage along this elaborate promotion pathway. It is this body that, while involving large numbers of the males directly in church government, is itself ruled authoritatively from the top down and rules the church as a theocracy. Since women are excluded from such priesthood councils, the church has developed auxiliary organizations in which they become active in church work.

The Work, Health, Recreation, and Education Complex

Mormon effort and attention were directed toward the here-and-now by the doctrine of an uncreated dynamic universe in which intelligences are advancing in power and perfection, together with the notion of the covenant and the gathering (and the consequent Zionism). The present life became a time of probation and advancement, in which man, by his own efforts and with God's help, would acquire experience in a new kind of material environment and thus hasten his development toward Godlike status. The result has been a vigorous and practical attitude toward daily life. "The Latter-day Saints believe not only in the gospel of spiritual salvation, but also in the gospel of temporal salvation." The importance of the present time is stressed. "To us the greatest day of all time is today, it is the algebraic sum of all our yesterdays and it holds the promise of all our tomorrows. 'If today is made great, tomorrow will be surpassingly greater.'"[49]

Mormonism transformed the earlier belief in the necessity of works for salvation into a doctrine of accomplishment. Knowledge and mastery, together with obedience to the church, constitute the foundation of progress in the present life and the preparation for "surpassingly greater" progress in that to come. Active effort is the fundamental characteristic of the Mormon attitude toward the tasks of everyday living. Through action, men will develop here below; through action, they will continue development beyond the grave; indeed, through action, God has developed to his present overwhelming supremacy. Mormonism represents a theological version of the American attitude of practical activism. It admonishes its adherents to be active and to be oriented toward accomplishment. "Drifting about in life" is dangerous. "It is dangerous both to the vocational and to the spiritual welfare of man."[50] Life is more than a vocation, more than a calling; it is an opportunity for deification through conquest, which is to be won through rational mastery of the environment and obedience to the ordinances of the church.

This doctrine, permeating individual and community life, is expressed today in a configuration of attitudes clustering around activity and development. This configuration represents an important aspect of the individual's integration into the life of the Mormon group, for it relates the striving of individuals to collectively prescribed ends. Moreover, since it is taught by exhortation and example from early childhood, this set of attitudes becomes second nature to those brought up in the Mormon home and community environment. It becomes the link between publicly preached and privately held versions of the Mormon heritage, so far as practical attitudes are concerned. We have called this set of attitudes "the work, health, recreation, and education complex."

It was proverbial among the Mormon pioneers that "there is no excellence without labor." "In obedience to God's command, man must devote himself to the work of subduing the earth." Every earthly task, "however apparently humble, however apparently remote from fundamental principles, has a spiritual counterpart, and is necessary for the completion of the plan under which man works. . . . All such tasks are proper, dignified and necessary parts of the Great Plan, and will lead man along the path of eternal progression." "All the capital there is upon the earth is the bone and sinew of working men and women." This emphasis is also applied to participation in church activities, for the Mormon church holds such participation as central to membership and does, in fact, achieve a very high degree of membership activity. Literally, "There is no place for the idler."[51]

"Complete living requires a sound body. The sound mind in the sound body is the first requisite of any person who desires to live happily and serve well."[52] As early as 1832, Joseph admonished the Saints in a revelation: "Cease to be idle; cease to be unclean; cease to find fault one with another; cease to sleep longer than is needful; retire to thy bed early, that ye may not be weary; arise early, that your bodies and your minds may be invigorated" (*D & C*, 88:124). Health of the body becomes a central religious concern in Mormonism, valued for itself and also as a necessary means for accomplishment and progress in the present life.

This concern for health was a popular idea when Mormonism was founded, and it was often expressed in dietary prescriptions. In 1833, at Kirtland, Ohio, Joseph Smith reported a revelation that is recorded as Section 89 of the *Doctrine and Covenants* and is known among the Mormons as the "Word of Wisdom." This revelation forbids smoking and drinking:

That inasmuch as any man drinketh wine or strong drink among you, behold it is not good, neither meet in the sight of your Father. . . .

And, again, strong drinks are not for the belly, but for the washing of your bodies.

And again, tobacco is not for the body, neither for the belly, and is not good for man, but is an herb for bruises and all sick cattle, to be used with judgment and skill.

And again, hot drinks are not for the body or belly [D & C, 89:5, 7–9].

It is typical of Mormonism not only that it should inherit the teetotalism of its circumstances of origin but that it should subordinate it to a general world view with which it was rendered consistent. Moreover, nineteenth-century notions of health became theological concerns and found their place in the Mormon religious teachings alongside Old Testament this-worldliness and apocalyptic anticipation. Although it was first given as counsel, this commandment has in recent decades become accepted as commandment and as such was sustained in a general conference of the church. Much effort is expended by the church to show the harmful effects of liquor and tobacco, while coffee and tea are held on almost the same level as alcoholic drinks.

The revelation continues, not only proscribing but commanding:

And again, verily I say unto you, all wholesome herbs God hath ordained for the constitution, nature, and use of man—

Every herb in the season thereof, and every fruit in the season thereof; all these to be used with prudence and thanksgiving.

Yea, flesh also of beasts and of the fowls of the air, I, the Lord, have ordained for the use of man with thanksgiving; nevertheless they are to be used sparingly;

And it is pleasing unto me that they should not be used, only in times of winter, or of cold, or famine.

All grain is ordained for the use of man and of beasts, to be the staff of life, not only for man but for the beasts of the field, and the fowls of heaven, and all wild animals that run or creep on the earth;

And these hath God made for the use of man only in times of famine and excess of hunger.

All grain is good for the food of man; as also the fruit of the vine; that which yieldeth fruit, whether in the ground or above the ground—

Nevertheless, wheat for man, and corn for the ox, and oats for the horse, and rye for the fowls and for swine, and for all beasts of the field, and barley for all useful animals, and for mild drinks, as also other grain [*D & C*, 89:10–17].

While the section of the Word of Wisdom prescribing dietary habits has not been made a requisite for full membership, as has the proscription of tobacco, coffee, tea, and liquor, it has had considerable influence upon Mormon life, and there exists in Salt Lake City a group known as "Eighty-Niners" who attempt to keep literally all of Section 89 of the *Doctrine and Covenants*. Admission to the temple and hence permission to take part in the ceremonies performed there—temple marriage, sealings, baptism for the dead—are denied to Mormons who do not abide by the proscription of smoking and the command to abstain from coffee, tea, and liquor. Moreover, this commandment has become for Mormons a most salient mark of their membership in the church. Together with tithing, it separates the loyal and fervent from the Jack Mormon and the halfhearted. Abstention from the practices forbidden in the Word of Wisdom appears to have replaced plural marriage as the badge of Zion, the sign of the gathered, in these days of accommodation to and integration into the larger gentile community. Frequently defended and rationalized in terms of bodily health and scientific hygiene, the Word of Wisdom is the symbol of Mormon concern with the things of this world.

Recreation—viewed as closely related to work and health—meets with strong Mormon approval and is seen as important in supporting and refreshing man for a more effective life, as well as for its own sake. It has become (especially since the accommodation that followed the manifesto of Wilford Woodruff ending plural marriage in 1890) an area in which the church has concentrated much of its organizational talent and a large share of its co-operative energy. It is today one of the important spheres of activity in which group action under church auspices engages the individual member in the active life of the church.

While this concern with organized recreation is an outstanding feature of postaccommodation Mormonism, there was very early an emphasis upon play and upon joy. The Mormon repudiation of religious pessimism found expression in the *Book of Mormon* notion that "men are that they might have joy" (II Nephi 2:25). Dancing and the theater were emphasized in early Utah and are given considerable attention today, and dancing was a typical

Mormon form of recreation even when they were crossing the plains. Beginning as spontaneous, unplanned, but approved activity, Mormon recreation has come to take place more and more within the context of church organization and sponsorship, especially through the auxiliary organizations that activate women and younger people.

In this process the Mormon church has drawn from many sources to develop a composite and many-sided recreational theory. Concern with developing group solidarity, health, leadership, culture, and self-expression has been important to Mormon recreational efforts, while Mormon theory has recognized social, rhythmic, dramatic, constructive, physical, and other urges as seeking satisfaction through recreation. The church program is characterized by a large degree of central planning and direction, and participation in church-sponsored recreation is considered a kind of religious activity.

It has been said: "The Mormons have spiritualized recreation. They have recognized the group factor in play: that the group not only enhances play, but is often the main motivating factor."[53] Recreation has become an important expression of Mormon activism and group solidarity, which it simultaneously reinforces. It is the natural context for the development of the Mormon child, and, together with the other activities of the church and its auxiliary organizations, it provides a most effective context for the learning of Mormon attitudes toward church and world. It is perhaps one of the areas in which genuine creativity has been shown by the Mormon group since the definitive ending of Mormon exclusiveness in 1890. On the whole, it is looked upon as an aid to eternal progression, as a lighter form of education, with which it is considered to be intimately related.

The Mormon definition of life makes the earthly sojourn basically an educative process. Knowledge is necessary to mastery, and the way to deification is through mastery, for not only does education aid man in fulfilling present tasks, it advances him in his eternal progress. The knowledge "we attain unto in this life," said Joseph Smith, "will rise with us in the resurrection," and "if a person gains more knowledge and intelligence in this life," he will, because of this knowledge, "have so much the advantage in the world to come" (*D & C*, 130:18–19). Mormonism had early been noted for its attempt to give rational answers to the religious problems of the burned-over district, and, in the midst of enthusiasm, the new religion sought converts through logical argument. The intellectuality of Mormonism is to be seen in the *Book of Mormon*, as well as in the revelations of the *Doctrine and Covenants*. Inheriting from its milieu the influence of the popular belief in education and the rationalism that found expression in Universalism and in Campbellite teachings, Mormonism again developed a currently accepted theme into a uniquely perceived part of a radically new theology. Proclaiming: "The glory of God is intelligence, or, in other words, light and truth" (*D & C*, 93:36), Joseph Smith had early admonished his followers: "Seek ye out of the best books words of wisdom; seek learning, even by study and also by faith" (*D & C*, 88:118).

An emphasis upon education appears early in Mormon history. Religious instruction both to children and to adults, the latter to be seen in the establishment of the Schools for Prophets in Ohio and Missouri, was expressive of this early interest. In Nauvoo, the Saints established a municipal university, where it has been claimed that modern and ancient languages, history, literature, and mathematics were taught, although how well we do not really know.

Again, in Utah, despite the exigencies of settlement, education was a concern of the pioneers. In 1850 it was decided to set aside $5,000 per year for twenty years to support a state university, and in that same year the University of Deseret, now the University of Utah, was founded. However, in the earlier years of settlement there was apparently a considerable gap between ideal and actuality. There was, moreover, as part of the intense Mormon-gentile conflict of the time, opposition from the Mormons to publicly supported free schools. At this time charges of obscurantism were leveled against the Saints, which were based on more than Mormon opposition to public schools, for it was the intention of the Saints to reorganize all knowledge in terms of their new world outlook. "The world of science was to be revolutionized, the theories of gravitation, repulsion, and attraction overthrown, the motion of atoms, whether single or in mass, being ascribed to the all-pervading presence of the holy spirit," according to the *Deseret News* of July 26, 1850.

The introduction of the Deseret alphabet was another Mormon innovation that aroused gentile suspicion and hostility. This strange experiment was a new phonetic sign system, whose only advantage seems to have been the prospect of quarantining the Mormon community against alien, gentile influences. In 1855 the legislature, with the approval of Brigham Young, appropriated $2,500 to make a type font bearing the new characters. The alphabet failed to catch on at the time, and, although it was revived after the Civil War, interest in it died out, and the project was given up.

Yet, despite the conflicts of territorial days, despite the inadequacies of practical application, despite the limitations imposed by a pioneer environment, the ideal of education as part of Mormon aspirations was preserved and enhanced. Instead of revolutionizing science and reorganizing knowledge in terms of Mormon beliefs and conceptions, the Saints accommodated themselves to science and learning and utilized them for their own community interests. Accommodation to and making use of the science and scholarship of the gentiles replaced earlier utopian ambitions. This attitude, which directs Mormons to look favorably upon education, remains, despite the fact that it led, even in pioneer days, to apostasy and continues to present such dangers to present-day Mormon students.

This official doctrinal emphasis has become a part of the spontaneous outlook of the Mormon people. The results can be seen in the high enrolment figures for high schools and colleges in Utah in recent years and in the proportion of the state budget devoted to education. Utah has more than its share of active scientists and of outstanding Americans in other fields.[54]

The dangers that secular thought presents to Mormon belief in the twentieth century have given rise to elaborate apologetics, while the dangers of the encroaching gentile milieu are met by a highly organized education program within the church. Ericksen, writing a generation ago, declared that such apologetics is "a sort of Mormon scholasticism which has, in recent years, engaged the attention of some of the educated members of the church. It has one purpose—that of justifying the Mormon dogmas. This peculiar rationalizing tendency has developed side by side with heresy which it is constantly endeavoring to silence by argument. Besides a large number of books written with this aim, the church theological classes are making use of this line of reasoning."[55]

Yet education remains of prime importance and, together with other components of this complicated network of practical orientations, provides a consistent and unified frame of reference for the activities of daily life, relating such activities to the central doctrines of the Mormon world view. The work, health, recreation, and education complex thus translates Mormon religious dogma and theoretical speculation into attitudes directing the tasks of daily life. It gives psychological reality to the implications of the practical activism of the Mormon outlook.

The Transcendentalism of Achievement

The central implication of Mormon theology is a definition of human life as a period of advancement through mastery. This is set within the elaborate framework of a developing universe in which God, gods, and other intelligences, including men, are increasingly developing themselves through progressively greater control over other uncreated elements. God himself is a developing being, and the orthodox Christian conception of a transcendent, unchanging God is replaced by a God who experiences continual growth, whose transcendence is relative and has been won through effort. This repudiation of creationist theology is at the same time a repudiation of spirituality in favor of materiality, a repudiation that Mormonism makes quite explicit. It does not, however, face up to the metaphysical problems (concerning being and change), the epistemological problems (concerning the nature of thought, ideas, and knowledge), and even the logical problems (concerning identity and unity) that such a view involves. The developing demiurge of Mormon theology is identified with the God of Judaic and Christian Scripture, as he is redefined in the new revelations of the Mormon scriptures.

The very notion of a new revelation in the fulness of time, upon which Mormonism was based, reflected the nineteenth-century conviction that its own age was one far in advance of any that had gone before. The acceptance of America as a chosen site for the reception of that new revelation reflected the general American belief that the New World had superseded the Old and was indeed the Old World's fulfilment. Mormonism gave theological expression to common sentiments not unlike those of Thoreau, who felt that he had been born in the "most estimable place in all the world and in the nick of time."

That such a revelation would consciously consecrate America as a promised land and, at the same time, proclaim a doctrine of eternal self-improvement is hardly surprising. That it would carry such notions beyond the limits that traditional Christianity, however liberally interpreted, would permit is a development congruent both with the spirit of secular thinking at the time and with the peculiar group experiences of the Mormon people. What Unitarianism had done in the cultured atmosphere of Harvard and Boston, in seeing Protestant Christianity in terms of a rationalism, itself becoming ever more scientific in its fundamental principles, Mormonism had done in the environment that it in part found and in part created for itself in the Middle West. If Unitarianism was more respectable and more in keeping with the intellectual standards of the university, Mormonism was more dynamic and more imaginative. Indeed, what Emerson did for Unitarianism, Mormonism did for itself. Where Emerson needed Eastern religion to give the commonplace American notion of self-reliance cosmic significance and extra-Christian implication, Mormonism developed such a conception itself.

However, where Unitarianism and Universalism looked to human perfectibility amid social amelioration, Mormonism combined such beliefs with older Protestant ideas associated with evangelical and enthusiastic religion. What was common to these developments was the extreme emphasis placed upon the efficacy of human effort and the tendency toward placing great reliance upon the human will. Mormonism, like the Puritanism of New England from which it was remotely descended, was voluntaristic and activistic. Mormonism, however, rearranged its theological principles to harmonize with the implications of activism in the expanding American society. Contemplative religion is even more foreign to Mormonism than it is to American Protestantism; it is as foreign to Mormon thinking as it is to American secular thought.

Like earlier Puritan and later secular thinking, the Mormon emphasis is upon action. Action, through what one Mormon thinker called a "vigorous exercise of the will," is central to Mormon conceptions. The tremendous emphasis upon rationality and knowledge that is so salient in Mormon thinking may obscure this dynamic voluntarism so basic to the Mormon position. Yet it must be seen that, from this viewpoint, knowledge is power, it is a means, and all action is fundamentally oriented toward goals. Such action is indefinitely prolonged through the doctrine of eternal progression. Mastery and control thereby become primary, and human growth—a growth that tends toward deification—is achieved through successful manipulation of and control over the material environment. God's supreme position is understood not in terms of his being First Necessary Being but rather as a result of a "conquest."

God's attitude toward the uncreated universe is a reflection of man's. He is not its source but rather its organizer. Like man, he is concerned with mastering it and increasing his control over it. In some way this process of continual external mastery either causes or parallels a continual internal metamorphosis. Through such conquest, God has become God; through it, men will become gods. It is not clear why mastery and conquest should bring deification; but the fact that this is how Mormon theology sees the problem underscores the importance of such mastery—based on extrinsic relations of utility—to the Mormon view.

What of the relationship between man and God? Mormons speak of loving God and use many of the terms appropriate to older, more orthodox conceptions. Yet insofar as Mormonism is consistent—and the spirit of the new conceptions permeates the entire configuration of Mormon beliefs—it sees God and man in terms of superior and subordinate engaged in gaining control over the world. Both God and man are part of this world, and their mastery is of the same type—an external, manipulative kind of mastery. The world is not a participation in the divine nature, neither an uncreated participation, as in Eastern religion, nor a created participation, as in orthodox Christianity. It is an eternal framework within which God and men work out their own development. Even its lawfulness and regularity are not derived from God but offer to God means and conditions for his own development.

Where in the context of this dynamic voluntarism do ethics belong? There is no doubt that, with the exception of plural marriage, Mormonism preserved the older Protestant morality. However, in relating the older morality to the central emphasis upon effort and development and the social doctrines of the gathering and the building of the kingdom, obedience to the law was often regarded as similar to knowing the regularities of nature and using them for utilitarian purposes. Revealed commandments convey information necessary to the progress of the individual. Yet this practical aspect of morality—that it is the embodiment of the

practical requirements of progress in this world and in the next—
is not the whole content of Mormon morals.

Mormonism preserves an older notion of obligation, a notion
that its Protestant founders never thought to repudiate because it
seemed so palpably natural to them. "Oughtness" remained a quality that characterized the Mormon attitude toward the commands
of God. In this connection, the tremendous Mormon emphasis
upon free will must be recalled. Mormonism conceives man as
free and sees him advancing to Godhood through the proper
use of that freedom. What is this proper use of liberty? From one
point of view it would appear to be the making of the correct
choice, in an almost scientific sense of "correctness." Knowledge
is necessary to make a proper choice; but, once the choice is
known, why would a free and rational being, such as Mormonism
conceives man to be, withhold assent?

At this juncture let us remember that Mormonism, in repudiat-
ing the vitiating effects of original sin, did not repudiate the conception of sin itself. Not only can man choose, but he may and
often does choose to do those things that God has forbidden him.
Such a choice is sinful. Hence man is bound to morality by a
genuine obligation, but at the same time the content of the obligation is seen as of practical utility in aiding man's development.
Since the Mormon God is not the creator, it is difficult to see why
his revelations would also be practical laws required for man's
progression, except that God, as a member of the same race as
men, is bound to them by a social tie, a kind of connaturality. He
is, in fact, conceived as a kind of Patriarch, the great Father of the
intelligences. Hence the tie binding men to him is that of subjects
to ruler. Authority is based upon this loyalty, which God's power,
not his ontological primacy, evokes and demands of men.

In this way Mormonism has preserved the older notions of sin
and guilt and combined them with the newer, frankly utilitarian
conceptions of the self-made God demanding loyalty from the
others in their common but unequal work. The patriarchal conception of Father is used to put these two notions together, although they do not fit together completely.

It is perfectly consistent with this voluntaristic utilitarianism,
however, that Mormonism would continue the radical, unsacra-
mental quality of the Protestantism in which it had its origin. Although the flesh and all nature are accepted as good in the Mor-

mon transvaluation of the older Puritanism, this goodness is seen largely as usefulness. Feeling the need for ceremony and mystery, Mormonism developed temple ceremonials, but these rituals, significantly called temple "work," are directed almost completely toward the accomplishment of ends. Mormonism is not characterized by symbolic richness, and it was derived from a background almost totally lacking in sacramentalism. A receptive, contemplative relationship to God is not found as part of Mormon prayer and worship. Rather, achievement is given the prominent part consistent with the basic activist orientation.

Freedom, rationality, the universe a world to conquer (a projection of the American continent to infinity), progress, self-improvement, mastery—these are the basic principles of Mormon theology. They are comprehended in terms of the advancement of intelligences toward perfection, an advancement in which one leading intelligence exerts authority over the rest. Authoritarian and centrally directed co-operation is the characteristic relationship between God and men, a relationship that is reflected in the closely knit church, authoritarian in structure, with its elaborate priesthood organization. Secular activity becomes of spiritual significance. In fact, Mormonism obliterates the line between secular and sacred through its theology of utility. But whether Mormonism represents a further secularization of American Protestantism or a sacralization of secular optimism and activism it is difficult to say. It is, in a sense, both. Mormonism has elaborated an American theology of self-deification through effort, an active transcendentalism of achievement.

CHAPTER SEVEN

Social Institutions: Authority and Government

The problem of authority is one that every human community must solve in some way, for the co-ordination of social life and its stability depend upon the solution. A religious community faces this in an intensified form; it must solve the problem of religious authority. Since religion is concerned with what is ultimate in the human situation—with man's orientation to what lies beyond the empirical here-and-now, beyond the purely human bases of existence—religious authority takes on a peculiar ultimacy and involves the foundation of all authority. Mormonism faced these problems, and it faced them in a special form derived from its own particular beliefs.

Mormonism was not only a religious body but a total community withdrawn and separated from the larger gentile community. It was also a religious community that posited its authority upon direct contemporary revelation and the leadership of a prophet believed to be divinely chosen and directed. Moreover, Mormonism was born in a democratic environment where people expected to govern themselves, or at least to be consulted about how they were to be governed. How could Mormonism reconcile such democratic predilections with the authority of a divinely inspired prophet? How were the special marks of a prophet, his charisma—that unusual character that enabled him to claim inspiration and supernatural powers—to be restrained and restricted? Such restriction was necessary, for if the special charisma of the prophetic office should be interpreted democratically as something available to every member or to any member who believed himself to possess such special gifts, prophetic authority would be dispersed, and the result would be a diffusion of authority and leadership. Even if the special prophetic gifts were successfully claimed only by a handful of leaders, the result would be faction and disunion. It was important for Mormonism to control and contain the very prophetic charisma upon which it was based.

Furthermore, how would Mormonism as a total human community distinguish and harmonize the civil and religious aspects of its authority structure? And, finally, how was Mormon authority, which claimed a divine origin, to be reconciled with the political authority of the larger community? Such problems present themselves in the history of Mormonism in three forms: the containment of charisma, the conflict between hierarchy and congregationalism, and the problems involved in the relations between church and state. Such problems had to be met by evolving Mormonism. Their solution involved the development of a set of social institutions insuring stability and durability.

The Containment of Charisma

Since the new church had been founded upon the claims of contemporary revelation, such revelation remained the basis of all its ecclesiastical authority. This meant that there were two possible paths of development open for the church. It could permit unrestrained prophecy and thereby splinter into smaller and smaller groups, finally breaking up into a Babel of private revelation. On the other hand, it could restrain prophetic gifts, restricting revelation and prophecy to one man, and develop a centrally directed organization about that one leader. Compromises between the two positions were, of course, possible but were likely to be unstable, at least until the original enthusiasm had dissipated itself. If more than one strong prophetic figure claimed revelation, it is hard to see how schism could have been avoided. The ideal of left-wing Protestantism as set forth in the *Book of Mormon* and discussed in our second chapter portrayed a profusion of prophecy and a plurality of prophets, combined with the ecumenical aspiration of one church united around that prophetic authority. Such an ideal was clearly impossible in real life.

Joseph Smith, having claimed charismatic gifts previous to his founding of a church, had almost limited his own gift to that of miraculous translation as early as the spring of 1829. In the months that followed he had, with difficulty, maintained his ascendancy over his amanuensis, Oliver Cowdery, whose series of flirtations with the notion of a prophetic calling of his own threatened Joseph's uniqueness. When the church was established in 1830, the two chief offices were those of Elder. Joseph had himself made First Elder and Cowdery, Second Elder. Moreover, Joseph's revelation explicitly stated that Joseph had been "called of God, and ordained an apostle of Jesus Christ," while Cowdery "was also called of God, an apostle of Jesus Christ . . . and ordained under his [Joseph's] hand" (*D & C*, 20:2–3).

Thus Joseph successfully maintained his priority to Oliver, both in terms of leadership position and as the channel of Oliver's ordination. Cowdery, however, remained very important. Joseph found it necessary to reinforce his own primacy almost immediately, and, in the first meeting after the legal incorporation of the church, he reported a revelation that gave him the titles of prophet, seer, and translator and stated that the members should receive his words as those of the Lord (*D & C*, 21:1, 4). Joseph also continued to use revelation to discipline his new band, e.g., to make the church support himself and Cowdery, to "magnify his office" (*D & C*, 24:3; §19), to admonish his wife Emma (*D & C*, §25), and to assign the Whitmers, an important family of early converts, to missionary tasks (*D & C*, §30). Joseph concentrated the charisma of prophecy upon himself by receiving revelations for other members of the church.

However, in September, 1830, Oliver Cowdery supported the claim of Hiram Page to have received revelations through a stone. Joseph again used revelation to admonish Cowdery that "no one shall be appointed to receive commandments and revelations in this church excepting my servant Joseph Smith, Jun.," who alone had been given "the keys of the mysteries, and the revelations which are sealed, until I shall appoint unto them another in his stead" (*D & C*, 28:2–7). Joseph sent both Cowdery and Page west to preach to the Indians (*D & C*, 28:14–16), although in a subsequent revelation Cowdery is again recognized as second only to Joseph (*D & C*, 30:7).

At this time Sidney Rigdon was converted, and he soon took Cowdery's place as second in command to Joseph (*D & C*, §35), to "watch over him" (*D & C*, 35:19) and to share his privileged position in the new church (*D & C*, 41:7–8). Cowdery was to remain important in Missouri, but he would never recover his previous position. In fact, he eventually lost in his rivalry with Rigdon and apostatized. He claimed revelation outside the church, in which Christ was said to have condemned Joseph's creation of an elaborate priesthood and repudiated his divine calling.[1] Rigdon, on the other hand, not only shared Joseph's leadership in Kirtland (*D & C*, §§37, 44, 49) but aided his new efforts at translation, this time of the Bible, at Hiram, Ohio (*D & C*, §71).

Early in 1831, Kirtland became a scene of much enthusiasm, and direct revelation continued to cause difficulty. So-called "apostolic gifts" of tongues, healing, etc., were approved (*D & C*, §46) but also restrained by Joseph, who set up a safeguard by giving the elders of the church the power to "discern all those gifts lest there shall be any among you professing and yet be not of God" (*D & C*, 46:27). A young boy, among others, produced revelations that caused Joseph to declare in the Lord's name that he alone was to receive revelations and no others unless "it be through him" (*D & C*, 43:4) and to discern and rebuke "false and deceiving spirits" (*D & C*, §52: Preamble, 14–21). Joseph met these problems in September by a revelation which declared that "the keys of the mysteries of the kingdom shall not be taken from my servant Joseph Smith, Jun." and, while admitting he had sinned, admonished the opposition to forgive him (*D & C*, 64:5–10).

That summer Joseph had made his first trip to Missouri to avoid opposition in Ohio, and that fall he removed to Hiram, Ohio, to work on further translations. In the spring of the next year, 1832, he was tarred and feathered, and Rigdon was beaten by a mob, with apostates responsible for both incidents. In 1833, while trouble with outsiders was breaking out in Missouri, internal dissent and unrestricted prophecy again caused difficulty in Kirtland. Joseph reported another revelation, declaring that only through him should "the oracles be given to another, yea, even unto the church" (*D & C*, 90:4).

After the prophet returned from Missouri, where he had gone with Zion's Camp to aid the Saints in Jackson County, he discovered that his position had further deteriorated, and he had to face trial before a church council. Members accused him of being a false prophet. However, he successfully asserted his leadership and organized Kirtland to build a temple. But, before the new house of worship was dedicated, a young woman who claimed to receive revelations through a black stone declared Joseph Smith a fallen prophet and revealed that David Whitmer would replace him. This prophetess was evidently a severe threat to Joseph's position at the time.

Although Joseph's leadership was precarious during much of this period, he successfully weathered all threats, thereby establishing three important precedents. First of all, he concentrated the right to receive revelations in his own person, defining himself as "prophet, seer and revelator." Second, he successfully dominated the first two duumvirates in church leadership. And, third, he had himself made president of the High Priesthood, which put him at the head of what was at that point the body of leading personnel, for the Presidency of the church was not established until the next year. Shortly after his election to the presidency of the High Priesthood, at Amherst, Ohio, in 1832, he was sustained in that position by a church conference in Jackson County, Missouri.

These precedents secured both the leadership of Joseph and the containment of charisma, and even the overwhelming unpopularity that he experienced after the Kirtland bank failure of 1837 could not upset what had been accomplished. The fact is that there was no way of getting rid of Joseph Smith without declaring him a fallen prophet, a decision that, if taken by the whole church, might have disrupted it, once and for all. It was upon his prophecy that the church was built, he was its foundation, and from this important function and position he was never really removed.

In fact, upon his death, imposters like Strang might claim to be his successors while lesser leaders would lead splinter sects away; but the two chief contenders, Sidney Rigdon and Brigham Young, did not really claim to replace him. Rigdon claimed merely the right to rule the church as guardian, while Brigham Young won the right to rule it as president of the Twelve. Only three years later, after his effective planning of the westward trek and his personal leadership of its first stages, did he assume the office of president with the title of "prophet, seer and revelator." Brigham ruled through strength of personality and the machinery of church organization, and neither the pretenses of Morris to renewed revelation nor the spiritualist claims of the Godbeite movement seriously threatened his position. Charisma had been successfully contained within the organized structure of the church and identified with the functions of church office. It had, in fact, to some extent been routinized, and organizational procedures under the direction of a strong authoritarian leader largely replaced visions and revelations, a process that had already started in the last days of Joseph's rule in Nauvoo.

Although taming and restricting private revelation, the church did not fully abandon it. It still recognizes that a member may have private revelation for the direction of his own life, but he cannot use it in any way for the guidance of the lives of others or of the church. Only the president of the church can receive revelation for the church, and about him the aura of charisma remains. He is considered God's spokesman and bears the title of "prophet, seer and revelator."

Hierarchical Structure versus Congregationalism

The recognition of prophetic leadership implies the development of a hierarchical church structure, with authority flowing from top to bottom, at least as soon as the informal master-disciple relationship among a small group is replaced by the more formal relationship of leadership and membership in a large church organization. The process of binding charisma within organizational forms was one aspect of the evolution of such a hierarchical structure, and the original relationship between the prophet and his disciples evolved into a relationship between the prophet and an oligarchy of leading elders, which merged into and exercised ascendancy over the rank and file of the membership.

At the same time the church inherited a tradition of congregationalism (*D & C*, 28:13; 26:2). However, church government by membership vote could be harmonized with authoritarian, prophetic leadership only if prophetic leadership could command the voluntary support and evoke the individual loyalties of the rank and file. This is, by and large, what happened, but the large amount of apostasy and the frequency of conflict testify to the difficulties involved. It appears that from 1831 to 1839 church government was marked by strong congregationalist tendencies, and the membership appear to have decided matters of church government for themselves. We have already seen that the prophet and his lieutenants faced much opposition from within the church, especially in Ohio and later in Illinois.

At first, elders were the only officers in the church, but soon the pressures toward centralization began to express themselves in organizational form. The need to contain charisma, the necessity to hold the organization under Joseph's leadership despite the factions and conflict that plagued Kirtland, and the pressure of external hostility in Missouri, all provided stimuli to centralization. In January, 1832, Joseph Smith was sustained and ordained president of the High Priesthood at Amherst, Ohio, and in April a conference in Missouri acknowledged and sustained him in office. In these events are revealed both the tendency toward centralization in the creation of the office and the expression of congregationalism in the manner of attaining membership approval. In March, 1833, the First Presidency of the church was established, with Joseph as president and Sidney Rigdon and Frederick G. Williams as his counselors (*D & C*, §90). In February, 1834, a High Council was set up in Kirtland while Joseph led Zion's Camp, a military relief expedition, to aid the Saints in Missouri. This council took over the control of church finances.

On September 24 of the same year Joseph had the High Council appoint a committee to "arrange the items of the doctrine of Jesus Christ for the government of the Church," which were to be taken from "the Bible, the *Book of Mormon* and the Revelations." Earlier, such action would have been initiated within a church conference, but, originating in the High Council, the action was now merely approved by such a conference. Moreover, Smith, who headed the committee, had earlier laid hands upon Sidney Rigdon and Oliver Cowdery, blessing them and assigning them the job of preparing "Church Covenants" for publication in the near future. The action of the High Council merely added Joseph himself and Frederick G. Williams to the pair, and this committee, together with its task, was then approved by a conference of the membership. Initiative was moving up the hierarchy, not indeed informally, but in terms of formal organization.

In August, 1835, a new scriptural work was produced by this committee. It was called the *Book of Doctrine and Covenants* and was, in fact, an edited and altered text of an earlier book of revelations called the *Book of Commandments*. This latter the church decided to publish in 1831 and had finally begun to print at its

Independence printing plant when the press was destroyed by a hostile mob in 1833. Some copies were struck off, and a few originals are still extant as collector's items.

The new book tended to register the centralizing changes in structure that had taken place. For example, three verses were added to an earlier section (*D & C*, 20:65–67) which recorded the higher offices of the priesthood that had been established in the recent period; the last of these three verses (*D & C*, 20:67) tended to equate the High Council and the general conference in regard to approval of ordination to offices in the higher priesthood. An earlier revelation that Joseph had received for Martin Harris had addressed Harris directly; this was now edited to address him through Joseph (*B of C*, IV, 2; *D & C*, 5:2). Moreover, Section 68 was changed to give the First Presidency the sole power to try bishops and high priests (*D & C*, 68:22). In February, 1835, the Quorum of the Twelve Apostles had been set up and made, at least nominally, of equal rank with the First Presidency (*D & C*, §107). It was the presidency of this body that later served Brigham Young as a steppingstone to supreme leadership. Two weeks later the Seventies, a larger priesthood quorum, was set up and ranked next below the Twelve (*D & C*, §107). A ranked and graded structure was evolving. In involving large numbers of members, this emerging hierarchical organization expressed the basic congregationalism in a new form that would really replace genuine congregationalism.

In 1834 fewer revelations were offered by Joseph, and, of those given, fewer were deemed publishable for the whole church. Furthermore, those published in 1835 and thereafter were entirely of a doctrinal and directory nature, commands to individuals apparently being discarded or kept private. The early charismatic spontaneity and indiscriminate publishing of prophecy was giving way to caution and discretion, while the chain of command was being made more formal and, in terms of formal structure, centered upon the prophet-president. The new *Doctrine and Covenants*, the method of its creation, and its acceptance by the church conference on August 17, 1835, reflected and formally registered the changes taking place.

The practical problems of the gathering and of construction required decision-making by a leading group who always derived their official authority from the prophet-president. Moreover, increase in size, together with concomitant changes in the nature of the decisions to be made and the number of persons affected by them, could not help making this system more authoritarian in practice. These developments took place in Nauvoo, which also saw a great increase in the intensity of the Mormon-gentile conflict and the authority of the leadership threatened by the desertion of Bennett and the dissent of Law and Foster; the tendencies toward centralization were further stimulated by these pressures. Since leaders of the church were also important civic leaders in the sizable city of Nauvoo, the separation of leaders and followers, together with concentration of power in the former, naturally followed. Yet open congregational action approved the acts of leadership, and the nearly absolute power of the prophet at this time has been characterized as "a willingly designated absolutism."[2]

It was at Nauvoo, in 1841, that Joseph Smith was elected "sole Trustee in Trust" for the church, to hold his office "during life" and "vested with plenary powers, as sole Trustee in Trust for the Church of Jesus Christ of Latter-day Saints, to receive, acquire, manage or convey property, real, personal, or mixed, for the sole use and benefit of said Church."[3] Joseph had indeed achieved absolute power in terms of formal structure, although he was still subject to the checks of his lieutenants.

The fact that the Saints in Ohio, Missouri, and Illinois had left their old habitations to join the gathering of the elect made the individual convert's fate almost totally dependent upon the group, which meant in practice upon the decisions of the leadership, a fact that became even more true in the isolation of Utah. Such dependence strengthened the ties between leaders and followers, and thus economic, social, and political factors joined the religious in strengthening group loyalties and enhancing the authority of the leaders. The growth of the Mormon community demanded initiative in decision-making and problem-solving, and, as leadership in decision-making is practiced and accepted, authority evolves naturally. This is especially true when it takes place, as it did among the Mormons, within the context of religious loyalty and the developing mentality of a peculiar and separate people.

The acceptance of Joseph Smith as a "true prophet of God" was and remains fundamental to an acceptance of Mormonism. The members of the leading oligarchy derived their authority from him. In a formal sense the church defined itself as a theocracy, as indeed it does today. In actual fact it was upon the acceptance of Joseph as a prophet by the rank and file that the legitimacy of the leading oligarchy depended, as well as the legitimacy of the structure in which they held their positions and the legitimacy of the restoration upon which it all rested. Accepting Joseph as a prophet and acting together for the achievement of the common ends that his prophetic leadership prescribed, the Latter-day Saints evolved a hierarchical structure which gave organizational expression to theocratic doctrine. Congregationalism, so much a part of the democratic habits of the converts, was important; but, however important it may have been, it had to become either the registering of assent to a leadership believed to be divinely inspired or rebellion.

There were, in fact, three possibilities: to apostatize (which was not infrequent), to attempt to persuade and limit authoritarian leadership by informal devices (which was done), or to claim that after some point in time Joseph (or Brigham) was a fallen prophet (which was also done). Informal devices to influence and limit the power of Joseph Smith, together with his own responsiveness to the expectations of his people and his lieutenants as he perceived these in the formal and informal contacts of daily life, were the really effective limitations on his power. The more these were successful, however, the more they strengthened the oligarchical structure of leadership and decision-making.

Had a fight between Joseph Smith and William Law developed out of the Seceders' church and the *Expositor* incident in Nauvoo, the third possibility—rebellion—might well have had its day. There seems little doubt that such a fight would have caused an exposure of plural marriage and thereby have found an issue that could split the church in two. Moreover, democracy in church government would certainly have been an issue. But Joseph's murder made a martyr of the prophet and thereby insured the dominance of the church Presidency and of the leadership loyal to him. The withdrawal of the Laws and their supporters and the further desertion of dissidents during the interregnum, together with the vigorous leadership supplied by Brigham Young in salvaging the organization and moving westward, greatly reinforced this dominance. In this the importance of Brigham's personality and ability must be emphasized.

Mormonism had attempted to reconcile prophetic leadership with congregationalism, an attempt that worked itself out in the context of common suffering and achievement. What had developed was a democracy of participation and an oligarchy of decision-making and command. As hierarchical bodies evolved, they were filled with men capable of exerting leadership. The development of a chain of command meant also the promotion of potential leaders from below. The tasks of life continued to demand initiative upon lower levels. Congregational action became more and more ceremonial, but initiative was not choked off, and men rising in the ranks remained capable of genuine leadership. Thus Mormon authoritarianism drew its leaders from the ranks, and the ranks supported such leaders. Genuine initiative on regionally or structurally subordinate levels remained a characteristic of Mormon ecclesiastical organization. There resulted an institutionalized structure embracing an elaborate network of priesthood and auxiliary organizations, activating a large proportion of the membership under centralized leadership.

Church and State

Perhaps no problem in the history of Mormonism is more complicated than the Mormon conception of church and state, on the one hand, and the problem of the relationship between the Mormon community and the United States, on the other. The idea of the "gathering" implied both a withdrawal of the elect from the gentile world and a separate community of the Saints. Since the gathering took place under the leadership of the restored church and its prophet-leader, the hierarchical leadership and the authoritarian rule implicit in it came to characterize the new community. The alternatives open to prophetic leadership were centralization or dissipation. Mormonism had chosen the former, but not without hesitation and difficulty.

As a result, the divinely appointed task of preparing for the Second Coming was accomplished under a more and more authoritarian guidance as time went on. In this millennial coming of the Lord, it was expected that he would reign from the New Jerusalem and govern the renewed earth. Such government would obviously be theocratic. Until then, the church government would also be theocratic, but the divine authority would flow into the general priesthood organizations through the prophet-president instead of coming directly from Christ, as expected in the Advent. The kingdom which the Saints were to prepare was an earthly kingdom, it was a this-worldly society, involving social, economic, and political aspects of life as well as religious. The New Jerusalem was a total community, and the Mormon separatism was not only theocratic in church government but also totalitarian, in the sense of encompassing the totality of human activity within its orbit and under the leadership of the church.

Thus it may be seen that the Zionism of Mormon millennial doctrine implied separation from the gentiles, theocracy, and authoritarian direction of the worldly activities involved in building the kingdom, and a total encompassing of life in a new society. The importance of the first is obvious, since practically all Mormon as well as schismatic Latter-day Saint activity took the form of building a separate community of the gathered. The importance of theocracy is no less clear. The Mormon church today defines its government as theocratic, and the establishment of a theocratic community was the main object of the schismatics. Strang became king of Zion on Beaver Island, Michigan. Hedrick hoped to set up a theocratic state during the Civil War, and Morris founded a theocratically governed schismatic colony in Utah. Moreover, such splinter groups as the Bickertonites and the Brewsterites had similar ambitions. The fact is that a separate community, based upon the ultimate authority of a leader of the church and in which church leadership exerted influence and took initiative in fields of endeavor far removed from religion and ecclesiastical affairs, was basic to all Mormon efforts. This indicates how all-embracing was the conception of the new society implied by Mormon ideals.

Moreover, together with hierarchical ecclesiastical government, which developed inevitably in the situation of a prophet-leader and a covenant people, there tended to emerge a trend toward monarchy. This appeared later than hierarchical government and under conditions of secrecy in the official church. In some of the schismatic groups, however, it came out into the open. Strang, as noted earlier, became King James in his Michigan Zion. Charles B. Thompson set himself up as king over his theocratic, socialistic group in Iowa. John C. Bennett is said to have brought "a well formuluated theocratic theory and plans for a military kingdom" to Strang, when he joined him four years after his expulsion from Nauvoo.[4] It has been suggested that such plans matured in Bennett's head in his last days of association with the Mormon prophet.

William Marks, Thompson, and others have reported that Joseph reigned secretly in Nauvoo, where he had established a kingdom and a Council of Fifty. It is interesting to note that among the things to which the Laws and Foster objected in the fateful Nauvoo *Expositor* incident was "any man as king or lawgiver in the church." It is not impossible that the tendency toward establishing a theocratic kingdom that came into the light of day in some of the schismatic groups went further toward realization in Nauvoo than Mormons today would admit or, in fact, than they know to be the case.

Yet the fact that church government began with marked congregationalist tendencies and that it retained them in some form throughout its career must also be reckoned with. At first, the conference of the membership was really the final governing body, and its position as a fundamental element in the Mormon church has remained. Yet a hierarchy of offices and councils came to exert leadership while membership vote both in general conference and in local church meetings became a matter of "sustaining" the decisions of the authorities. It became a matter more of expression of assent than a process of choice. Yet discussion and initiative were not shut off in local church councils and committees. While Brigham Young became something very close to an absolute leader in one sense, the fact is that his lieutenants were capable of initiative and his people in large numbers gave their assent willingly. Today, sustaining the authorities is a formality and is, in fact, a requirement for full membership. One of the questions to which one must answer in the affirmative before being allowed to enter a temple concerns whether or not one sustains the general authorities of the church. Yet the congregationalist tradition has been real and finds expression in such diverse forms as wide membership participation and, in some circles, opposition to authoritarianism among the leaders.

The Saints had always recognized the legitimacy of civil government, despite the theocratic nature of the church and its totalitarian claims. Was this recognition only because the exigencies of the situation demanded that the Mormons meet the requirements of civil law? Certainly, taking part in politics in Missouri and Illinois, application for statehood in Utah, and the subsequent acceptance of territorial status, all implied an acceptance of civil government; and these acts were obvious conditions for survival in the circumstances. The Nauvoo Charter was the way to self-government, and territoriality was a move to control the gentiles who were being attracted by California gold and to forestall their dominance in the region.

There can be no doubt that it was in the interests of the Mormon leadership and the Mormon group as a whole to recognize and to participate in the civil state. This involved recognition of the separation of church and state, at least in a formal sense. Yet the theocratic implications of Mormon beliefs found expression not only in the supervision of civil life by ecclesiastical government, as in the early days of territorial settlement in Utah, but also in the statements of the Mormon leaders at an earlier period. In his candidacy for the Presidency of the United States in 1844, Joseph Smith favored "theo-democracy," advocating the joint rule of God and man, while his brother Hyrum saw political parties as superfluous and spoke in favor of a one-party state. Was not Mormonism advocating a change of the secular republic into a sacred despotism?

But this is far from the whole answer. There is strong reason to believe that the Mormon founders and converts naturally thought in terms of republican political forms, that in seeking their own interests they would naturally make use of them, and in governing themselves would just as naturally set them up. The *Book of Mormon* had early given republicanism a strongly preferential treatment. Moreover, in 1835 a general conference of the church at Kirtland, Ohio, the same one that approved the new *Doctrine and Covenants* and a more centralized church government, approved a "Declaration of Belief regarding Governments and Laws in general" (*D & C*, §134). This declaration took a thoroughly Lockian position on the limited nature of religious societies, supported freedom of worship, and opposed it as unjust to "mingle religious influence with the civil government, whereby one religious society is fostered and another proscribed."[5]

In its quarrel in Missouri the Mormon leadership went so far to appease its enemies that it denied the charge of abolitionism leveled against the church by what amounted to an acceptance of the institution of slavery. This was also the position taken by the 1835 declaration, which did "not believe it right to interfere with bond-servants" or to convert them "contrary to the will and wish of their masters, nor to meddle with or influence them in the least to cause them to be dissatisfied with their situations in this life" (*D & C*, 134:12). While this attitude must have gone against the grain with many of the Yorker, Ohio, and Yankee converts, the general attitude toward government institutions must have seemed natural enough, and, while attempting to convince outsiders that the rumors of Mormon illegality and crime were without foundation, the document must have reassured those who may have been worried about the tendency toward centralization of the church government.

Moreover, it must be recalled that the Mormon idea of America as a promised land included an official recognition of American political institutions as divinely appointed. The Mormon church saw in the discovery of this continent and its settlement the preparation for the restoration of which it claimed itself to be the institutional embodiment. The free political institutions of the United States were seen as strategically important in this regard, and the Saints believed and today still believe that the Constitution was divinely inspired. Certainly, Joseph's several attempts to seek redress of grievances from state and federal governments and his candidacy for election to the Presidency of the United States would seem to support the notion of his constitutionalism. Extra-constitutional methods were not a Mormon monopoly in the unsettled West; but, like most pioneers, the Mormon founders and converts seem to have been quite permeated by the democratic notions of government characteristic of their time and place. It is interesting to note that, in defending themselves at the very height of the polygamy fight in Utah, the Mormon leadership appealed to the First Amendment. Obeying the laws of the land was a constant Mormon admonition and has become a proverbial statement among the Saints. It was the basis upon which Wilford Woodruff acceded to the antipolygamy laws in his "Official Declaration."

Yet the fact is that both Jackson County and Far West were each to have been a New Jerusalem. How would this have been integrated into the larger gentile political structure? Nauvoo attempted this on the basis of the unusual Nauvoo Charter. Yet the Missouri and Illinois experiences demonstrated that it was impossible to be both a special covenant people building a separate community and an integral part of a larger secular commonwealth.

The situation was bound to lead to conflict, and it led to violence in the semisettled regions of those two states.

Joseph Smith, near the end of his life, came to realize that he had been attempting the impossible and began to think in terms of westward movement. Experience had demonstrated that Zion could not be gathered in the midst of Babylon. It must physically remove itself from the gentiles more completely than it had done. Brigham Young carried out what Joseph also had been coming to understand as necessary in his last days. He took his people west to the isolation of the Rocky Mountains in the territory of the Republic of Mexico. Did he intend to carry separation to the point of a politically independent Mormon nation? Would he establish a theocratic civil-ecclesiastical government on this virgin land?

There was a good deal of anti–United States feeling among the Saints after the expulsion from Nauvoo, but Brigham still sought federal aid and even enlisted 500 men in the military service of the United States and would have offered a larger number, had the government been willing. While the idea of getting out of United States territory must have been seductive indeed in the light of past experiences, Brigham certainly understood the mission of the Mormon Battalion in marching to California to take that area from Mexico and, shrewd as he was, could hardly have failed to read aright its significance for the Great Basin. On arrival in Utah in 1847, the Mormons unfurled the Stars and Stripes, and in 1850 applied for admission to the Union. Certainly these moves were tied up with such projects as the Mormon corridor to the sea and the settlement of the San Bernardino Valley in California, obviously designed to give the Saints control in the area.

Yet Mormon loyalty to the older sovereignty was not lacking. If one is to emphasize the self-interested motives for Mormon loyalty, one must also register the shock caused by the announcement in 1857 of the sending of Johnston's army against them by President Buchanan. Mormon separatism in the Utah Mormon War became an open threat, but it was not unprovoked. Moreover, the tendency to expect and demand federal aid at one time and to consider secession at another characterized other western groups. Even a fight with federal officials was not peculiarly a Mormon experience. Mormonism was experiencing the usual concomitants of westward settlement, but it was experiencing them in its own special way, in terms of its unique history and point of view. Separateness was implied in the groundwork of the Mormon gospel, and separateness itself implied, especially given the circumstances of the time and the characteristics of the group, a tendency toward political independence.

The fact is that the Mormons never worked out consistently the political implications of their religious philosophy. Its theocratic and separatist aspects were counterbalanced by democratic and patriotic motives which were equally genuine and equally well grounded in Mormon doctrine. If the former were based upon the ideal of Zion, the latter followed from the Mormon definition of man and had, besides, the support of popular bias. Moreover, acting upon these somewhat contradictory conceptions, the Mormons unintentionally created the situations that drove them toward separation, while causing their internal structure to develop the hierarchical and authoritarian implications of its prophetic basis. The ambiguity of Mormon ideals with regard to church and state, an ambiguity that was not fully recognized, was reinforced by the ambivalence toward the United States that conflict had brought into existence.

The conflict itself was partly the result of the original orientations and partly the fruit of Mormon attempts to implement them in action. Other circumstances could obviously have brought other results. Gold was discovered at Sutter's Mill by Mormons who had been demobilized from the Battalion and were on their way back to Utah. Ironical though it may be, the discovery merely hastened an inevitable development, the settlement of the West by gentiles and the forced integration of the mountain Zion into the larger American commonwealth. The Mormons were not uninfluenced by their American patriotism at any point in this long struggle, and since accommodation they have emphasized and even exaggerated their belief in America as a chosen nation. Even Joseph Smith had said a few months before his death, "The whole of America is Zion itself from north to south."[6]

As for the separation of church and state, it came naturally enough to have real meaning after statehood was achieved and the Mormon and gentile communities in Utah began to develop some genuine co-operation. Since all male Mormons are members of the priesthood, there is a considerable overlap of personnel, and top leaders, such as the Apostles, have accepted top legislative and executive positions, even in the national cabinet.

Politics

Mormonism, together with its acceptance of civil government, was, almost from the start, involved in politics. Mormon voting had set off one anti-Mormon riot in Missouri, and in Illinois, bloc voting by the Mormon community, together with resentment of Mormon political influence in Springfield, was a source of gentile fears and suspicions. Joseph Smith had been both mayor of the city and president of the church at the time of his death, and Brigham Young held both the territorial governorship and the church Presidency simultaneously and had run for and accepted the governorship of the "Provisional State of Deseret." He held the gubernatorial position for years in the Deseret "shadow government" that met alongside the territorial government, the legislatures of the two coinciding.

If this last gesture expressed possible separationist tendencies, it also signified the willingness of the church to enter into politics. In the Mormon-gentile conflict of territorial days, the Mormons had formed the People's party and took an active part in political struggle. When in 1890 President Woodruff issued his "Official Declaration" ending church approval of plural marriage and when, a few days later, President Harrison pardoned those who had been imprisoned for polygamy, the old line-up of People's party versus Liberal party in Utah began to disintegrate. In place of the local parties, national political party labels were imported. Mormons, at the direction of the church, became identified with both the Republican and the Democratic parties, but immediately after statehood most of the church leadership leaned to the Democratic side. Very soon, however, the leadership changed its political sentiments and became, by and large, Republican. It has since remained largely on the side of the Grand Old Party, especially, perhaps, sympathizing with the more conservative wing, although the Utah vote has not been controlled by conservative churchmen in this respect.

When Reed Smoot was elected to the Senate in 1902, an important Mormon churchman for the first time entered the higher echelons of the national government. He had been appointed an Apostle in 1900, and after his election Utah opposition took the form of a protest against his being seated. The Mormon-gentile conflict was reopened on the national scene. Led by Protestant ministers of Salt Lake City, the objectors, who had successfully eliminated Brigham H. Roberts from the House of Representatives in 1900, forwarded their petition to the Senate.

Joseph Fielding Smith has commented on the hearing which followed: "It was apparent from the beginning that it was the Church of Jesus Christ of Latter-day Saints that was on trial before the nation, not Senator Reed Smoot." Petitions supporting the hostile opposition poured in from the country. Polygamy and the church's "supreme authority in all things temporal and spiritual" were urged as objections against Smoot's acceptance.[7] Church leaders had to testify, and, finally, after a majority committee report against Smoot, the Senate voted. There were 28 yeas, 42 nays, and 20 abstentions. The resolution, which required two-thirds approval, was defeated, and the Utah senator took his seat. The last major flareup of the Mormon-gentile conflict on a national scale had ended in a Mormon victory.

In the years that followed, both Republican and Democrat, Mormon and gentile, shared the political offices of the new state, but the Republicans held something of an edge. In 1933, with the coming of the New Deal under President Roosevelt, the Mormon leadership saw in the program of government controls a threat to the values of individual initiative and hard work. As a result, the majority of church leaders became even more confirmed supporters of the Republican party. Yet in 1932, Roosevelt carried Utah, and Reed Smoot, Apostle and senator for almost a generation, was defeated by Elbert Thomas, another Mormon, who had fulfilled a Mormon mission in Japan and who was a professor of political science at the University of Utah. The Democratic party, despite the opposition of the church paper, the *Deseret News*, which was outspokenly anti–New Deal, remained dominant in Utah until 1946. Senator Thomas was defeated in 1950 by another Mormon Republican, who had strong support from the church leadership.

The political trends in Utah are, in general, similar to those nationally, which suggests that the church leadership cannot and does not control the vote. Analysis of local figures supports this suggestion. In fact, while exerting political influence, the church leadership often points with pride to the fact that it does not control the vote, an interesting reaction conditioned by generations of gentile resentment and suspicion on this score.

The Organization of the Mormon Church

The Mormon church is governed by a complex priesthood hierarchy, which involves "all worthy males" in some capacity. There is no professional clergy, but there is a conception of the priesthood as involving a "principle of power, of intelligence through which divine work and purposes are achieved."[8] Thus has Mormonism articulated the anticlerical tendencies of its original milieu with the notion of priestly power inherent in the basic conception of the restoration.

Mormonism originated in a time when lay responsibility in church government was widespread and developed in circumstances that demanded lay participation for the survival of the group and the carrying-out of its program. The natural tendency of converts in a new and somewhat sectarian group was to participate in the governmental, proselytizing, and other activities of the new church. When efforts to build the New Jerusalem began, such participation would naturally expand. If western conditions caused older and established churches to make use of laymen, a new and struggling religious movement had all the more reason to do so, and no inhibiting traditions.

Yet Mormonism maintained this high degree of active participation by the membership while at the same time setting forth and developing a concept of priestly office. The lay priesthood of the Mormon church compromised and combined anticlericalism with priestly function. Unlike the Disciples, who also obliterated the distinction between the clergy and the laity by holding that no man be called priest, Mormonism accomplished the same thing by making every man a priest and giving him the titles of office. Moreover, since the Mormon priesthood rested upon the genuineness of the prophet by whose agency it was brought about, its organization became hierarchical in structure, a tendency that was increased, as has been seen, by the demands of building Zion and the conditions of conflict. The combination of anticlericalism and priestly office was at the same time an organizational expression of the compromise between democracy and authority as a democracy of participation and an authoritarian structure of control.

The elaborate priesthood organization is divided into two orders or subdivisions. The lower, called the Aaronic or Levitical priesthood, is believed to have been restored through the miraculous ordination of Joseph Smith and Oliver Cowdery by John the Baptist in 1829 (*D & C*, §13),[9] while the higher or Melchizedek priesthood is believed to have been restored through the miraculous intervention of Peter, James, and John, the time of which is uncertain (*D & C*, §27; §128; 76:57; 68:19; 84:14–20; §107; 124:123). Consistent with the concept of the priest as holding a divine office, ordinations are by the laying on of hands, and there is a theory of "Apostolic Succession," for the holders of these offices in the Mormon church are given certificates tracing their ordination through several generations of such laying on of hands, going back to the original miraculous events.

These two priesthood orders are further subdivided into councils or quorums, which are age-graded, and together form a promotion ladder by which the Mormon boy advances to adult status in the church. These ranks and the corresponding age grades are as follows:

THE AARONIC OR LEVITICAL PRIESTHOOD

Deacon, twelve to fifteen years of age
Teacher, fifteen to eighteen years of age
Priest, eighteen to twenty years of age

THE MELCHIZEDEK PRIESTHOOD

Elder, twenty years of age
Seventy, not age-graded in a formal sense
    but usually mature men in middle life
High Priest, not age-graded, but usually
    mature men in middle life

The faithful Mormon boy is admitted to the Aaronic priesthood at the age of twelve, when he is ordained a deacon. It is usual for him to remain in this rank for about three years, during which time he serves in an auxiliary capacity to senior members of the Aaronic priesthood and to the members of the higher priesthood. Twelve deacons form a quorum or council, at the head of which is a president and two counselors. The quorum also has a clerk. The young boy is thus introduced at an early age to the characteristic organization and functioning of the church.

After about three years as deacon, the young boy is advanced to the rank of teacher. Officially, this rank has the duty "to watch over the church always, and be with and strengthen them; and see that there is no iniquity in the church, neither hardness with each other, neither lying, backbiting, nor evil speaking; and see that the church meet together often, and also see that all the members do their duty. And he is to take the lead of meetings in the absence of the elder or priest" (*D & C*, 20:53–56). These duties, laid down in 1830, were obviously not intended for members in the present adolescent age bracket. The original function of the teachers—to contribute to the internal peace of the local church organization and keep the bishop informed on the condition of his flock as well as to discuss doctrine—is still carried out. It is not, however, left to boys of this young age; rather, the teachers merely participate in these activities, accompanying older men, members of the higher priesthood. This experience is a sort of apprenticeship for the boys in the church today, who, together with their older mentors, are supposed to visit the entire local membership monthly and inform the bishops of cases of need, marital troubles, and similar problems requiring their attention.

At the age of seventeen or eighteen, after some five or six years as a deacon and teacher, the boy is ordained a priest, whose "duty is to preach, teach, expound, exhort, and baptize, and administer the sacrament" (*D & C*, 20:46). The priests actually assist elders and visit the homes of members at the suggestion of the bishop. They are also organized into a quorum or council consisting of forty-eight members, which is headed by a high priest.

The highest office in the Aaronic priesthood is that of bishop, which must be filled by a member of the higher order with the rank of high priest. This office may be filled also by a literal descendant of Aaron, but apparently this requirement has never been met in the church. The bishop is assisted by two counselors, making up the typical Mormon executive body of a chief and two assistants, and these two counselors must also be high priests. There are in the church both general and local bishops, the general including the Presiding Bishop, who is over all bishops and all Aaronic priesthood quorums or councils in the church. The local bishops are the administrative heads of wards, are, in fact, unpaid local pastors, and are selected by the First Presidency of the church on the advice of the stake presidency and council, regional authorities to be discussed later.

The Melchizedek priesthood is the higher order and also has three ranks—elder, seventy, and high priest. When a young man is ordained to the higher priesthood, he is made an elder. This rank marks the arrival at full adult status, and its holder is believed to possess all the supernatural powers of the Melchizedek priesthood as a body capable of administering divine ordinances on earth. Such powers, however, may be used legitimately only in their proper organizational context. Thus the charismatic priesthood is contained within the organizational structure and controlled by the discipline of the church. The elders, who are ordained around the age of twenty, are organized into a council or quorum, which, when completely filled, consists of ninety-six members and is presided over by a president and his two counselors, who are also elders and members of the same quorum.

Above the elders is the rank of seventy. The seventies are elders who are called to be traveling missionaries and who work under the direction of the Council of the Twelve. Most members are ordained to this rank after they are called by the First Presidency of the church to go on a mission. The usual age for missionaries is around twenty-one. It is customary for many Mormon youths to go on missions to foreign countries or to other parts of the United States for two years at their own expense. This is looked upon as important character training for the young man, and it is after this mission that he is usually made a seventy. The quorums of the seventies are made up of seventy members and are presided over by seven presidents, each of whom is supposed to have equal authority with any of the others. The senior member presides, and this quorum may extend over two or more stakes (territorial divisions to be discussed later).

At the top of this ascending ladder of priestly office is the rank of high priest. The members of this rank hold most of the leading offices in the church, locally and on a general level. The First President and his two counselors, the Twelve, bishops, and stake presidents are all high priests. Mission presidents and the seven presidents of Seventies need not be high priests.

Authority in this priesthood organization is from the top downward and responsibility from the bottom up. The President of the church is still the divinely inspired prophet, seer, and revelator of the restored dispensation. All the local, regional, and church-wide functions of the church are managed by this non-professional priesthood under the leadership of the top officials. The top leadership consists of a body of men called the "General Authorities." There are twenty-six members, and they are the occupants of the major offices: the First Presidency, consisting of the President and his two counselors, the Council or Quorum of the Twelve, the Patriarch of the church, the First Council or Seven Presidents of Seventy, and the Presiding Bishopric, consisting of the Presiding Bishop and two counselors. They are given here in order of importance. They also appoint assistants to aid them in their tasks.

The Presiding Bishopric is composed of the Presiding Bishop and his two counselors and has authority over the lesser or Aaronic priesthood. It also has charge of all church business not directly controlled by the First Presidency. The traditional job of the bishop is to manage the "temporal affairs" of the church. The Presiding Bishopric, together with the twelve high priests who act as its special counselors but are not members of the General Authorities, acts as a court to try a member of the First Presidency against whom charges may have been brought. The First Presidency has sole power to appoint members of the Presiding Bishopric.

The First Council of the Seventy, with seven members, presides over the quorums of seventies in the church and is a traveling high council in charge of missionary work and any other work assigned to it by the First Presidency. When traveling, its members are considered representatives of the First Presidency and the Council of the Twelve.

The office of Patriarch is somewhat different from the others and stands a little to one side in the hierarchy of leadership. It is hereditary, although the person appointed, who has a hereditary right to be a candidate, like other officers must be sustained by a general conference of the church. The jurisdiction of the Patriarch is general, extending throughout the church. He bestows blessings and declares lineages, the latter believed to be by inspiration of the Holy Spirit. There are also regional patriarchs with similar functions. The patriarchal blessing has often been a means of encouragement in times of stress and has thus helped to hold the community together. It is through the declarations of lineage that ancestry is traced back to the tribes of Israel.

The Council or Quorum of the Twelve, whose members are called "Apostles," is believed to hold the restored office of the original Apostles. The members of this body elect the First President of the church, choosing their senior member (a precedent started by Brigham Young). The Apostles travel throughout the church, handle administrative business, and comprise a kind of executive high council.

The most important office in the church is that of First President, the position held by Joseph Smith and Brigham Young. The other presidents have been John Taylor, who was with Joseph at the time of his death and was a firm defender of plural marriage in Utah; Wilford Woodruff, who yielded to the federal government in making his famous "Official Declaration" ending church sanction of polygamy; Lorenzo Snow, who had been ordained an Apostle by Heber C. Kimball; Joseph F. Smith, who was born in Far West, Missouri, a collateral descendant of the prophet (whose direct descendants continue to hold the chief offices in the schismatic Reorganized Church), and who had been made an Apostle by Brigham Young; Heber J. Grant, who had been made an Apostle by George Q. Cannon and who was the first church president to be born in Utah; George Albert Smith, also related to the family of the founder and born in Utah; and David O. McKay, the present head of the church. The president is still considered the divinely inspired prophet, seer, and revelator, although revelation has been undramatic and almost unofficial. Of all the statements on policy made by the presidents since Joseph Smith, only two have been added to the *Doctrine and Covenants*, the order of Brigham Young in Nebraska preparing the westward trek (*D & C*, §136) and the Official Declaration ending polygamy, which, however, has not been given a section number but has merely been appended.

The president is assisted by two counselors, and together these three men constitute the First Presidency. The president calls and appoints bishops (*D & C*, 68:15, 19, 20), may officiate in all offices of the church (*D & C*, 107:9), and may with his counselors try difficult cases of church discipline (*D & C*, 107:78–80). He appoints all other members of the General Authorities. All offices are subject to approval by the sustaining vote of the general conference of the church. Such general conferences are held twice a year in Salt Lake City, in April (called the "annual conference") and in October (called the "semiannual conference"). To these, all members may come, and bishops and many others do come in from all over Mormondom, and interest in them is genuine. Yet such meetings have no genuine legislative function. They are rather mechanisms to facilitate communication between the central and the local and regional leadership and to cement relations between leaders and members.

Under the General Authorities, who govern the general body of the church, are the stake and ward organizations, roughly comparable to the older diocese and parish, except that the Mormon units are usually smaller. The membership of a stake varies from 2,000 to 10,000, although some smaller than 2,000 were reported in 1949, when the average size was 5,000. The stake is presided over by a stake presidency made up of a president and his two counselors, and the high council, really an advisory group to the stake presidency, which usually has 12 but sometimes 15 members. There is also a stake clerk.

The stake president is chosen by the General Authorities of the church, by the First Presidency, or by the Council of the Twelve. All priesthood and auxiliary organizations of the church have divisions at the stake level. A stake patriarch is appointed by the First Presidency or the Council of the Twelve. Stake conferences are held quarterly, usually on Saturday and Sunday, and a representative of the General Authorities, often an Apostle, attends.

The stake is subdivided into wards, and the ward is the basic geographical unit of Mormon church life. There are usually from 200 to 1,800 persons in a ward. Nelson estimated the median figure for ward membership at 450, and in 1949 the average ward size was 631.[10] Some few are under 100 members. The church considers 750 as the ideal size for a ward; it is felt that, when a ward exceeds that figure by very much, a portion of the congregation will become mere onlookers, and this conflicts with the basic Mormon conceptions of active participation. As a result, there is a continual subdivision of wards within the church, especially in the urban areas and particularly in Salt Lake City. In these expanding areas, a new ward is frequently established by fission, and two wards continue to meet in the old meeting house while a new one is being built for the new ward. This principle of subdivision to insure participation also holds on the stake level.

The ward has local priesthood organizations in all the ranks of the two priesthood orders. These groups meet locally each week, and the groups of the Melchizedek priesthood meet with their stake quorums quarterly. The ward is presided over by a bishop, an unpaid part-time official, who supervises all ward organizations with the aid of his two counselors. He has sole power of appointment of local church officers; this is, however, carried out in close consultation with and with the approval of the organization concerned. Such appointments are sustained by a vote of the membership. In the ward, a bishop's court, composed of the bishop and his two counselors, is at least potentially possible, although in many wards such courts have not met for years. The church courts were of the utmost importance in the early days of settlement, when Mormons avoided the courts presided over by hostile federal officials. The church courts counseled conciliation and were a potent force making for harmony and integration of the group.

All members of the church, including the members of the General Authorities, must belong to a ward organization and are bound in local matters to the authority of the bishop. Wards are supposed to keep a filing system on their members, which is kept up to date on the basis of the monthly visits of ward teachers to the homes of the members. Every five years a complete census is taken and forwarded to Salt Lake City. All important statistics on the membership are supposed to be kept in the ward. The importance attached to keeping records in the Mormon church is tremendous.

The stake presidency nominates the ward bishops in its jurisdiction, forwarding its suggestions to the First Presidency of the church for confirmation. There were 179 stakes in 1950 in the United States, Mexico, and the Hawaiian Islands. The number of wards in a stake varies from five to ten, and in 1949 the average number was eight. In that same year there were nearly fourteen hundred wards in the church.

In the missionary areas, both at home and abroad, the stake and ward organizations are replaced by districts and branches. A district is headed by a president and two counselors, as is a branch. These officials are likely to be young men serving on their voluntary two-year mission, who do not have to be high priests. These mission organizations are integrated into a larger territorial organization called "the Mission," which is also headed by a presidency. There were forty-two missions in the church in 1950, twenty-six of them outside the United States.

The church has a number of auxiliary organizations whose role it is to activate those not members of the priesthood councils, mostly women and young people, and to carry out special tasks not handled by those bodies. Several of them fulfil these requirements by activating various age and sex groups within the church. These bodies are organized on a ward, stake, regional, and general basis, their structures meshing with the structure of the church on all these levels. Their officers are appointed by the church leadership, after consulting the group concerned, and locally by the ward bishop. It is in the context of these structures that church education, highly organized and effective, takes place; that the remarkable program of Mormon recreation is carried on; and that the relief of the poor is effected and many other church programs carried out.

The largest auxiliary is the Deseret Sunday School Union, which in 1949 had 406,850 members and which conducts religious education. It is not solely a children's or young people's affair but includes men and women of all ages in the church. It has graded classes for various age levels.

Next in importance, if not, indeed, more important, is the Women's Relief Society, which in 1949 had 121,910 members. It is in and through this organization that the mature women of the church are activated. Founded in 1842 in Nauvoo, Illinois, by 18 women under the direction of Joseph Smith, the Relief Society has evoked the support and activity of Mormon women for over a century. Family relief, maternal and child welfare classes, and aiding the Church Welfare Plan have been among its activities. It has no written constitution and by-laws but works under the direction of the priesthood and on the basis of its own precedents. It has supplied the feminine equivalent of the priesthood activities for men.

The large-scale recreational programs of the church are carried out to a great extent by the auxiliary organizations of the younger people: the Young Men's Mutual Improvement Association, the Young Women's Mutual Improvement Association, and the Primary. The first two are organizations of adolescents and young adults of the church, and the last is made up of children under twelve years of age. All carry on educational and recreational activities. In 1949 their membership was as follows: YMMIA, 69,200; YWMIA, 82,000; and Primary, 135,000.

Many of the older people of the church are active in the Genealogical Society, which devotes itself to genealogical research in preparation for vicarious temple work for the dead. It publishes a genealogical magazine and runs a genealogical library at Salt Lake City. The two Mutual Improvement Associations, together with other church agencies, such as the Department of Education, the Music Committee, and the Ward Teachers, publish the *Improvement Era*, a monthly, now over half a century old. The Sunday School Union publishes another monthly, *The Instructor*, now in its eighty-eighth year, and the women's organization issues its own monthly, *The Relief Society Magazine*, now over forty years old.

The church maintains a Department of Education, which carries on, among other activities concerned with church education, the institutes and seminaries that the church has erected and maintains next to colleges, junior colleges, and high schools throughout the intermountain West. The church has used these to meet the threat of secularism in education. In 1949–50 some five thousand students participated in the sixteen institutes for college students. In the fall of 1950 three new institutes were opened. Much larger numbers took part in the seminaries, similar organizations for the high schools, of which there are about a hundred and twenty. Both institutes and seminaries maintain buildings and facilities, often at tremendous expense, such as the Institute of Religion at Salt Lake. Utah high schools may allow credit for the Bible courses given at the seminaries. The church maintains Brigham Young University at Provo, Utah, a large, reputable, and expanding institution of higher learning, and a business college at Salt Lake City. At one time the church maintained junior colleges throughout the state, but these have now long since been sold to the state government, which operates them.

The Church Welfare Plan organization, discussed in detail in the next chapter, has of recent years activated thousands of Saints who have seen in it a recrudescence of the old co-operative spirit and answered with enthusiasm its call to co-operative activity in the economic field.

The degree of active participation achieved through these organizations is phenomenal. In 1949 the church estimated that it would take nearly 350,000 men and women, or about 55 per cent of the membership twelve years of age and over, to fill the volunteer offices required by the functioning of the church organizations; over 50,000 of them needed to fill the priesthood offices and committees alone; and some 250,000 required for ward organizations.[11] In that same year, of some 350,000 males twelve years of age and over, more than 250,000 were "bearers" of the priesthood. The Sunday School Union registered 400,000 members in 1949. Yet these figures involve some, and in certain cases considerable, duplication. The church has provided a job for everyone to do and, perhaps more important, has provided a formal context in which it is to be done. The result is a wide distribution of activity, responsibility, and prestige.

However, while there is no professional clergy, the General Authorities and others whom they appoint as their assistants do receive stipends that enable them to live at a very respectable standard. A small amount, about $10 a month, is allowed to ward bishops and stake presidents for expenses. Most church leaders continue with their own private businesses, but there are also full-time employees in important positions and a large white-collar staff of several hundred persons. Thus a "bureaucracy" has developed with paid and professional administration to make this complicated organization work.

The bishops and stake presidents are apparently somewhat older than one might expect in such an active organization. Nelson found in an incomplete survey that the median age for both stake presidents and bishops in 1935 was 47.2 years. Comparatively few stake presidents were found under forty. There was considerable occupational diversity shown in the same survey, but farmers accounted for half the ward bishops. There is reason to believe that businessmen and professionals are important in the cities in local and stake leadership. The tendency to have men of advanced age in the top positions has long been noticeable in the church.

Yet, despite the tremendous activism of the Mormon group, an activism that conveys an impression of great vitality to the observer and that involves an unusually high number in responsible participation, there are those who are inactive or only marginally or periodically active. There is a tendency for church tasks to overburden some members while others are not involved. There are also young men who do not advance in the usual priesthood promotions because they are not considered "worthy," often meaning that they smoke or drink. These men stay in the Aaronic priesthood and are known as "adult Aaronics." There is also a sizable number of "Jack Mormons," who do not participate at all. These lukewarm to cold varieties do not fit into any neat categories. Sometimes some of them become active in one program or another. Others contribute money even when they do not participate. Somewhere between one-third and one-half of the church membership of one million might be a fair estimate of those active, but it must be recalled that the inactive may come to life sporadically or in special campaigns of one kind or another.

This complicated organization, with responsibility going from the bottom up and authority coming from the top down, with lateral cohesion provided by quorums and auxiliary organizations, based upon the territorial organizations in wards and stakes, imbued with a tremendous activism, and involving a large percentage of its membership in many-sided activities, is the contemporary church—the product of a century and a quarter of experience, including struggle against man and nature and co-operation to build the Kingdom of God. The organization developed in the difficulties of Ohio, the enthusiastic construction and bitter conflict of Missouri and Illinois, and the westward march and conquest of the arid Basin for American civilization is a truly amazing sociological mechanism. It embodies the ideals of the Mormon people as made explicit in their theology and in the loyalty and devotion they have shown their leadership. Of this dynamic popular theocracy one can best, perhaps, recall the words of that pioneer student of Mormon economic activity, Richard T. Ely, when he said over half a century ago: "So far as I can judge from what I have seen, the organization of the Mormons is the most nearly perfect piece of social mechanism with which I have ever, in any way, come into contact, excepting the German Army alone."[12]

CHAPTER EIGHT

Social Institutions: Co-operation
and Mastery

The religious beliefs embraced by the Mormon converts—the gathering and the building-up of the New Jerusalem—required co-operation; and the situations in which the Saints found themselves, in crossing the Atlantic or the plains, in establishing Zion in the Mississippi Valley or in Utah, made co-operative behavior imperative. Their intense consciousness of a special group character, which derived from the concrete combination of belief and experience, in turn strengthened religious convictions.

Their predilection for co-operative endeavor was formalized and given theological expression early, in a revelation relating directly to economic activity. This revelation in turn set the tone of Mormon economic life for decades; for, despite the fact that its concrete prescriptions proved unworkable, its fundamental ideal gave substance to a peculiar set of Mormon conceptions with regard to co-operation and property.

Mormonism had not been untouched by the general utopianism that characterized so many sects and permeated the nation in a more diffuse form, in this period when Emerson said every literate man had a plan for a new society in his waistcoat pocket. Various connections have been shown between Mormon economic ideas and the sectarian socialism of that day. An obvious link is supplied by the conversion of Sidney Rigdon, a man who was favorably impressed by such experimental efforts. There are less obvious connections, such as Leman Copley, who had been converted from Shakerism. Yet the implications of Mormon doctrine and the demands of the Mormon situation required that economic relations not remain outside the orbit of consecrated action. The notion of a "land of promise," which had already been explicit in the *Book of Mormon,* was soon made concrete in terms of the special destiny of the Mormon church and its peculiar mission. A new way of life for Zion seemed a logical development.

Joseph Smith disapproved of "The Family" at Kirtland, in which Rigdon and his followers held "all things common," and almost immediately suggested instead a "more perfect law of the Lord."[1] On February 9, 1831, a few days after his first statement, he offered this higher law to the church. Perhaps he intended to reconcile the socialism of Ohio with an individualism from New York, or perhaps he merely wanted to suggest an alternative to "The Family" to hasten the latter's demise. It is entirely possible that he was motivated by the desire to aid the New York Saints who, after his exhortation, had followed him to Ohio; and it is not impossible that he wished to lay down a new rule of life for the religious community he was founding. In his complicated situation the young prophet, still untried in leadership, may have been moved by all four motives.

The complexity of the situation suggests such a compound genesis. For not only did Joseph Smith succeed in reconciling the contrarieties then animating the little flock at Kirtland; he also brought together in a single social pattern two important tendencies in the behavior of western America: hardy, self-reliant individualism and the friendly urge toward mutual helpfulness. Yet there were important differences between the Mormon doctrine and the prevailing attitudes. First of all, the new revelation gave overwhelming dominance to co-operation, though not repressing certain individualistic aspects of economic life, while outside the church co-operative endeavor remained the informal accompaniment of a vigorous, and even a strident, individualism.

The idea that the earth was the Lord's and that it was held in stewardship by men derived from biblical origins. This doctrine, of apostolic lineage, blended with Greek and Roman notions of the public good to become a basic Christian conception in Patristic times. It found clear formulation in the thirteenth century in the scholastic doctrine that property may be rightfully owned by individual persons but that its use is subject to the stringent requirements of the common good. Such a doctrine became the commonplace, first of pulpit and later of pamphlet, as economic change upset Europe in early modern times. It was a doctrine extolled by the humanists and proclaimed by leaders of the Protestant Reformation as well as those of the Catholic counterreform; it was as palpably right to Latimer as it had been to More, as much at home in Salamanca as in Geneva. It had been somewhat eclipsed, driven with religion itself from the market place to the less influential spheres of human endeavor by the steady secularization of economic life in the Western countries, especially in the eighteenth and nineteenth centuries.

Heroic sects there were, of course, and not least in New York and Ohio. But what is notable about the new law of Joseph Smith is that, in place of heroic sectarian communism, it proposed to establish, as an institutional form within the context of the new church and its Zion in America, the older notion of the relation between individual ownership and the common weal. In this it failed; but it succeeded in re-creating the older concept of property within the vigorous new Israel that would soon go west. Calvin's heritage in Massachusetts had not completely dissipated itself across the years and the miles that numbered naturalization and westward movement. It would see a new life in Utah's deserts.

The new revelation, referred to as the "Law of Consecration," the "United Order," the "Order of Enoch," and the "Order of Stewardships," was not limited in its influence to the orthodox Brighamite church. The Reorganized Church, led by the family of Joseph Smith, Joseph Smith III becoming its president in 1860, gathered those Mormons of Illinois and southern Iowa who did not follow Brigham west. It did not come together for some years, and it took another decade after the acceptance of the presidency by the prophet's son before it acted on the doctrine of the gathering. Yet in 1870 Decatur County, Iowa, was chosen as the scene of the gathering, and for the next ten years Saints who considered themselves "Josephite" but not "Brighamite" quietly came to the region in southern Iowa, not far from Independence, the original and final Zion of the millennium. Here the church purchased over 3,000 acres, and the Saints settled upon this tract that belonged to the Order of Enoch, which became the rule of life. The town of Lamoni was later founded and remained the headquarters of the church until its removal back to Independence.

Strang also established the Order of Enoch, and smaller groups seem to have practiced communism of some form. Those who followed Lyman Wight to Texas, after the assassination of Joseph, evidently practiced both communism and polygamy. Thompson's group in Iowa was socialistic. Morris' short-lived Zion in Utah was based upon a consecration of the property of members to the church. Clark[2] reported in 1937 that the Cutlerites, who had only twenty-four members, practiced community of property. In 1873 in Utah, where co-operation had made settlement possible, Brigham Young went over to teaching communism. Like the notion of contemporary revelation itself, the idea of economic reform in a co-operative or communistic direction was typical not only of the orthodox Brighamite church but also of the splinter groups and the larger dissenting body.

The Law of Consecration

The new economic ethic, purportedly revealed to Joseph Smith from on high and announced by him on February 9, 1831, contained these lines:

. . . and behold, thou shalt consecrate all thy properties, that which thou hast unto me, with a covenant and a deed which cannot be broken; and they shall be laid before the bishop of my church, and two of the elders, such as he shall appoint and set apart for that purpose.

And it shall come to pass, that the bishop of my church, after that he has received the properties of my church, that it cannot be taken from the church, he shall appoint every man a steward over his own property, or that which he has received, inasmuch as is sufficient for himself and family:

And the residue shall be kept to administer to him who has not, that every man may receive according as he stands in need:

And the residue shall be kept in my storehouse, to administer to the poor and needy, as shall be appointed by the elders of the church and the bishop; and for the purpose of purchasing lands, and the building up of the New Jerusalem, which is hereafter to be revealed; that my covenant people may be gathered in one, in the day that I shall come to my temple:

And this I do for the salvation of my people.[3]

This new law sought to make it the rule of the church that "every man may receive according as he stands in need," which meant, in the circumstances of the gathering, to bring about something approaching economic equality among the converted. It sought, moreover, to socialize the surplus over and above what a man received as "sufficient for himself and family." This social-ized surplus, turned over to the bishop's storehouse, would serve two purposes. It would, first of all, place such surpluses at the disposal of the church to grant to the landless or those inade-quately provisioned. It would, in addition, offer a means of sup-port to the new church and provide it with a treasury to buy lands and build up the New Jerusalem. The new economic ethic of the Saints was to be an integral part of the gathering of the covenant people and was preparatory for the millennial coming of the Lord. This was, moreover, a saving revelation, offered for "the salvation of my people." Social and economic welfare was a part of the salvation offered by the new and restored church to its believers. It was also an aim of the new revelation to make the community of the elect self-sufficient. This desire for autarchy, implicit in the conception of a separate community, became an important part of Mormon economic thinking. It was of the first significance in territorial days and is still very much alive in Mor-mon thinking today.

Yet private enterprise remained. The member of the church was to be appointed "a steward over his own property, or that which he has received," and was to work it himself as a private farm or commercial establishment. This was not a communal plan, nor yet a collective method of farming or production. The family farm, run by the individual farm family, was to remain the basic unit of Mormon economy. Moreover, capitalistic relationships were to be the rule; market conditions would prevail; the decisions as to crops, marketing, or similar problems in non-agricultural enterprise were to be made by the stewards on their private initiative.

The plan was intended to work in the following manner: The convert was to give all his possessions, land and other property, over to the bishop, with a deed making the latter the legal owner. The bishop would hold such goods as a trustee for the church. The individual would then receive back from the bishop a parcel of land and an amount of property (or non-agricultural equiva-lents, in the case of consecration of commercial enterprise) suffi-cient for the support of his family. This might be the same as what he originally consecrated, or it might be more or less than the original amount. Moreover, to assure the equalization intended in the first measures, the consecrating member was to turn over his "surplus," the amount produced over that needed for his family, to the bishop each year, to be kept in the latter's storehouse for the relief of the poor and for church purposes (*D & C*, 42:32–33, 55; 72:16–19; 104:11–13).

The property returned or given out of the church's store to the individual member—his "stewardship" or "portion" or "inheritance" (*D & C*, 42:32; 51:4; 72:3; 82:17; 104:11)—was not worked in common but by the individual. Although it was intended from the first that individual management would remain and thus incorporate an important aspect of private initiative into the socially oriented institution, it was not the original intention to have the member receive legal title in fee simple for his "portion." The church through the bishop was to retain the legal title to the reconveyed "stewardship." This, together with the problem of how large a "portion" should be, caused trouble in Jackson County.

Bishop Partridge, who had charge of instituting the new order in Missouri, held that inheritances ought to be tentative and provisional, entitling each steward to the right of use only, with a "lease and loan . . . binding during the life" of the member "unless he transgresses, and is not deemed worthy by the authority of the Church, according to its laws, to belong to the Church." In case of such transgression the steward was to "acknowledge that I forfeit all claim to the above described leased and loaned property, and hereby bind myself to give back the lease, and also pay an equivalent for the loaned articles, for the benefit of said Church."[4] This system would give the bishop disciplinary power to be used against the lazy and at the same time allow him some flexibility in caring for new members, through a readjustment of older portions. This method would, furthermore, guard against the insincere and discourage apostasy. It would insure that "the wealth of the community would never be lost to apostates, 'trouble-makers,' or idlers."[5]

This policy met with resistance, and apostates succeeded in gaining ownership of their portions in the state courts. Although in April, 1832, the church was still trying to make the old system work, a year later Joseph advised Bishop Partridge that "you are bound by the law of the Lord to give a deed, securing to him who receives inheritances, his inheritance for an everlasting inheritance, or in other words to be his individual property, his private stewardship, and if he is found a transgressor and should be cut off, out of the church, his inheritance is his still."[6] Thus the church bowed to the frontier and the general American biases toward private property and gave the stewards deeds, returning them their portions to be held in fee simple.

In the original plan it was intended that, should a man die in fellowship, the bishop was bound to recognize the widow's claim, and similar arrangements were made in case of "inability in consequence of infirmity or old age."[7] It was provided, however, that if the steward apostatized or was excommunicated, the case was to be different. The widow would apparently have claim if she was a church member, but otherwise the claim would lapse. The children would have claim only if the parents had been faithful; otherwise "the claim of the children, as above described, is null and void." The new arrangements changed these regulations also. The edited 1835 edition of the *Doctrine and Covenants*, which the Saints hold officially to have been changed by inspiration, incorporates these revisions—which, in fact, were the results of harsh necessity. Thus the directive of Joseph Smith given in April, 1832, in which the widow's claim depended on the husband's faithfulness at death, seems to have been altered to include the accommodated rules (*D & C*, 83:1–4).[8]

The original revelation provided that the portions turned back to a man should be as large as necessary "for himself and family." The criteria proposed by revelation later in the spring of 1831 were a man's "family," his "circumstances," and his "wants and needs."[9] The deed of stewardship drawn up by Bishop Partridge for Titus Billings of Jackson County spoke of what "is needful for the support and comfort of myself and family" in defining the surplus that he should pay yearly into the bishop's storehouse. The problem that arose in practice was one of authorizing a final arbiter, in case the specific meaning of such terms could not be agreed upon. Bishop Partridge, not unnaturally, felt that the bishop should determine what was sufficient for support and comfort. This position was not acceptable to many in the church.

Joseph again intervened, and in June, 1833, about two months after his settling of the stewardship problem, he counseled Partridge that "the matter of consecration must be done by the mutual consent," that "every man must be his own judge how much he should receive, and how much he should suffer to remain in the hands of the Bishop." Joseph stated that sole power in the hands of bishops would be intolerably despotic, "giving to the Bishop more power than a king has," but added that, "upon the other hand, to let every man say how much he needs, and the Bishop be obliged to comply with his judgment, is to throw Zion into confusion, and make a slave of the Bishop." He concluded that there "must be a balance or equilibrium" between the two. Reasonable negotiation was Joseph's solution, with stalemates to be settled by the high council, on which the bishop must not sit as a member.[10]

Not only in the Missouri Zion but also in Kirtland, Ohio, and in nearby Thompson, where the Saints from Colesville, New York, had settled, this revelation was put into operation. Its basic content has been well summarized by Joseph A. Geddes, although Geddes' study is based upon the version given in the 1835 edition of the *Doctrine and Covenants*. In this version the revelations had been edited to include the changes that circumstances made necessary and also to suggest that the main purpose of the law was to care for the poor, possibly to avoid the accusation of socialistic experimentation, for which the Saints had apparently been ridiculed. Geddes' summary presents the final form of the law, the form in which it has affected the later Mormon economic outlook in many ways:

1. The earth is the Lord's.
2. The people are stewards only over their possessions which are to be known as stewardships or inheritances, but each steward is to have a deed to his stewardship.
3. Those who have surplus property, i.e., more than is required to provide a frugal living for the family, are to consecrate it by deed to the church, for the benefit of the poor. Surplus production beyond family needs from each stewardship is to be turned over to the Bishop's Storehouse.
4. The bishop is to apportion the inheritances among the people on the following basis:
   a) Equal according to their families
   b) Equal according to their circumstances
   c) Equal according to their wants and needs.
5. Those who are either excommunicated from the church or themselves leave it, keep the inheritances deeded to them, but do not receive back the surplus that has been consecrated to the poor.
6. In other respects, business relations are to be carried on in the usual manner under the competitive, capitalistic system. Simplicity, frugality, cleanliness, industry and honesty are enjoined.[11]

This new revelation was not successful. Problems arose concerning the transfer of property from individuals entering the order. Moreover, collection of the surplus as well as division of land caused difficulty. Hamilton Gardner, in his study of Mormon economic experimentation, concludes from the available evidence that the great majority of the Saints in Jackson County did consecrate their property.[12] Yet, as Leonard Arrington has noted, the revelations and correspondence of Joseph Smith point toward the palpable fact that the plan operated very imperfectly during the years 1831–34. He suggests poverty of the converts, lack of liquid church resources, persecution, opposition of the civil courts, idleness, and unfaithfulness of the converts in making initial and annual consecrations as the basic factors explaining why the plan did not work. It was Gardner's opinion that it failed because it was thrust upon the people without their having been adequately prepared for it. J. Reuben Clark, Jr., who studied the writings of Joseph Smith on this question, declared that the reproofs and calls to repentance contained therein show why it was "not possible for such a group of Saints to live up to the law of consecration and the United Order."[13]

In June, 1834, Joseph Smith, who had arrived in Missouri with Zion's Camp (a semimilitary relief expedition that lived according to the "law"), revealed a withdrawal of the United Order. In this revelation he reports the chastisement of the Lord for the Saints' unfaithfulness:

. . . they have not learned to be obedient to the things which I required at their hands, but are full of all manner of evil, and do not impart of their substance, as becometh saints, to the poor and afflicted among them;

And are not united according to the union required by the law of the celestial kingdom [D & C, 105:3–4].

Since "Zion cannot be built up unless it is by the principles of the law of the celestial kingdom" (D & C, 105:5) and "in consequence of the transgressions of my people, it is expedient in me that mine elders should wait for a little season for the redemption of Zion—that they themselves may be prepared . . ." (D & C, 105:9–10), Joseph used this occasion to urge the building of a temple in Kirtland as a main objective and had the Lord add: "Let those commandments which I have given concerning Zion and her law be executed and fulfilled, after her redemption" (D & C,

105:34). Thus the summer of 1834 saw the abandonment of the unsuccessful Law of Consecration or First United Order.

In 1838, another revelation was given by Joseph to the Saints at Far West, requiring "all their surplus property to be put into the hands of the bishop of my church in Zion, for the building of mine house, and for the laying of the foundation of Zion and for the priesthood, and for the debts of the Presidency of my Church" (*D & C*, 119:1–2). It continued: "And this shall be the beginning of the tithing of my people" (*D & C*, 119:3), and they "shall pay one-tenth of all their interest annually," declaring that "this shall be a standing law unto them forever, for my holy priesthood" (*D & C*, 119:4).

In practice this new law seems to have worked much as did the old. The convert did not turn his entire possessions over to the church and receive back an inheritance but rather consecrated the surplus immediately and thereby "obviated the transfer and reverse transfer." Ten per cent was set for the yearly surplus. Arrington concluded that in basic respects "the law was precisely the same in effect as the 1831 law of consecration." It is difficult to determine how much consecration actually took place at Far West.[14] Brigham Young, who was in Far West, later declared that it was hard to find anyone who would admit to having a surplus, although "once in a while you would find a man who had a cow which he considered surplus, but generally she was of the class that would kick a person's hat off, or eyes out, or the wolves had eaten off her teats," or a man "who had a horse that he considered surplus, but at the same time he had the ringbone, was broken-winded, spavined in both legs, and had the pole evil at one end of the neck and a fistula at the other, and both knees sprung."[15] Yet obviously some property was consecrated. It has been said that considerable pressure was put on the reluctant, in those days when the Saints were in a state of alert and alarm, but that soon Joseph went over to the substitute idea of large co-operatives.[16]

It is important to note that both the 1831 Law of Consecration and the so-called "inferior law" of 1838 are not to be explained as adaptations to the Missouri environment. On this point Gardner correctly concluded that

it must be laid down as indisputable that the Mormon enterprise of communism stood in no relation of effect and cause with the physical conditions obtaining where its practice was essayed. Nothing can be pointed

to in connection with the soil, climate, or physiographical characteristics of western Missouri which tended to produce communism rather
than some other form of economic life. Nor is the fact that agriculture
formed the basis of the system of controlling weight, for such would
have been the case elsewhere. Again, it is apparent that the order was
not evolved from any unique qualities of the Mormon people. Their
records disclose no intimation that any impulse had existed theretofore
on their part toward communistic endeavor, or any effort been made
to try it. Of course, the close cohesion of the Mormons, arising from
their religious system, together with their amenability to church discipline, formed most favorable factors towards the unity and centralized
control so necessary to communistic success; but these circumstances
alone, without extraneous action upon them, would have produced no
results whatever in this connection. The conclusion is inevitable that
the genesis of the United Order must be accounted for on grounds
separate from the physical conditions of western Missouri and the social
nature of the Mormons. The fact is that it was a scheme superimposed
upon these factors by the fiat of Joseph Smith, possibly because of their
adaptability to what he intended, but in its origin entirely foreign to
both of them.[17]

Perhaps Gardner places too much emphasis upon the independent
innovation of the leader, important as that may be, for certainly
the group atmosphere and the already existing common notions
of the gathering and the kingdom were closely related to and
found expression in the United Order. Yet the importance of innovation is correctly emphasized. The Mormon ethic originated
out of the spirit of the people, but it was not an obvious and auto-
matic response to environmental challenge and was a creative pro-
posal imposed upon the going community.

Perhaps this imposition in part explains its failure, while the
congruity of the law with the social structure and basic notions
of the group explains how it came to embody the Mormon economic ideal after it ceased to work in practice. Arrington attributes
failure in the final analysis to the rapid growth of the body and
sees the failure as a condition for further increase in size. Rigid
adherence would have slowed down expansion, on the one hand,
and growth bringing heterogeneity did cause internal difficulties
in the working of the plan, on the other. Yet, as Arrington points
out, the ideas of stewardship remained, and the Law of Consecration is to this day the ideal of the Mormon church—its "blueprint"
of a Christian society to be achieved eventually, when the Saints
are worthy of it. Gardner suggests that, had "adequate preparation" been made for it, the new law might have worked in the
period 1831–34.[18]

In Nauvoo, neither the law of 1831 nor the inferior law of 1838 was applied. It was here, in 1841, that the law of tithing was established as the substitute for co-operative economic activity and the means for support of the church.[19] Although collection does not seem to have been very regular at first, tithing became the basic Mormon method of money-raising. It has also become an important symbol of loyalty. In 1900, Joseph F. Smith, then president of the church, said: "By this test the loyalty of the people of this Church shall be put to the test. By this principle it shall be known who is for the kingdom of God and who is against it."[20] Tithes are today paid to the ward bishop, and the member is given a receipt. The bishop forwards the money to the Presiding Bishop of the church. Here it is budgeted by the General Authorities for church expenses, and some of it is returned to the wards and stakes. A ward organization is allowed 65 per cent "of the cost of janitorial service, heat, water, light, telephone, and building repair and renovation"[21] out of tithing money.

With its practical failure and its consequent withdrawal, the Law of Consecration became an ideal rather than a commandment. It was no longer to prescribe the details of Mormon communalism, but, what was to be more effective by far, it was to hold before the Saints an ideal to inspire their efforts and evoke their moral aspirations, while permitting them to develop in a flexible way the methods of co-operation appropriate to the concrete circumstances of effort. The idea that the earth and all the wealth contained therein were the Lord's and that man held his earthly possessions in trust, acting as a steward accountable to the Lord, gave the older classical and Christian notions a depth of meaning based upon Mormon group experience and integrally related to the total Mormon view of their mission and of themselves. It produced in them a sense of property in which the rights of the individual were subordinate to the requirements of the common good, a conception of property rights as "limited, tentative, and temporary," to be seen as "derivative and subordinate"—in short, as "a conditional trust." "The very heart of the United Order—the conception of property ownership as a life-lease subject to beneficial use and social direction—continued to govern the thinking of Church members and the directives of Church leaders."[22] The Utah experience would further incline Mormon thought in the same directions.

Irrigation

On arrival in Utah, the requirements of survival, the established economic ethic, the cohesion of the group, and the physical characteristics of the terrain, all combined to produce a version of the Mormon conception of property even more oriented toward the public welfare. Brigham Young's early regulations forbade any man to buy or sell land and permitted a man to own, for both city and farming purposes, only what he could till or otherwise use; these edicts befitted the conception of Zion and were demanded by the realities of colonization.

On the day after his arrival in the Valley, Brigham issued a statement of policy which proclaimed that there "would be no private ownership of streams of water. . . ." Arrington's study has shown that in early territorial days in Utah, Mormon policy made "property rights [depend] upon use," made "basic natural resources . . . subject to public rather than private ownership," and "sometimes asked [members] to sacrifice property rights in favor of projects sponsored by Church leaders to facilitate the agricultural and industrial development of the region."[23] Grazing lands, timber, and other natural resources were made common property by the pioneers, but it was in the co-operative control and management of water—the urgent prerequisite of life in Utah —that Mormon co-operation found its most impressive expression.

Mormon settlers had no previous experience with irrigation, although it appears that the leaders knew that it would be required for survival in the Great Basin. In the Valley, the Saints followed the advice of Brigham Young and constructed a community ditch to carry water. This was used at first as a source of culinary water for the fort built by the pioneers, but the following year it irrigated gardens within the fort. In September, 1848, Brigham conceived the idea of building a canal to the east of Salt Lake City. Naturally, the first efforts of the colonizers were agricultural, since food was an absolute necessity and, moreover, it was the idea of the leadership to base a Mormon society upon farming. For this latter reason, mining was avoided. In agricultural work, in the construction of houses, and in the water-provision measures necessitated by farming, there was much associative endeavor in the first months and years in the Valley.

This was a natural continuation of the working together that had enabled the Saints to get out of Nauvoo and cross the plains and, like their migration itself, was under the authoritarian direction of Brigham and the priesthood. Yet it was in connection with irrigation, which became the most important of these co-operative activities, that the characteristic Mormon tendency to work together developed into a social technique and issued in permanent cooperative institutions. Moreover, out of the democracy of participation also characteristic of Mormon activities, there developed a set of democratic institutions for the control and distribution of water. These techniques and the subsequently developed institutions provided the Mormons with the social and technical tools required for subduing the cheerless wastes of the Great Basin.

It has been said that a "destitute people, having no resources save the genius of their leader and the labor of their own hands, resolved to associate and organize their efforts to bring the water on, as the people of Holland were compelled to cooperate to keep the water out."[24] Yet the resolution to associate and organize was a natural response for a group whose explicit religious beliefs and previous experience had combined to restrict individualism and emphasize collective action. If Utah demanded irrigation, it does not follow that any group going there would have developed it or, having developed it, would have had the social organization, the group loyalty, and the discipline requisite for its success. Mormon belief and Mormon action had prepared the Saints to meet the challenge of the new environment. While the situational factors in Utah precluded a variety of possible responses, the Mormon group was ideally prepared by its beliefs and experience to answer its narrow and stringent demands.

Gardner's analysis has suggested: "Three elements have stood out as the underlying causes: first, the physiographic conditions; second, the religious organization of the Mormons; and third, Brigham Young."[25] On the first he has commented:

But the mere physical conditions could not alone have been responsible for the cooperative system which arose. Other parts of the arid West have since been reclaimed without bringing forth such a method. The existence of cooperation in early Utah and its absence in neighboring states when physical conditions were identical must be accounted for by a difference in social structure. In near-by states the colonists acted individually and were not connected with each other by any particular interest, while in Utah there existed a compact social body, closely united by common ties and easily capable of being used as a vehicle to cope with general needs. This common bond was the peculiar church organization and religion of the Mormon people.[26]

Gardner is quite right in emphasizing the tremendous importance of beliefs and social structure in influencing Mormon settlement in Utah. Nowhere is the role of these two factors more evident than in the handling of water and resources by the Latterday Saints. Yet the effect of geographic conditions in demanding and eliciting co-operation among the non-Mormon settlers and later residents in the arid West is both obvious and important. Turner referred to the Far West as a social frontier, stating: "No conquest was possible by the old individual pioneer method. . . . In a word, the physiographic province itself decreed that the destiny of this frontier should be social rather than individual."[27] Vincent Ostrom has told how Major John W. Powell anticipated as early as 1878 "the creation of new patterns of community organization to provide 'cooperative labor and capital' " for the utilization of natural resources in western conditions and how William E. Smythe later saw the necessity of a new kind of associative living in the West.[28]

Stockgrowers' associations, the cattle roundup, and brand enforcement are early examples of such co-operation, and later instances are evident in the proliferation of institutional forms—local, regional, and national—for the conservation, control, and distribution of water in the arid area of the West. Moreover, secular utopian settlement was also to be found in the West, as in Greeley, Colorado. Yet the Mormons were pioneers in such co-operation, and their values and social structure predisposed them to co-operative activity.

Early settlers in Utah and Southern California organized the mutual water companies as semi-public agencies to provide irrigation water for farming communities on a cooperative basis. C. C. Teague has indicated that the mutual water companies were the origin of the agricultural cooperative movement in California. "From cooperation in mutual water companies it was just another step to the development of nonprofit, grower-owned and grower-controlled cooperative marketing organizations and cooperative purchasing agencies."[29]

Whatever the influence of the mutual company as a co-operative form in California, the fact is that, long before Major Powell's prediction, the Mormons were using co-operative techniques in the control of water. Both in Salt Lake City and in the many villages planted in the irrigable valleys of the Great Basin, the Latter-day Saints developed irrigation techniques. Within each settlement there grew up both a church ward organization and an informal water association, two hardly distinguishable aspects of the community. In these villages the whole group worked together to construct the irrigation system. First they erected a dam to store the water in an artificial reservoir or, if there was a stream nearby, a headgate to divert it to the planted fields. The next step was to dig the canal to carry the water from its source, and then the ditches and subditches that brought on the water from the canal to the individual holdings of the settlers and into the gardens to supply the growing crops. The building of this system was supervised by the bishop. Repair was similarly handled, and the announcement of work to be done would be made by the bishop at sacrament meeting on Sunday, together with orders for men and teams to appear on the spot for work during the following week. Such work was, of course, without cash remuneration, for cash was scarce and often useless in the early days. Instead of pay, each man was allowed the use of water in an amount proportionate to the labor he and his draft animals had put in on construction. The right to continue this use depended upon a man's utilization of the water. This dependence of right upon use was later formalized in law as "beneficial use."

A water master was often appointed, who was given charge of the distribution of water to plowed fields. Such an official was named in Salt Lake City on August 22, 1847, a month after arrival. When in February, 1849, the new city was divided into nineteen church wards, the bishop of each ward was put in charge of water distribution, as was done in many outlying villages for over a generation. With the organization of city government in Salt Lake in 1853, ecclesiastical supervision gave way to civil administration, and a general water master was appointed by the city council. The church ward remained, however, the area of local supervision, and water masters were appointed in each ward to serve under the city water master.

Under this early system in the conditions of settlement, the needs of a family and the amount of labor it could contribute to building irrigation installations differed but little from family to family. With the quantity of water based upon the labor contribution and subject to continued use, there was, in such conditions, a fairly equal division of rights to its use. Since a man was also limited in the amount of land he could own by his capacity to use it, there was considerable economic equality among the settlers. Moreover, no one man or small group could gain control and exploit the others. The equity of the system is as striking as its equality. Both these characteristics were, by and large, preserved in the later, formal, legal, and institutional rules and bodies set up in the water code and the mutual irrigation company. Certainly, if the Mormon leadership simply wished to make private fortunes, nothing offered a better chance for speculation than the Utah water supply. If some top Mormon leaders made personal fortunes, they also watched over the collective welfare. They had other business in mind, the building-up of Zion on the basis of co-operation and fellowship.

By 1865, there were already 1,043 miles of canals in Utah, irrigating 153,949 acres and valued, including the dams, at $1,766,939, with another $877,730 worth in the process of construction.[30] The thousands of miles of canals and ditches, the dams and the reservoirs and other installations of early Utahan irrigation "were built by the farmers, owned by the farmers and operated by the farmers. In fact they constitute one of the greatest and most successful community or cooperative undertakings in the history of America."[31] The human relations required for the efficient operation of irrigation necessitated the discovery of new practices and the discarding of old ones by the Mormon settlers. The development of irrigation on a large scale as the basis for community life required that older legal precedent based upon generations of experience in humid climates had to go.

The Mormons, consequently, working out the requirements in their own experience and following the general outlines of their economic ethic of co-operation and their strong conception of the public aspects of property, rejected the older law of riparian rights, which provided that a stream should run its course undiminished in quantity and unpolluted in quality. The doctrine of riparian rights provided that each riparian owner should have the right of the full natural flow of the stream, subject to the reasonable use of other riparian owners.[32] This older system was replaced by a new one in which beneficial use of flowing water would determine the rights on the stream. The term "beneficial use" became the key phrase in the subsequent Utah law, which was based upon the Spanish Doctrine of Appropriation. This new notion was implied in Brigham Young's first proclamations in the Valley but was given more formal statement by the territorial legislature in 1852, which declared: "The county court shall have control of all timber, water privileges, or any water course or creek, to grant mill sites, and exercise such powers as in their judgment shall best preserve the timber and subserve the interest of the settlement in the distribution of water for irrigation or other purposes."[33]

The first incorporation of irrigation companies was based upon a law passed by the territorial legislature in 1865. Changes in the law in 1880 gave more rights to private ownership. The Utah experience with water control in connection with arid agriculture was summarized and codified in the Water Code passed by the state legislature in 1903. According to this law, which remains, with some subsequent changes, the basic water regulation, beneficial use is the "basis, the measure, and limit of the right" of water use.[34] Water flowing in a natural stream is not subject to private ownership, but individuals are permitted to own rights of diversion and use. In territorial days and in the early years of statehood, a stream could be diverted without filing application with the state, but the 1903 legislation laid down procedures to formalize such application, while recognizing the previously existing rights.

On this basis was Mormon farming sustained, which in turn sustained the Mormon commonwealth in the West. Today in Utah there are approximately 700 irrigation companies of all kinds, and these possess more than 8,750 miles of unlined earth canals, 410 pumping plants, 1,973 diversion dams, and nearly 400 storage dams. The storage dams have a capacity of more than 3,400,000 acre-feet of water. These works represented a capital investment of $42,000,000 in 1946, and at least $1,500,000 are spent each year on their maintenance. "Irrigation companies have the major responsibility for safe maintenance and efficient operation of Utah's dams, canals, spillways, wasteways, flumes, inverted siphons, head gates and lateral gates—the structures with which irrigation water is stored, diverted, and conveyed to 1.3 million acres of productive land in the state. Clearly, the task of the irrigation companies is huge; its performance vital."[35] Of Utah's 52,701,440 acres of land, only 1,800,000 are farmed, and, of those, only

500,000 acres are dry-farmed. The remaining 1,300,000 acres are dependent upon irrigation.

The irrigation companies vary greatly in size, from small units serving less than 100 acres to large ones serving thousands of acres. The average company irrigates about 1,600 acres. Throughout the state, 509 companies serve over 300 acres of ground each, while 179 irrigate a smaller area. There are four types of companies: commercial companies, which are not important and irrigate less than 100,000 acres of land; individually owned irrigation projects, which serve less than 200,000 acres; irrigation districts, which have been organized in some parts of the state, often in connection with reclamation projects, and which often serve a large number of mutual companies; and the mutual company, "a non-profit association established for the purpose of distributing water at cost and performing other functions incident thereto for the benefit of the members."[36]

The mutual company is the product of Mormon co-operative experience and today serves about 80 per cent of the irrigated land in the state. It holds legal title to the water rights and distribution facilities and is responsible for the maintenance of the latter. The expenses involved are met through an assessment on the company stock, which often includes a labor charge to be worked out by the members; this charge is usually made on an annual basis, although there often are special assessments to cover unusual repairs and innovations. Early water rights based on labor contributions were converted to shares of stock on incorporation. At an earlier period co-operative labor was the basis of company maintenance, and this is still the case in many areas, although payment in money is also permitted and often made at the present time.

Officers are elected once a year, the usual rules of corporate voting stock prevailing, although in some cases elections are held every two and even every three years. It is not uncommon for the president and secretary to be returned to office for a long period. There are usually five directors, among whom are typically a president, vice-president, and secretary-treasurer, although the number of directors varies from three to nine. Many companies hire attorneys, and some employ full-time engineers.

The methods of water delivery differ according to the amount of water available. They are three: demand or call, under which the water master, who is appointed by the directors, turns on the water at the request of a member; continuous flow, possibly only where there is an abundance of water; and rotation, the most common method, used by over 400 companies in Utah to irrigate over 750,000 acres. Under the last method, the water is put into streams or ditches, the users taking their streams for a certain period of time proportionate to the amount of stock they own and in a pre-arranged order. This was the method that emerged in pioneer days, and it is a monument to the Mormon capacity for disciplined co-operation. It has, on the whole, resulted in equitable distribution, although too long an interval between deliveries may inconvenience a small stockholder and the hour of delivery is often inconvenient. In Utah, 41 companies have adequate storage facilities to use the demand and call system to irrigate some 160,000 acres, while 42 companies use continuous flow to irrigate over 100,000 acres.

New legal definitions in formal codes, new co-operative forms on the level of village life, and a generally more socially conscious attitude toward the public domain—these were the Mormon contribution to Utah's social outlook. At the same time the experiences of Utah drove home the earlier lessons and increased both Mormon group consciousness and the co-operative economic ideal that was so much a part of it. The conquest of the desert increased an already strong emphasis upon mastery in Mormon theology and popular awareness. The earth experience with matter was made concrete in the conquest of the arid West, and the development of the individual through mastery took the highly communal form of group victory over Utah's difficult terrain. Co-operation and mastery were further integrated into the Mormon outlook and, together with an orientation to hard work, came to characterize Mormon practical attitudes.

Further Co-operation in Utah

The middle years of the 1850's in Utah saw a short-lived attempt to revive the Law of Consecration. People were asked to place their property at the disposal of the president of the church, and several thousands made over title of their possessions to Brigham Young. However, nothing ever came of this movement, and the consecrations never went through. The leaders of the church explained the whole affair as a test to try the faith of the Saints.

Nearly twenty years later, there developed a recrudescence of the United Order. Brigham Young preached the revival himself and took an active part in its organization, also keeping up a correspondence with local groups in which he offered advice on practical problems. His intention was to "organize the Latter-day Saints, every man, woman and child among them, who has a desire to be organized, into this holy order," whose object was "to labor for the benefit of the whole."[37] Thrift, as always with Brigham, was a moving idea, as was retrenchment in the economic situation of that time. Self-sufficiency was also of first importance to him, for the ideal of autarchy had remained prominent in Mormon thinking. Recent events had, if anything, increased such concern, since there is no doubt that the second United Order was in part a response to the panic of 1873.

Joseph Smith had organized joint-stock companies in the church. A prominent example was the Central Council that he placed over the United Orders of both Missouri and Ohio. He set this body up as a "United Firm," in which the members pooled their resources. This "United Firm" or "United Order" operated a sawmill, ran a tannery, managed a printing office, and owned legal title to much real property. It was intended to promote commerce and to have a monopoly over Mormon trade in both Ohio and Missouri. There were also small businesses that, although legally owned by a private partnership, were actually United Firms or consecrated enterprises. Moreover, at Far West the church organized four large co-operatives, which apparently were intended to dominate large spheres of economic life. Such ideas had not died out in Utah. Informal co-operation had been very much alive in the first days of settlement, and success in irrigation over a far-flung region testified to Mormon co-operative abilities. Apostle Lorenzo Snow had organized a successful co-operative venture in northern Utah, called the "Brigham City Cooperative Mercantile and Manufacturing Company," from which Brigham possibly took his immediate inspiration, while co-operative stores were operating succesfully in many parts of Mormondom.

Starting in the year 1873, church leaders formed United Orders throughout the Mormon region, creating over a hundred of them, which means one in almost every settlement of any importance. Brigham Young personally organized the United Order at St. George in southwestern Utah, his "winter capital," and, as he moved north to Salt Lake City in the spring of 1874, he established Orders in community after community on the way.

In this second United Order, which appears to have been more successful in the younger settlements than in the older towns, the chief economic enterprises were undertaken on a communal basis, but in the great majority private ownership remained in homes, cattle, and even in some businesses. Dissensions appeared immediately. Laziness and shirking as well as the neglect of common tasks caused difficulties. Moreover, "the jealousies and envy inherent in human nature flashed out," and the "net result was that the corporations soon began to crumble and dissolve, and the members reverted to their former manner of individualistic economic life."[38] Some of the Orders went far in the direction of what Joseph Smith had earlier condemned as the "folly of common stock."

Of the hundred or more local groups formed, seven became communistic—"only the United Orders of Bunkerville, Nevada; Sunset, Allen's Camp (St. Joseph), and Woodruff, Arizona; and Orderville, Kingston, and Springdale, Utah, followed, at least for a period, the pattern of apostolic communism."[39] These experimental communities were soon given up. Some lasted only a month or two, others endured for six or eight months, but, by the end of 1874, practically all had disappeared. It has been observed that "in less than a year after its installation, all that remained of the United Order in Utah was a memory."[40] Said a participant, "the practical workings of the principle not proving satisfactory to the people in general, in a few months, the companies were nearly all dissolved."[41]

Yet there were important exceptions. Orderville and Bunkerville seem to have had success. There is no doubt that Orderville greatly improved the economic position of its members in the midst of general poverty. This group was established when the Mount Carmel United Order fell to quarreling. Twenty-four families, desiring to continue with the new system, "unanimously concluded to remove from Mt. Carmel and found a new settlement." Here there was common property, and "all things" were done "by common consent" and through common labor. Vegetables, grains, lumber, wool, cotton, and leather were produced, as well as "the manufactures obtained from them."[42] From 1875 to 1877 members received neither wages nor wage credits but rather took from the common storehouse according to their needs. From 1875 to 1880 common meals were served in the common dining hall, which was located in the center of the square around which the village was built.[43] "Early in 1877, however, on the advice of Brigham Young, the Order inaugurated a system of bookkeeping which awarded compensation in the form of book credit for all work done."[44] Wages were set up for men, women, and children, without any differentials for skill within the age and sex categories. After 1877, a price system was in operation.

There were thirty-three different departments in the group, handling farming, grazing, manufacturing, and repair through common labor. The group became almost completely self-sufficient. Said one student of the community: "Orderville prospered. It is conceded that this village, built from scratch, became more nearly self-sustaining than any other community in the Church."[45] Said another: "As a result of the labor of the community, the assets of the Order rose from $21,550.57 in 1875 to $69,562.22 in 1879 and $79,577.29 in 1883. While their circumstances were modest, their production was amazingly high, and in terms of present [1954] values averaged several hundred thousand dollars worth of goods per year."[46] The community also attracted new members, and between 1875 and 1880 the group grew from 150 to over 700.

Yet apparently all was not smooth sailing. Early forced to abandon complete communism for wages and a price system, some members accumulated credits while others went into debt. In 1880 measures were taken to make those with surpluses consecrate them to the Order, while the debts of those who owed were wiped out. These changes, adopted as a yearly procedure and accepted on the advice of the General Authorities of the church, re-established and maintained economic equality. Religious and moral qualifications had been emphasized in admitting new members, but in the late 1870's leniency on financial requirements for membership in the midst of the general poverty in southern Utah let in people who did not pull their weight. This increased discontent within the group. With recovery from the panic, the local discovery of silver, the coming of the railroad, and the appearance of eastern store clothes in the region, the Orderville Saints took on an archaic look that further marked them off as separate from their neighbors. This, together with their poor homes and frugal life, exposed them to ridicule.

Their difficulties increased when their own children began to reach adolescence. Young people wanted the store articles that the non-co-operating youth possessed. Moreover, the young were further alienated by the almost complete impossibility of becoming members of the Order without goods to consecrate. Opportunity outside was greater for the rising generation. This alone would have doomed the experiment in time unless it was changed.

Further problems continued to arise. Communal dining was given up in 1880. In 1883 a wage differential was introduced. In the same year, enterprises owned by the Order were leased to foremen and managers in an attempt to increase incentives, and farming was placed on "a semi-profit basis," with a record kept of expenses, receipts, and profit for various persons involved, although the income remained communal property.[47] Apostle Erastus Snow, seeing the internal conflict within the Order, chose to emphasize the experimental nature of the group and compared the Order to co-operative stores and similar institutions. In July, 1883, he told the Orderville Saints that their way was not the one way of the Lord, an impression they had gathered from Brigham Young. This was quite a blow to some members, who went to Salt Lake to see the First Presidency. At the center they were given similar advice, the authorities apparently wanting to hold the group together, partly as an example, even at the expense of giving up many of its institutions that were causing conflict.

In 1884 the First Presidency of the church at Salt Lake City attempted to solve the Order's problems. It counseled a return to the old system of equal labor and disbursements, stating that differentials only increased selfishness. Moreover, it suggested a plan whereby the youth might be given shares in the Order on coming of age and another to allow personal tastes to be gratified and reduce regimentation. The immediate effect of the intervention was temporarily to stop agitation for dissolution. The equality of work and credit was not, however, re-established, although by this time most families had some privately owned possessions and these were increased with the division of nearby fields into five- and ten-acre plots. Yet, despite the internal stresses and strains, the agitation for breaking up, and the changes toward individualism, the Orderville United Order was an economic success and was prosperous and expanding when it was finally disbanded.

In fact, southern Utah people suggest that such prosperity and expansion may have been an important reason for its dissolution.

There was much jealousy and envy on the part of non-co-operators, and many complaints went in to Salt Lake City, complaints that may finally have dampened the enthusiasm of President Taylor and the General Authorities. Arrington places the final responsibility for disbanding upon the Edmunds Law. Since the community leaders practiced plural marriage, this law sent them into hiding and some of them to jail. At any rate, in 1885 the General Authorities counseled disbanding, and the members, apparently with reluctance, voted to dissolve. Said Bishop Esplin: "I did not go into it for this, I thought I would always live in the United Order."[48] It took years to liquidate the company completely, but by 1900 it had been entirely accomplished. "Today Orderville is a farming and grazing community of four hundred people and is hardly distinguishable from dozens of other southern Utah villages except for the ruins of its 'factories' and its memories of Utopia."[49]

Some years before the experiments with the second United Order in Utah, the Saints applied to commerce and even to industry the co-operative techniques they had worked out in other spheres of action, especially in the control and management of water. The incentive for this was in part derived from the conditions of the Mormon-gentile conflict. In 1849 the first store in Utah had been established by two non-Mormons. Other merchants came, and in time there were also Mormon merchants, some of whom had large businesses for the time and place. In the 1860's, when national sentiment was running high against the Mormons and hostility was marked in the Territory, also when Congress was debating anti-Mormon legislation and the House of Representatives passed the Cullom Bill, the church leaders decided that it was time that Mormon money stopped going into the pockets of the enemies of Mormonism. These problems were brought to a head by the approach of the railroad.

Earlier, General Patrick Edward Connor had sought to develop the mines of Utah as a way of bringing about "a large Gentile and loyal population sufficient by peaceful means and through the ballot-box to overwhelm the Mormons by mere force of numbers, and thus wrest from the Church—disloyal and traitorous to the core—the absolute and tyrannical control of temporal and civil affairs."[50] Now it was generally anticipated among the non-Mormons that the railroad would put an end to Mormon domination and even to the church itself. Mormon leaders recognized the threat in both its political and its economic forms. The influx of a large population of gentiles, following upon the stimulated growth of mining activities, would challenge the Mormon numerical superiority, while the separate community of Mormondom, based upon small and expensive irrigation agriculture and small local industry, would be replaced by specialization of products and labor, import of eastern capital, and other features integrating Utah as a mere segment into the larger capitalistic American economy. This would destroy the economic base of the separated Mormon community.

Brigham Young had ridiculed gentile hopes for Mormon destruction, saying that it was a poor religion that could not stand a railroad, but he also took strong measures to meet the challenge. These measures were not unanimously accepted at the time. The boycott that the church established, forbidding Mormons to trade with outsiders, reflected a heightened cohesiveness and awareness in the midst of conflict, but it also showed up certain crevices in that coherence. The "New Movement" of Godbe, Kelsey, Stenhouse, and others, which fought Young on these economic and other, religious, matters, was in part an objection to the economic measures of the dominant church leadership. The Godbeites wished to come to terms with the gentile business community and its individual ethics and to end the exclusiveness of the gathered. They also wanted to develop mining, which Brigham had restrained, holding that it should be developed only as required for Utahan needs. The opposition, like the gentiles, felt that mining should be developed to meet the needs of the national economy. Mormondom as a separate economic entity or the American capitalistic economy—this was the choice offered, and the Godbeites took the latter. The majority of Saints, under the leadership of Brigham and the priesthood, took the former and set themselves the task of defending local industry, the particularist basis of their sacred commonwealth, against the onslaught of the national "big-business" economy. The autonomy of a diversified economy was seen as requisite for a continuation of Mormon ambitions.

Brigham Young mobilized the Mormon community to meet the problem. In a remarkable study of the implementation of Mormon economic policy in these years, Leonard J. Arrington has shown how Brigham Young revived the School of the Prophets, an earlier discussion forum that Joseph had organized first in Kirtland.[51] From 1868 to 1872 and especially in 1868–69, following the coming of the railroad, this group promoted Mormon resistance to the new economic pressures. The organization, which had over 900 members in Salt Lake City and branches in other settlements, held general meetings and discussed the current problems, including enforcement of the boycott, the Godbeite opposition, and the promotion of local industry. The 1865–66 boycott against hostile merchants, which had elicited from them an offer to sell their goods and leave the Territory on terms that the church turned down, was now extended to all gentiles.

The School of the Prophets developed policies and techniques of implementation to protect Utah home industry against industrial competition from the east and to contain mining within bounds in order to prevent disintegration of the established Mormon community. Such efforts as building part of the railroad line and branch lines into the Territory, deflating reports of mineral wealth, manufacturing farm machinery and furniture, setting up a woolen and silk industry, and protecting Mormon lands along the railroad were undertaken by the school. It was, in fact, the mobilized leadership of the Mormon church and local communities. Perhaps its most important, or at least most spectacular, effort was in the institution of co-operative trade in the Territory. This effort, often treated in isolation, Arrington has shown to be a part of the school's activities.

The episode of the School of the Prophets in Utah is an example of the strength of Mormon group loyalties and self-consciousness and testifies to the extent to which co-operation, flexibly applied, had become a standard Mormon response in situations where either harsh nature or hostile men erected barriers to the fulfilment of sacred tasks. It also offers clear evidence of the Mormon design to erect a realistic economic base for a genuinely separated community. Mormon Utah desired statehood, and Utah Mormons would have tolerated gentiles if only the latter had responded reciprocally. But social separatism was a requisite of the gathering, and it had to have an economic base. It is small wonder that the Mormon community, anticipating with the coming of the railroad in 1869 the re-establishment on a larger scale of the old, fatal situation of a gathered Zion surrounded by an unrepentant Babylon, would have reached new heights of co-operation to forestall coming dangers. The School of the Prophets also testifies to the alertness and initiative of secondary leaders and shows that the leadership in its hierarchical structure could mobilize widespread initiative.

It was in these circumstances that Brigham Young, acting through the School of the Prophets, founded Zion's Cooperative Mercantile Institution (Z.C.M.I.). At this time, some 150 co-operative stores were set up throughout the Territory supplied from Z.C.M.I., although much later they were permitted to buy stock from other houses as well. The Mercantile Institution was not a genuine co-operative venture itself, although it was in a real sense part of the Mormon group effort to achieve self-sufficiency and economic independence of its enemies. The original articles of incorporation drawn up in 1870 showed that Z.C.M.I. was a closely owned company. Of a total of 1,990 shares, owned by 21 shareholders, 1,772 were in the hands of four men. Brigham Young owned 772 and William Jennings owned 790. Fourteen stockholders owned fewer than 21 shares each. Yet the Z.C.M.I. did keep prices down and did supply outlying co-operatives. Moreover, Z.C.M.I. was accompanied by real co-operation, and the stores in the outlying areas were genuinely co-operative, although they distributed profit on the basis of shares and not purchases, as do co-operatives of the Rochdale type. Voting was also weighted according to shares.

In 1872 the School of the Prophets was disbanded. Evidently its work was done. It had not prevented the integration of Utah's economy into that of the nation, but it had slowed down disruptive processes and had maintained the position of the community of the Saints. Cultural homogeneity and economic self-sufficiency were successfully defended, and Mormon accommodation would not come until the defeat of the church on the issue of plural marriage and Utah's final integration into the national whole. Strict mercantile exclusiveness was not, however, maintained, and in time the country stores fell into the hands of a few well-to-do men. Said Gardner in 1917: "To a limited degree the shares of the country institutions have come to be concentrated in the hands of the more shrewd, resourceful, and powerful stockholders."[52] Said a member of an important Mormon family in 1950: "There were real co-operatives in Utah when I was a boy, but they were bought out by rich men. I know because my father was one of them."

The church also made use of co-operative techniques and the spirit of the gathered so conducive to their application, in establishing the Perpetual Emigrating Fund Company, which helped many immigrants to come to Zion in the nineteenth century. In 1870 the co-operative ideal found expression in the encouragement of manufacturing and markets and in co-ordinating Mormon economic efforts generally. The institutional form for these activities was Zion's Board of Trade, composed of businessmen. The church had a great influence upon this body, of which President Taylor was the presiding officer. "Unlike the United Order movement of 1874, the boards of trade did not require the participation of all (or most) of the people in each community. They coordinated the leadership and channeled the activities of the strategic few in ways which, it was hoped, would result in the economic expansion of Mormondom."[53] This new form was connected with the effort to build up industry in northern Utah and was an example of President Taylor's flexibility in economic matters. He did not believe in economic blueprints and sought (and believed he saw) in this new combined effort the way to promote Mormon economic welfare. This was not an antigentile measure but rather a positive attempt to build up the resources of the Mormon community. Arrington has characterized it as a "Third United Order."

Such Mormon efforts to develop industry continued after 1890 in fields as far apart as sugar and insurance. The development of the beet-sugar industry and the related stimulus to farming constitute a good example of the social role of church leadership at the time. Although the industry was taken over by eastern capital for a period, it is today under Utah control, with the Mormon church a very substantial stockholder. It is, however, no longer genuinely co-operative, as it was at first. In the early days of the depression the church invested over $900,000 to keep the industry from going under, thereby preventing calamitous results for the economy of the region.

The ideal of co-operation to be seen from the very inception of the church was reinforced in terms of Mormon commitment and at the same time made flexible in application by the experiences, often bitter and discouraging, of the Mormon people.

Working together, often under central direction, group loyalty, self-sufficiency and independence, aid to the needy and mutual help—these remained constant features of Mormon activities and ideals. After 1890 the tendency to experiment with social forms, familial or economic, was curtailed. In time, co-operative institutions declined.

The most striking aspect of the Mormon experience is the flexibility with which a co-operative attitude was brought to bear in concrete situations. So naturally did co-operation follow from the fellowship of the restored gospel—a fellowship deepened by common suffering—that it was not confined to narrow rules and rigid formulas. The failures of its first attempts to find expression in institutional forms, together with the defeats of the Saints in Ohio, Missouri, and Illinois, forcing them each time to start over again in their Zionist project, increased the flexibility of this ethic of co-operation. Doctrinaire commitment was made difficult by the very fact of rapid growth. Yet in the diversity of forms tried under various circumstances can be discerned the central content of the original Law of Consecration—the reconciliation of individual enterprise and co-operation within the larger context of the common weal.

The Church Welfare Plan

Although the accommodation of 1890 was followed by a period of compromise and integration into the gentile community, the Mormon church retained its structure and its conviction of peculiarity. In this new situation, the building of Zion was postponed and to some extent made abstract in a manner that obviated the necessity of concrete attachment to a given piece of ground or a particular social effort. All tasks became of significance in a religious sense, although the older memories remained. The church continued to be interested in its own business investments and in the development of the region, although no longer with its former hegemony in such matters. The basic pattern of life in the Mormon communities appeared to have set. What Geddes has called Mormon "objections to selfishness in the capitalistic system,"[54] seen, for example, in earlier experimentation and in the counsel of the General Authorities to the Orderville Saints in the 1880's, no longer acted as an important inspiration to Mormon policies.

Accommodation and withdrawal from social experimentation were part of the general trend toward conservatism that seemed to characterize Mormon leadership. Institutions formed in an earlier day carried on, but a certain amount of "fixity and mechanization"[55] was to be seen in their functioning. Social differentiation proceeded, and an urban middle class increased in importance, while well-to-do families emerged in the villages. Only in education and in recreation were genuine innovation and real co-operation to be seen. The people of the covenant had come to terms with Babylon, although the old tradition lingered on.

That old tradition, built deeply into Mormon social structure and Mormon consciousness, was to return after its period of latency. Following upon more than a generation of quiescence, it again came forth to give evidence of its tremendous vitality. The time was the 1930's, and the occasion was the depression, which evoked so much interest in social and economic experimentation throughout the nation. Mormon experimentation was less pragmatic than that of other groups, based as it was upon a century of tradition and a continuing church organization. The Mormon answer to the challenge of the depression contains an apparent irony, but one that testifies to the strength of the co-operative tradition. The Mormon answer was based upon the principles of co-operation, and it was proposed by the conservatives in the leadership of the church.

Testifying to the vitality of its belief in temporal salvation, the church came forward in 1936 with its Welfare Plan, a communal project to aid the needy among its members. Its basic principles were as old as the church. When Utah was hit by the economic slump of the thirties, the leadership recalled the words of Brigham Young when facing comparable problems earlier: "Set the poor to work—setting out orchards, splitting rails, digging ditches, making fences or anything useful. . . ."[56] The conservatives who dominated the officialdom did not look with favor upon the efforts of the federal government along this line and objected to Saints being on public relief, which appeared to strike at the moral roots of the community.[57] The Republican predilections of many in the leadership may have contributed some anti–New Deal motivation, as unquestionably was the case with certain prominent initiators of the plan. But the tradition of self-sufficiency, of mutual help and co-operation, predisposed the membership to receive the plan with enthusiasm. If J. Reuben Clark, Jr., spoke for the conservatives when he said, "No man is politically free who depends upon the state for his sustenance," he spoke for a much larger group in saying, "We Mormons have cared for the essential needs of our own in the past; we can do it now."[58]

The responsibility of caring for its own poor had remained a concern of the church; but, as settlement gave way to permanent habitation, there were often no poor in Utah to be aided, and the Fast Offerings, taken up once a month at sacrament meetings for such purposes, dwindled. The sharp economic decline of the early thirties altered this situation radically, and in 1933 the First Presidency of the church made an attempt to meet the new conditions. Letters were sent out to stake presidents asking for a census of resources available to meet the emergency and urging them to stimulate self-help and mutual aid and to try to find employment for the needy. Such measures soon proved hopelessly inadequate. After earlier attempts to bring forward an effective program, in the April conference of 1936 the First Presidency launched a church-wide, centrally directed effort. This plan was accepted with enthusiasm, and many considered it the result of divine revelation guiding the church leadership.

The Welfare Plan was given organizational form with the Presidency, the Council of the Twelve, and the Presiding Bishopric at its head; these were to work through the ward and stake organizations to put the new program into effect. To these established bodies was added a General Welfare Committee, which, working under the General Authorities, became the administrative body of the project, although it did not become a policy-making group. Recommendations on policy growing out of the experience of the Welfare Committee still have to be brought before the General Authorities for approval, which may or may not be given. Once approval is given, the committee is the executive organ charged with implementation.

The General Welfare Committee is subdivided into a number of subcommittees with special areas of competence.[59] When these committees were first established, programs were set afoot through the church organization and the auxiliary organizations on local, regional, and church-wide bases to provide needed goods and employment. By 1939, after three years of operation, it was estimated that 14,000 persons had acted in supervisory capacities and that over 100,000 members were active in the work of the Plan. Wards and stakes set up their own operations and, in fact, some of them had anticipated the plan and had established storehouses. In one place three wards had jointly bought a farm. Both the foundation of the Z.C.M.I. and the earlier United Order had been anticipated and partly inspired by such local initiative.

Once taken up by the leadership, such activities were to become general throughout the church. As the Plan moved into high gear, every ward in the church made estimates of its annual need in advance, and on that basis an over-all production plan was formulated by the General Welfare Committee, which was prorated back to the wards. The operations were regularized, and the organization on a local basis came to be handled by stake and ward welfare committees, composed of heads of local priesthood councils and auxiliary organizations. Most of the work was actually done without compensation, although a few experts had to be employed. Many worked in return for relief.

The response of the membership was overwhelming. Many who felt opposed to the conservatism of the leadership found themselves responding with enthusiasm. Members of university and college faculties, businessmen, lawyers, and people in similar walks of life plowed fields, planted crops, and went out in the morning to pick vegetables before going to their own jobs. When a call went out to build a grain elevator at Welfare Square—the central storage area of the program in Salt Lake City—an overabundance of labor responded, and the construction time was half the engineers' original estimate. The production figures were large indeed. By the 1944 April conference the Plan had fixed assets, such as canning factories, farms, and a coal mine, valued at $2,500,000. A central storehouse in Salt Lake City became a clearing house, and a modern canning factory there produced at one period 30,000 cans of food daily. By 1947 the Plan had completed 1,500 projects and aided almost 300,000 persons. These projects were not confined to Utah but were also located in other states of the intermountain West; in California, where the Los Angeles Plan group purchased the Louis B. Mayer ranch; and even in eastern cities where Saints resided. It has been estimated that the Welfare Plan farms 35,000 acres of land.

The new program also carried on rehabilitation work. This was mainly of two kinds: placing members in welfare jobs where they could learn new skills and lending money. For the latter, a central agency, the Cooperative Security Corporation, an incorporated non-profit organization, was established under the Finance Subcommittee of the General Welfare Committee. Loans were made to individuals and to church organizations, the latter continuing an old policy of the General Authorities of giving financial aid to local projects and of helping to meet local needs. Individuals were given loans only if they had no collateral. Such "character loans" were and are granted on the recommendation of a person's bishop, quorum president, and stake president. In eight years of operation, only about 2¼ per cent of the loans have been defaulted out of a half-million dollars lent. The Plan continues today and is one of the most important auxiliary organizations of the church.

The Plan suffered many of the drawbacks of voluntary organization: lack of skill in handling relief distribution, inappropriateness of projects established, and the like. Yet in certain respects it was a tremendous success. It did not take all the Saints off federal relief, nor did it make federal grants of money unnecessary for public projects, including the repair of irrigation facilities in rural villages. The attempts of some conservative Mormons to give an impression that it did so are a little less than candid. Moreover, the Plan has been criticized by persons within the church who favored a more community-oriented expression of the tradition of Mormon co-operation as against an exclusively Mormon form. It has also, not without reason, been called economically anachronistic. Yet, on the whole, it has called forth tremendous enthusiasm from the Mormon group.

As to eligibility for Welfare Plan relief, "Clearly the Church Plan does not include the care of non-members as lying within its duty or obligation,"[60] although it has aided some non-Mormons. It is held in traditional Mormon fashion that the first responsibility for aiding a needy person devolves upon his relatives. This is in keeping with the Mormon emphasis upon the family. If the family cannot provide, then the church steps in. Those who are "worthy," that is, those who have paid tithes and been faithful to other church duties, are eligible without question. Other cases are considered on their merits.

Together with the Plan has gone a policy on the part of church officialdom to encourage people to store food a year or more ahead. This has met with a good response, as well it might in a people predominantly agrarian or from more or less recent rural backgrounds. It has connotations that stir memories of past hardship shared as a separate people and is suggestive of coming crisis and the advent of the millennium. J. Reuben Clark, Jr., has been particularly emphatic in stressing the "save a year in advance" idea. Millennialism, self-sufficiency, thrift, peculiarity, and co-operation form a meaningful context for such efforts.

The Welfare Plan continues in the present the Mormon co-operative tradition and attempts to find a solution to current problems in terms of the ethic of co-operation and the doctrine of the gathering. It has given the Mormon group a special task and thereby embodied the older idea of the kingdom in contemporary common effort, once again rendering it concrete. Despite the criticism of liberals, who object to its exclusiveness and its economic backwardness, it is, precisely because of these things, the genuine expression of Mormon convictions of peculiarity and the rejection of Babylon.

How it affects the actual integration of the Mormon group into the larger community and their unlimited participation in government, business, and the professions is another question. Church leadership evidently follows implicitly a policy of parallelism. The good Mormon will be a leader of his business community, which will include non-Mormons; of his political party, which will (outside Utah, at least) be predominantly a gentile organization; and of his professional groups, but he will also be gathered unto Zion and will participate in an exclusively Mormon social context when it comes to co-operation to meet such problems as a national depression. He may then easily oppose other forms of co-operation and relief that seem to resemble his own in everything but their gentile quality. Accepting an unlimited church, he can become a strong advocate of the limited state.

Such parallelism seems to work, but there are those among the Saints today who think that a better Mormon contribution might be to blend the special Mormon co-operative tradition with the general community and assert a brotherhood that transcends the gathered. Such a course might be more appropriate to the situation of the Mormon people outside the rural areas, where they have overwhelming numerical dominance; but what will such a policy do to the notion of the special people gathered unto Zion? Parallelism is the contemporary expression and working compromise of the conflict caused by being gathered in the midst of Babylon.

Co-operation is still the expression of group solidarity; yet, while it is an integral part of the ethic of mastery for the individual—advancing him along the path of eternal progression and relating him in fellowship to his community—for the Mormon group as a whole co-operation has been adjusted to the expectations of the gentile community while preserving a degree of exclusiveness and peculiarity. This complex of co-operation and mastery is part of a living tradition and may yet demonstrate in the face of future problems the institutional inventiveness that it has displayed in the past.

CHAPTER NINE

Sources of Strain and Conflict

The Latter-day Saints have successfully created a Mormon community with its own values and social structure, although it is no longer a separate entity but is rather very much a part, both geographically and sentimentally, of the larger secular society of the United States. Yet Mormonism retains much of its old peculiarity, and Mormondom remains in many respects a society in its own right and, as such, has been subject to a number of stresses and strains within its own structure. These sources of conflict have created grave problems for the Mormon movement, and some of them are even now capable of severe threats to its welfare. The ideas and values that provided an adequate basis for the successful establishment of its social institutions also contained elements of conflict and dilemma that in time emerged and challenged Mormonism's spiritual and intellectual resources. Some of these strains may be seen to have arisen directly as a result of Mormon beliefs and their implications. Others, deriving from such beliefs, are the result of relationships to the world of men and of inanimate nature.

Perhaps Mormonism's greatest and most significant problem is its encounter with modern secular thought. This encounter presents itself in terms of a specific dilemma that may be phrased, "education versus apostasy," and has created an unhappy intellectual group among the Mormons today. Closely related to this fundamental problem are two other dilemmas. Mormonism's insistence upon reason and the implicit rationality of its tenets come into conflict with its equally emphasized belief in the miraculous and give rise to what we may call the dilemma of "rationality versus charisma." In addition, Mormonism's concern with both authority and individualism presents another problem.

This third dilemma of "authority and obedience versus democracy and individualism" leads into the whole problem of Mormonism and the governing of men. We shall examine this issue especially in terms of the balance between consent and coercion involved in Mormon authority and leadership. Next we shall turn to polygamy, which for long was a source of so much difficulty for the Mormons, both within their own group and in relation to outsiders. The problems of polygamy live on in terms of an excommunicated and persecuted polygamous tradition of "Fundamentalists" whose existence raises the related conflict over the right of the church to alter basic beliefs. Within the church itself, plural marriage expressed patriarchal ideals of marriage, ideals that survived as theoretically preferred, even with the rejection of polygamy itself. We shall also consider the present status of such ideals.

Another dilemma faced by Mormonism has been that created by its simultaneous acceptance of progress as defining human meaningful effort and of agriculture as the proper basis for community life. In the context of today's industrial society, what problems are raised by these orientations? Not unrelated is the conflict between political conservativism and social idealism. Moreover, as a separate and peculiar group integrated into the general American community, to which they have great loyalty, the Mormons face possible strain from a conflict between patriotism and group particularism. This has indeed been important at times in Mormon history. Important also has been the relation between Mormon orientations to convert the Indians and their pioneer attitude of condescension and suspicion, as well of rivalry, toward them. This issue, important in all western settlement, remains important in the Southwest, where Mormons and Indians still live close together. Finally, we shall see that Mormon beliefs have at times caused Mormons to do those very things that have resulted in difficulty in the concrete setting of Mormon life. In Utah, Mormon emphasis upon the family has led to the migration of surplus youth. This migration raises in another way the issue of Mormonism's confrontation of the larger gentile world. It is with this issue in its most significant form that we shall begin this examination of the dilemmas that have confronted the Mormon development through the years, some of which still challenge its successful continuance.

The Mormon Encounter with Modern Secular Thought

A Salt Lake City Mormon intellectual once remarked to me that the Mormon religion has provided the basis for a satisfying life to the great majority of its followers. He added: "Only the questioning intellectual is unhappy."

The situation of the intellectual is likely to be somewhat ambiguous in any society, and he is generally the object not only of esteem but also of suspicion. In fact, the difficulty of the intellectual in this respect is simply an expression of a fundamental tension between thought and life. The intellectual in his creative aspects is necessary to the maintenance and progress of society, for it is he as creator who produces widely shared and appreciated benefits, ranging from the realm of values to that of physical comforts. Yet the intellectual is also given to reflection and criticism; he also questions. As a questioner and critic, he not only annoys conservatives but may come to threaten, or at least appear to threaten, cherished beliefs, values, and institutions. As creator and preserver, the intellectual is esteemed; as critic and questioner, he is suspect. In submitting established mores to historical, rational, and ethical criticism, the intellectual often makes himself resented and becomes a target for aggression. Mormonism succeeded in evolving an intellectual group from its own native roots, an accomplishment of note, doing credit to its tradition, but one that introduces the ambiguity of intellectual conflict into the Mormon society. To the general ambiguity of the intellectual's position, Mormonism contributes some specific aspects of its own.

Moreover, the intellectual in modern times has frequently been in the vanguard of that complicated historical process that is sometimes referred to as the "secularization of culture." From the sixteenth century to our own day the general trend of Western thought has, under the influence of science and rationalism, tended more and more to relegate religion to a position of secondary importance and to challenge its fundamental viewpoints. Modern man has come to take an increasingly this-worldly view of his own significance. The intellectual has often been the chief agent in the furtherance of this process of secularization. The development of a native Mormon intelligentsia meant the production of a group within Mormonism that would be particularly vulnerable to the secularization of Western thought and in the closest communication with the general intellectual life of the larger civilization.

Under these conditions, it is quite obvious that the return of Mormonism to full participation in the general life of the American republic would, of necessity, involve an encounter with modern thought. Such an encounter would bring peculiarly Mormon beliefs and values into touch with critical ideas and approaches that would test the former's viability in a way different from that of any previous challenge. The Mormon attitude toward education and learning would make this challenge even more important and increase the difficulty in meeting it. From their earliest beginnings, the Latter-day Saints have placed great emphasis upon education. They studied Hebrew in Kirtland in order to understand the Scriptures better; in Nauvoo they founded one of the first municipal universities, if not the first; they founded the University of Utah (then called the University of Deseret) three years after settlement, and it celebrated its one-hundredth anniversary in 1950 and is said to be the oldest university west of the Mississippi. They did all this because they had supreme confidence in man's ability to master his environment and build a good society through knowledge and effort. They intended to use such knowledge in constructing the ideal religious commonwealth, for which they believed the Lord held them as specially consecrated. Little did they realize that in placing their hopes in education they were at the same time creating the "transmission belt" that would bring into Zion all the doubts and uncertainties that, in another century, were to beset the gentile world. Once again we see, as so often in human history, the latent consequences of social action producing results unintended and unforeseen by human actors. What problems has this historic irony created for the Mormon church?

The church was based upon the idea of modern revelation, upon the belief in the restoration in our time of what had been lost through the sinfulness and apostasy of man. Arising at a time of great confusion, the new church offered to its followers clarification on the basis of a new revelation, thereby resolving, on what seemed to be the highest authority, many of the important issues about which other denominations could only quote an ambiguous scripture. It was an age when most believing Christians in America still held to a literal acceptance of the Bible as the content and rule of faith. A new revelation that seemed consistent with older beliefs and arguments based thereon had great cogency and appeal to the early converts who came from such a background. The explicitness of the new Mormon revelation addressed itself to the very points about which contemporary religious thinking puzzled without conclusion. From a new revelation so explicit; from a modern scripture so timely, whose translation was a divine work and therefore uncorrupted; from scriptures given by God himself to chosen people in the latter days, a literal reading of the word would certainly offer solution to any important religious problems.

Therefore, despite Joseph Smith's recognition that the Bible need not necessarily be taken literally in all cases, the modern scriptures were certainly to be so understood. Literalism became and has largely remained characteristic of the Mormon approach to the text of modern revelation. The Bible, recopied for generations, translated over the centuries into various languages, may be unclear, may even be seriously corrupted, but the scriptures presented to the world in our own time by a man who talked with God, translated by a modern prophet through divine inspiration and miraculous assistance—these scriptures must be literally true, or the very foundations of Mormon faith are threatened.

Thus it was a very literalist kind of religion, on the whole, basing its claim to divinity and veracity upon the status of its revelations and their literal meaning, that was placed in close relation to and communication with modern thought by the reincorporation of Mormondom into secular American life. This confrontation contained the great possibility that acquaintance with modern learning by thoughtful Mormons would lead to apostasy. Quite obviously, by encouraging education and giving it a central place in both its own activities and its world view, Mormonism exposed itself more vulnerably to the danger. This is especially the case, since the Mormon appreciation of education emphasized higher education and thereby encouraged contact between Mormon youth and those very elements in modern thought that are bound to act as a solvent on certain aspects of Mormon beliefs. The Mormon youth, who usually comes from a background of rural and quite literal Mormonism, finds that his entrance into the university is an introduction to the doubt and confusion that his first real encounter with secular culture entails. He has been taught by the Mormon faith to seek knowledge and to value it; yet it is precisely this course, so acceptable to and so honored by his religion, that is bound to bring religious crisis to him and profound danger to his religious belief. The college undergraduate curriculum becomes the first line of danger to Mormonism in its encounter with modern learning.

The church has not been unaware of this threat, nor has it failed to respond to the danger. The most striking of its efforts in this direction is the Institute and Seminary system. This highly organized and generously financed program has included the building of L.D.S. institutes near colleges and seminaries near high schools, where religion is taught and where students can participate in church-sponsored religious and social activities. In the school year 1949–50, some five thousand students participated in the sixteen Institutes of Religion maintained by the Mormon church adjacent to colleges, junior colleges, and universities in Arizona, California, Idaho, Utah, and Wyoming. In the fall of 1950, three new institutes were opened—at Reno, Nevada, for the Mormon students at the University of Nevada; at Albion, Idaho, for those at the Idaho College of Education; and at Price, Utah, for the students at Carbon Junior College.

The Institute program began in the mid-twenties when the first Institute was established at Moscow, Idaho, for the Mormon students attending the University of Idaho. By 1935, four were functioning, at Moscow and Pocatello, Idaho, and at Salt Lake City and Logan, Utah; this figure was to grow to thirteen in the next three years. The program of the institutes is not rigidly fixed, and in many places their Bible courses are given academic credit by the university or college nearby. At some institutes there are classes on such subjects as courtship and marriage, church history, missionary training, etc. Often question-and-answer classes are held, to aid the student to orient himself in his new intellectual situation.

Together with the Institute religious and educational program, there is also a social program carried on by an organization of Mormon students called Lambda Delta Sigma. Besides its purely social affairs, this organization takes part in such work as the distribution of Christmas baskets and other community activities.

Besides this, there is usually a chapter of Delta Phi, an organization of Mormon youth who have returned from serving two-year church missions, meeting at the institutes. In their educational program, the institutes often give certificates for the completion of their own curriculum during the college years. In areas where there are only a few Mormon students and where there is no Institute, Deseret Clubs are formed. A short time ago such a club was disbanded at Berkeley when an Institute was established there, at the University of California.

The Seminary system is similarly carried on adjacent to high schools in the intermountain West. There are now about 120 of these seminaries, and, like many of the institutes, their Bible courses are often given credit by the public school system. Even in Ogden, Utah, which, as an industrial and railroad town, has a large gentile population, the school board has granted such credit. It is interesting to note that at the University of Utah, in Salt Lake City, no such accrediting of Institute courses has taken place. The church does run a very large and very impressive Institute near the campus, but it has not achieved official recognition in terms of course credit. This appears to be due to Protestant opposition and to that of the Masons, who are strongly represented at the university and who in Salt Lake City are reputed to be of vigorous anti-Mormon sentiment.

For the Mormon student to come directly to a college or university without the possibility of seeking help at these institutes would be for him to come from a high-pressure chamber to the open air without passing through a series of decompression chambers. The Institute system provides able teaching, most often by men who themselves are intellectuals and who are aware of the kind of problem the student faces and the sort of help he needs.[1] It also provides Mormon recreation and social activities that strengthen the ties with his church for the youth away from home. This system is expensive, and the church spends freely, almost lavishly, upon it; and there is evidence that it has salvaged many apostates. The later return in tithes to the church may exceed the original cost of supporting the system, although that is not, of course, the motivation of the church.

The church has its own university, established for the furtherance of education among the Saints in 1875 at Provo, Utah. While the institutes and seminaries have been manned by people who often tend toward a liberal position or at least have a conservative-liberal attitude in theology, the Division of Religion at Brigham Young University has of late years been conservative. Recently it has produced an erudite, scholarly, and even esoteric scholasticism, to support conservative literal theology of a most fundamentalist nature.[2] Yet Brigham Young University has not been free from those currents of modern thought that we have characterized earlier, and a few years ago such opposition led to open conflict.

It is difficult to gauge the attitudes of the authorities of the church toward the Institute and Seminary system, which is subject to strong liberal, or at least conservative-liberal, influence. The church gives generous support, and the good work of the system in keeping youth in the church is recognized. It is interesting to note that the chairman of the executive committee of the Church Board of Education is Joseph Fielding Smith, the grandson of Hyrum, the prophet's brother, who was killed with him in Carthage, Illinois. Smith, unquestionably one of the top leaders of contemporary Mormonism, a man of great courage and personal integrity, is at the same time one of the most literalist of Mormon writers and thinkers.[3] Yet Joseph Fielding Smith has had much to do with the great expenditures made by the church in supporting the Institute and Seminary system.

The Institute system is the way the church has developed to meet the threat of apostasy involved in Mormonism's encounter with secular education. How adequate is that response? The answer to this question involves a more fundamental issue. Upon the way the Mormon church can meet this more basic dilemma posed for it by its relation to modern learning will depend the final outcome of its attempt to give organized educational support to the faith of its college youth. Can the church make the accommodation to modern thought necessary to satisfy the concern with truth that its own teachings have created in its more intellectual members and, at the same time, maintain the basic articles of faith without which it will certainly cease to survive in its present form?

There are, in fact, two aspects of this issue, each of which creates its own peculiar difficulty for the church. It will be recalled that the government of the church, though marked by strong authoritative characteristics, is a government by laymen. There is no clergy in the professional sense of that term. In the early days of the church this was indeed a great source of strength, and the widespread lay participation that has resulted from it is still an important aspect of Mormon organizational vitality. Yet this preponderance of non-professionals affects the church's formation of its basic outlook and creates added difficulties in connection with the present problem. Despite the fact that the small group of the General Authorities do receive a stipend, the church leaders are not professionals in the sense of having received the special educational formation and training in philosophy and theology that the education of a clergy would involve. This means that the church has, with few exceptions, no theologically qualified leaders who can guide it in its encounter with secular thought. Members of the higher councils may be educated men, but they are usually not educated in those subjects that would be helpful to religious leaders facing these problems. In terms of theology, the church is governed not only by laymen but also by amateurs.

If we add to this the general policy of promoting in the higher reaches of the hierarchy on the principle of seniority, we see that older and therefore usually more conservative men tend to get into these influential positions. Moreover, the other bases of choice for active church positions often have to do with faithfulness to the church, loyalty to its moral code, activity in church organizations, and proven administrative ability rather than with the kind of education and background that would prepare the leaders for the difficult and subtle philosophical and theological problems to be faced here. The one group of men who could come near to meeting the challenge of secular learning are those involved in the Institute and Seminary system and others like them in education and related professions. But the present bases of selection and promotion make the possibility of many of these men advancing to membership in leading bodies and especially in the General Authorities a very slim one indeed.

The conservative, literalist, fundamentalist group seems now to control the church, and these principles of church organization— lay leadership, seniority as the basis of promotion, selection on other bases than theological learning, and control of appointments by conservative elements—make the advancement of liberals into church leadership very unlikely in the next several years. Yet it is these very liberals, shut out from leadership, who in the church's educational system are saving many of the youth from apostasy.

Can the church remain in this kind of halfway house, and, if so, how long?

Quite recent events suggest a more favorable turn in their direction than most liberals would have felt likely at the time when this study was originally made. The accession of David O. McKay to the First Presidency of the church has signaled and not improbably caused a considerable decrease in the influence of the most conservative elements. President McKay, while a man genuinely respected by all groups within the church, is not unfriendly to the liberals. His policies appear to have curtailed dogmatizing by members of the General Authorities and to have introduced a degree of flexibility in religious thought into the sphere of official acceptability. Yet, because the Mormon church cannot state a minimum religious position required for membership, for reasons we shall discuss later, such flexibility may actually lead to a dilution of Mormon doctrine in the long run.

Moreover, it must not be overlooked that the church leadership needs the intellectuals. It needs them not only to man the church's educational institutions but, perhaps more important, to prevent the kind of open rift between the Mormon church and modern learning and higher education that would involve intellectual embarrassment and loss of respectability. Thus it must seem wiser to many among the church leaders to seek unvoiced compromises and to avoid embarrassing confrontations. To this fact must be added the observation that the new leadership at Brigham Young University, while certainly conservative in theological matters, seems to be seriously concerned with academic standards and not shy about hiring persons of liberal religious opinions in seeking professional quality. When these developments are considered against the background of the intellectual atmosphere in the country today—one marked far less by sharp cleavages and well-defined differences than was the case a few years ago and exhibiting a general trend toward social conservatism—we are impressed by the possibility of a slow drift toward a dilution of belief. Such a drift, which may be well started, is certainly far from the flood. It could issue in a victory for religious and theological liberalism without any crisis or showdown. Although age and conservatism control the top bodies, youth, as is often tritely remarked, possesses the future, and the youth incline away from the older literalism to the extent that they become intellectuals or are influenced by the intellectuals in the church's educational system. There is no reason to suppose such a drift will not continue.

Such a slow infiltration of liberal notions may, in its own undramatic way, prove as fatal to Mormonism as a religious system as would a severe crisis. Mormon beliefs and their ability to answer the needs of men today may be put to the test and found wanting without any outer signs of controversy, although the inner crises and conflicts with which we shall deal later remain an important aspect of private lives. Moreover, a new generation may be able to discover new compromises and find that it can make compromises more easily than did an older group. To this, only the future can offer the definitive answer; present indications are too scant.

The possibility of a crisis must not be completely written off, however. Certainly a reversal of the present trend that mildly favors the liberals, or at least a serious challenge to it, is quite possible. The order of succession to the presidency makes it likely that the next man to hold the First Presidency of the church will be a conservative. Should that happen, a crisis may well develop. Yet the fact that the Mormon intellectual has accustomed himself to living in a prolonged and normalized state of crisis in relation to literal Mormon beliefs and to church authority as their embodiment seriously qualifies any dramatic prognosis.

Unquestionably, there is a tendency privately to accept more liberal views—or something several degrees more liberal than the old conservative and literalist Mormonism—on the part of many who support and sustain the General Authorities and defend the Mormon tradition. It is difficult to gauge such a trend, which, together with the more outspoken liberalism, may contribute an important element to the present and future composition of the Mormon picture and may represent a subtle secularization within the ranks. The structure of the church is such that it is difficult to meet the problems posed by apostasy in any way except in terms of suffering slowly festering discontent, or a slow drift to liberalism under the cover of orthodox phrases and genuine loyalty to the organization, or some combination of the two.

There are aspects of the church's fundamental doctrine that make the problem involved here even more difficult. This second side of the question is equally as important as that which we have just examined. The conflict in the minds of the intellectuals is one of liberalism versus literalism in theology. Many Mormon intellectuals would like to follow the example of liberal Protestantism, and yet they seem to realize that it would be impossible for the church to sustain them in this position. The problem is complicated for them because they often have tremendous loyalty to the values of Mormonism, despite their inability to accept the literal interpretation of Mormon revelation. Furthermore, they have considerable group pride and feel a strong solidarity with their own backgrounds.

Mormonism, as we have seen, was the child—the stepchild may be more accurate—of nineteenth-century American Protestantism. Its early appeal lay in the fact that its restoration of divine revelation in the latter days answered the problems about which the older denominations could only quarrel. Thus the church must hold to its latter-day revelations literally or lose the theological and charismatic basis of its legitimacy. Because of the great conviction on the part of Mormons that they are close to a generation especially chosen by God and that their immediate ancestors talked with God—a belief that is supplemented in our day by the supposed presence of miraculous works and prophecies—there has never arisen any distinction in Mormon thinking between the natural and the historic elements of its beliefs, on the one hand, and the supernatural and transcendent elements, on the other. With any distinction between absolute or relative aspects ruled out, it has been impossible for a middle position to emerge between literalism and liberalism. There is actually no room in Mormonism for philosophy as distinct from theology.

Furthermore, the immediacy and explicitness of Mormon revelation make that theology a very literalist one. This immediacy and explicitness and the doctrine that there is no fundamental difference between the spiritual and the material or between the temporal and the eternal leave little legitimate room in Mormon thinking for what some Mormon leaders call "the philosophies of men." These latter are seen as vain and invalid, presuming to answer problems for which official Mormonism has divinely inspired and explicit answers. The origin of the earth, the destiny of man here below as well as in eternity, the temporal significance of contemporary events, the basic attitudes toward governmental forms, even the origin of the American Indians—all these are an-

swered so explicitly in Mormon scripture and with such immediacy to a divine source that there is little place for a religiously
oriented, though not divinely inspired, philosophy. Mormonism
can have only a theology, for its theology monopolizes the field
that philosophy would seek to develop.

As this theology is literal and fundamentalist, the liberal can
choose only between submission and personal disquietude or apostasy and suffering the guilt of deserting the tradition in which he
has been reared and to which he feels great attachment. The
church was founded upon a new opening of the heavens in our
day, and it cannot easily, a mere century later, refuse to accept
literally the words spoken by God himself to its founders. Yet if
it were not for the fact that Mormonism arose in literal Protestantism and took this attitude into its own outlook, we wonder if
there would not be room for reinterpretation, which, while moving away from literalness, would retain what is held to be the
divinely inspired essence of the revelations to the modern prophet.
The nature of modern revelation itself seriously restricts the
sphere of such interpretation; the lay leadership of the church
makes its appearance unlikely even in that restricted sphere.

The position of the church, to recapitulate, is briefly this: With
its fundamentalist theology, it faces the threat of apostasy on the
part of its intellectuals, who cannot accept such a position. The
kind of *rapprochement* necessary to satisfy such people is possible
on two bases. The first is to go over to liberalism in theology,
which would destroy the basis of the peculiar Mormon claim to
legitimacy. The second is to take the position that some have
called "pre-fundamentalist," that is, to state certain essential articles of faith, adherence to which is necessary for church membership, and to leave the rest of the area open to non-literal interpretation. The Catholic position offers an outstanding example. But
there has been no attempt by Mormon leaders to separate a central core of dogma from the latter-day revelation, because of two
factors. First, all has been held equally important because of its
immediateness to a divine source and the explicitness of the statement of modern Mormon revelation and because the spirit of
Protestant literalness has been carried over into Mormon thinking.
Second, the basic organization of the church, involving as it does
the principle of lay leadership, has not produced a specialized
corps of theologians who would be professionally prepared to
grapple with the problems involved.

The Mormon intellectual often perceives this problem as close-ly related to that of conservatism in politics on the part of church leaders and that of authoritarianism versus congregationalism in the government of the church. It has not been uncommon for the intellectual to be a political liberal where the orthodox is con-servative, to be a liberal in theology where the orthodox is literal-ist, and to be in favor of a return to the earlier congregationalism in church government where the orthodox has a strong convic-tion of the rightness of obedience to divinely constituted author-ity. While these three orientations are not necessarily always found together, some intellectuals seem to see in the knotty prob-lem of literal versus liberal theology only the result of the dis-liked authoritarian structure of the church. This seems to result in part from contemporary American values, which are to a con-siderable degree derived from those branches of Protestantism that played down established authority and in part from the tend-ency so common among intellectuals to see in certain liberal re-forms the solution of all problems.

These people seem to forget that the authoritarianism of Mor-monism is not at all new and that unorthodox and even radical experiments, first in theology and later in the sphere of family relations and socioeconomic institutions, have been carried out in the past under authoritarian leadership. Moreover, it is erroneous to think that the establishment of full congregational government would have an immediate effect in theology to the liberals' liking. The ideas of the General Authorities on such questions are com-pletely supported by the rural membership and to a large extent by the urban middle-class membership, which has recently emerged from rural conditions. There is hardly to be found in the whole country any organization that displays greater agree-ment on basic questions, and from this arises the vitality of Mor-monism that is so impressive to many eastern visitors to the inter-mountain West. While the growth of congregationalism in the church would unquestionably have an eventual effect on church policies, there is every reason to believe that its immediate results would be disappointing in the extreme to the liberals. In fact, those who advance into church leadership are remarkably repre-sentative of the general membership, especially of the active mem-bership, and it is to be seriously doubted whether the most radical congregationalism would bring any basic changes for some time.

Clearly, the dilemma of education versus apostasy is one to

which Mormonism has as yet found no genuine solution. The church remains, however, committed to the encouragement of education, and it attempts in the ways we have indicated to meet the complications that such education brings in its wake. Mormonism as a way of life has to its credit that it has created a genuine intellectual group of considerable proportions in relation to the general size and rural composition of the community as a whole. But these intellectuals find themselves very often in a condition of inner conflict. Torn between a loyalty to the Mormon tradition and a commitment to modern thought, affected by both a genuine attachment to their own group and its way of life and the intellectual dispositions of the modern temper, these men find their own Mormonism a great problem to themselves.

In frank discussion, their profound difficulties come to the fore. I was told by one that "a day of reckoning is coming, because of the church's insistence on fundamentalism." He compared the church to a train rushing down the track without an engineer. Another declared that the liberals in the church were "doomed to defeat," that the liberal idea of a Mormon church that gave up certain theological tenets, such as the uniqueness of the Mormon people, modern revelation, and the like, and embraced instead social idealism was unworkable, as it would destroy the motivation of the rank and file. This man stated that the destruction of orthodox theology would mean the destruction of the church. He added that the leadership knew this and hence fought liberalism. Another Mormon intellectual in Salt Lake City took the position that there was actually much room for liberal thinking in the church if one abstained from smoking and drinking and thereby gave tangible evidence of loyalty. When I suggested this possibility to another, he replied, "Are we not compromising when we sit in church and say nothing?"

I was assured by one man that the leaders of the church have to keep in the church both people who are quite liberal and those who are quite conservative; he said that, inasmuch as the leaders are facing the real situation, it is not so easy for them as for their critics. He declared: "We are making progress. I don't see an awful lot of priestcraft; there is a little tendency in that direction." Yet the same man spoke very seriously of the danger of being cut off from the church if he published a book to which the church objected. Another man who spoke favorably of the church to me and urged me to get close to the Mormon people and see the Mormon point of view from the inside said to me later, "We are priest-ridden and we are politics-ridden."

In these remarks we begin to get the feel of the intellectual's predicament and of his attitude toward authority and theological orthodoxy. His objections are usually held within the context of strong loyalty to Mormon institutions and values. There is much pride in the accomplishments of Mormon settlement, and, despite the fact that its theological foundations have vanished for them, many of these intellectuals feel strongly identified with the very peculiarity of Mormonism that derived originally from those foundations. The result is conflict. The man who expresses antagonism to some aspect of the church will express admiration of another and rise in defense of the Mormon value system if necessary.

This can be seen most clearly in the remarks of one man who stated: "There are three types of Mormon intellectuals: the sophisticated, who call attention to the mythology and the stupidities; the apologists, who are ready at any time to preach a sermon on the fine things in Mormonism; and the evasive, who are neither aggressively for nor against." He said that Mormonism needed the first two, but, he added: "To paraphrase St. Paul, the worst of these is the third." He went on to point out that the community needed its intellectuals and that they should be contributing to its growth and success. To him, Mormonism represented a socially vital force, and it was important for the intellectual not to destroy the basis of the community's values.

He paid high tribute to the humanistic content of much of Mormon theology, saying that it brought God and man closer together. He admitted that he thought this was often done crudely, and he said: "You know of the California philosophy professor who introduced a Mormon student to one of his colleagues and said, 'This man is from Utah. He believes that God has hair on his back.'" But, despite this crudity, he continued, Mormonism has given the basis for a happy and successful community life and made the accomplishments of Utah settlement possible. He then spoke unfavorably of those who dig up facts to "expose" the basis of the Mormon tradition. He said with some emphasis: "Are we concerned with the conservation of values or with facts?" He said that two points of view clashed here: one was the concern with these values which are the basis of the community, and the other was the concern with historical fact. He said: "Can we say, though Zion fall, let's get at the roots?" I asked him whether if a man had some facts unfavorable to the preservation of Mormon values he should not publish them. He replied with some emphasis, "By all means, publish!"

Such an example merely points up the struggle that is real to many, the internal conflict between loyalty to the values of the church and a belief in the untenability of the church's theology. Few have seen here any "third alternative" to the liberalism-literalism dilemma. One man who was unusually perceptive in that regard did talk to me about the vast potentialities for development that he saw in Mormon theology because of the great variety of its doctrinal sources—the Old and New Testaments, the *Book of Mormon*, the *Doctrine and Covenants*, and the *Pearl of Great Price*. It was possible, he continued, to draw on these and develop what was best in them, laying special emphasis upon what was best in the teachings of the prophets and of Christ. He emphasized the importance of the belief in a personal God who communicated with men—"a living God"—and in the personal immortality of man. He especially stressed the centrality of Christ and the importance of reorienting Mormon teachings with respect to present-day problems on the basis of the teachings of Christ.

Another pointed to the possibilities of continuing the break with orthodox Christianity that Mormon innovations in faith and theology in the nineteenth century had already initiated and developed. This man saw the hope of Mormonism to lie in the extra-Christian elements that Joseph Smith had introduced into its beliefs. He stated that "the theologians, not the theology," were at fault; that they were timid about developing the potential of the theology itself. He felt that such a development would in some respects be like that of Unitarianism but stated that, "unlike the Unitarians, the Mormons could do it on a solid theistic basis."

That there is loyalty to the Mormon tradition among the intellectuals may be seen in their frequent return to Utah. Writing in 1945, Maurine Whipple said: "We come back because Zion is worth occasional discomfort. We come back because Zion is the most unpredictable, exciting, satisfying place in the world to live in. We come back because Utah is a foreign-land-gone-American."[4] In recent years some of the most prominent members of the faculty of the University of Utah have returned to teach there, often from illustrious eastern universities, at reductions in their salaries. I have talked to some of these men, and all feel happier to be back. Their reasons may be different in each case, but they all testify to a strong loyalty to their own people and their own traditions.

Despite this confusion, despite these conflicts, the liberal Mormon intellectual remains a churchgoing man; university wards of the Mormon church have unusually large attendance. He remains a loyal but troubled opposition. His loyalty and opposition differ in degree from individual to individual; yet in all there is loyalty, and in many there is opposition. These people not only go to church, they are engaged in church activities; they often rise up with enthusiasm to answer a call, such as those sent out by the Welfare Plan program. They contribute as best they can to church and community. Yet the question must be raised: Is there not here a great likelihood of a permanent alienation of the intellectual from the community? If the intellectual does not rebel, is not his frustration costly to the community, which could make far better use of his special talents? Will not some eventually rebel? What of the children of such parents? Will not the Mormon regard for education make this problem more and more pressing for the church?

It is a curious fact that, despite the importance of the conflict between science and religion in earlier years, today it is not physical science so much as the humanities and social sciences that seem to offer a threat to religion. In fact, the encouragement of physical science offers one way of sidestepping the education versus apostasy dilemma. Certain aspects of Mormon theology, in stressing rational mastery over nature as an important human goal, are quite congenial to natural science. Among the leading Mormon intellectuals to whom I talked was a man most orthodox in religious belief who was also a physical scientist of note. The erection of a large, costly, and excellently equipped science building on the upper campus of Brigham Young University, which was completed in the fall of 1950, offers another example. Yet the fact is that Mormon students, in their selection of college courses, are also attracted by the humanities and the social sciences. The Mormon emphasis upon reason and upon community seems to be an important background fact in this respect.

We can only conclude that the encounter of Mormonism and modern secular learning is one that is still taking place. It is a spectacle of the present, of which no history can as yet be written. Upon its outcome will depend in a deeper sense the future of Mormonism. A final loss of the intellectual would be a wound from which the church could hardly recover. A liberalization of belief and an abandonment of traditional positions in faith would transform, if not destroy, Mormonism. These potentialities slumber fitfully and insecurely within the present state of prolonged but regularized crisis.

In the meantime the conflict in the minds of the liberal Mormon intellectual remains real indeed. For many of them, their discontent and their loyalty are a burden they cannot lay down. They do not see any clear way out. They are, of course, statistically a small part of the community, and yet, despite their small number, they are not without crucial importance. Their alienation would be of great consequence. They express their conflict in private discussions and at times in published books. In the former, their great dilemma often expresses itself in contradictory statements. Their group loyalty is strong; their pride in the accomplishments of their people, great; their respect for the values of their faith, genuine; but they are unable to accept an orthodox literal theology which for most of their fellow churchmen is the basis of all the other cherished values. Some of them at times apostatize; most of them go on co-operating as best they can. Perhaps a long-term drift toward liberalism may solve their problems for them. Utah's three institutions of higher learning in the meantime offer them a meaningful context for intellectual activity, and the situation with respect to intellectual freedom in church educational institutions should not be a cause of major difficulty.

Yet they may well ask themselves what such a drift toward liberalism will leave of Mormonism as a religious ideology. Upon the answer to that question may depend their own evaluations of their present activity and function. Mormonism, which a hundred years ago began with such high hopes for education as a solution to the problems of mankind, finds itself today with uneasy intellectuals in Zion itself. They have followed the admonition of their prophet and sought wisdom, but the result of their quest has placed them in opposition to many of his most important doctrines.

Rationality versus Charisma

Closely related to the difficulties involved in the confrontation of Mormonism and modern secular thought is the related conflict between two inherent tendencies within Mormon doctrine itself, which may be called the dilemma of rationality versus charisma. Mormonism has been inclined toward rationality from the start, and this has long been related to a certain utilitarianism in the general Mormon outlook. This can be seen in the intellectual emphasis of the *Book of Mormon* and also of the later *Doctrine and Covenants*. Even in the Book of Abraham (*Pearl of Great Price*), where the astronomical discussion is naïve and obviously erroneous, the emphasis is upon an intellectual appeal. Argument rather than emotion plays an important part in Mormon proselytizing. Moreover, as men of action, Mormons have shown themselves eminently practical. One result of this side of Mormon thinking has been a kind of rationalistic apologetics to meet the problems raised by secular thought and science. A generation ago, one group of more intellectual church leaders thought that this approach was successfully meeting the challenge.

At the same time, charismatic phenomena were common throughout Mormon history. At Kirtland there were extremes of religious enthusiasm, and there even Brigham Young spoke with tongues, while Joseph Smith, who disapproved of such excesses, accepted them from such an impressive member and pronounced them to be the pure "Adamic language." Today private revelations are still claimed, and the laying on of hands and anointing with oil for healing remain constant Mormon practices. These "healing ordinances" are performed by two elders, and the sick person and others present are asked to have faith. Writing in 1950, Nelson said: "There is scarcely a faithful member of the Church in a Mormon community who cannot testify to having been healed from an illness in this way."[5]

There has been a routinization of revelation in Utah, a fact for which the Utah group has been chided by the Reorganized Church. The latter still maintains its claim to revelation in a form reminiscent of the first years under the prophet Joseph. Although this has caused some inner conflict, revelations are still being added to the Reorganized Church's edition of the *Doctrine and Covenants*. The 1950 edition contains a statement, numbered Section 142 and signed by the president, Israel A. Smith, which includes the following: "I have earnestly sought divine guidance, and it is with gratitude that I am able to transmit to the church, through the appointed channels, the following as the will of the Lord."[6] While the reference to "appointed channels" suggests some degree of routinization, yet the revelation continues: "The voice of inspiration directs me to say," and is followed by five statements including two nominations to office.[7] This is a far cry from the Utah church leadership, although many devout Mormons consider the messages of the First Presidency to be inspired. Yet they are not added to the standard works of Mormon scripture.

Nevertheless, the emphasis upon charismatic phenomena in popular Mormonism is considerable. Such an attitude offers obstacles to the beliefs and loyalties of the more rationalistic, who follow out one side of the implications of the Mormon position and of Mormon training, a side further encouraged by secular thought and education. Yet the disappearance of such phenomena or its repudiation would disappoint the more literally inclined and give rise to serious doubts on their part.

Authority and Obedience versus Democracy and Individualism

Furthermore, as we have seen, the encounter of Mormonism with modern thought is further complicated by another dilemma characteristic of the Mormon outlook—that between authority and obedience, on the one hand, and democracy and individualism, on the other. Taking its origin from several sources and developing under conditions peculiar to itself, Mormonism gave its own interpretations to what it took from its many roots. As a result, it has often set up beliefs and values whose implications were in some respects mutually contradictory or at least lent themselves to contradictory interpretations. Such contrarieties became sources of strain.

The emphasis upon the free agency of man, upon man's development through his own effort, and upon the possibility of the individual's achieving Godlike status continued under specifically Mormon conditions and in Mormon theological terms the earlier Christian emphasis upon the importance of the human person. Such an emphasis contained both democratic and individualistic implications. Carrying with it much of the spirit of the early New England Protestantism from which it originated, Mormonism did not remain uninfluenced by these implications. Yet, as a church claiming descent from the rule of a specially chosen prophet-founder and embodying a hierarchy of office and decision-making, the Mormon body established an authoritarian structure and demanded obedience to its officials as the context of Mormon religious life. These two tendencies demanded some kind of accommodation to each other if serious conflict was to be avoided. In terms of church government, there has resulted a democracy of participation within the context of hierarchical organization and authoritarian operation. On the whole, the accommodation between these two tendencies has worked well enough, as we have seen. It certainly has worked out sufficiently well to permit effective operation of the church organization. Yet it remains a potential source of strain, and for the intellectuals it is an actual source of difficulty.

Consent versus Coercion

The whole question of Mormonism and authority and in a larger sense of Mormonism and the governing of men has been one that has agitated both Mormons and gentiles throughout the years of Mormon history. It has unquestionably been one of the major problems in the Mormon story. From the point of view of operation, government rests upon two foundations—consent and coercion. The hostile critics of Mormonism have interpreted government in Mormon settlements and in the Mormon ecclesiastical organization in terms that gave great prominence to coercion, and as a result they have tended to see important community efforts involving group discipline and obedience to ecclesiastical leadership in terms of coercion and exploitation of the rank and file.

The main trouble with such explanations of Mormon authority is that they obscure precisely what needs to be explained. In the first place, they conceal the positive aspect of Mormon leadership, based upon an acceptance of Joseph Smith as a prophet, and the consequent consent to the established government of the church. The body of beliefs and values accepted upon conversion, or in the course of maturation in the case of those born of Mormon families, implies the legitimacy of church government. In the second place, interpretations that magnify coercion tend to play down by implication the important comparative fact that coercion as a method of government is not confined to new and unconventional movements. The existence of police forces, the use of armed force against the Confederacy during the Civil War, the raising of armies to defend the Republic by universal conscription, and the measures that the federal government finally took against the Mormon church—all these testify to the importance of coercion as a part of constitutional government even in the established communities of the mid-nineteenth century. Yet in the larger instance of the United States, it would appear that the majority of citizens gave their consent—many perhaps in a quite passive way—to these measures or at least granted the right of the government to make use of them. The success of the Mormon movement in so many undertakings and Mormon cohesiveness in the face of failure suggest that, in the smaller case as well, the position of leadership rested ultimately upon consent. The new movement certainly made use of force, but the terror against enemies and apostates in Missouri, in Illinois, and in Utah must be seen as subsidiary to and derived from a community of consent based upon common acceptance of the new religion. The importance of such measures must not be minimized in either larger or smaller cases, but it must not be magnified in such a way as to conceal the vast and fundamental role of consent.

The exact proportion of consent to coercion in the operation of any government is difficult to gauge and does not permit of quantitative measurement. Yet it may be safely assumed that, unless leadership, decision-making, and the enforcement of standards in the group can be carried out by loyal men, the community is doomed, and such loyalty must ultimately rest upon consent. The recruitment of active loyal forces requires at least passive loyalty from some of the people, and in a new movement engaged in conflict and without the benefit of the stability that comes of age and custom the membership must have been largely loyal. Apostasy, while creating enemies without, acted as a purgative within. The Mormon leadership would seem to have rested, first of all, on consent and to have made use of coercion as a supplement. In this it does not appear to have differed in its fundamental working from all leadership and all government.

Despite the case of the Laws and Foster in Nauvoo or that of the refusal of the Godbeites to go along with the religious, ecclesiastical, and economic measures of Brigham Young in Utah, the fact is that leadership was, in the last analysis, based upon general consent. All communities draw a line against dissent somewhere. Mormonism drew it in Utah against those who opposed cultural autonomy and economic self-sufficiency and fought the dominant position of Brigham Young. The nature of Mormonism as it evolved demanded a certain rigidity both as a formalization of its charismatic leadership and for the fulfilment of its tasks. Yet under the hierarchical leadership that derived from the authority of Brigham Young, the work of western settlement and the need for local and regional leadership combined to make considerable individual initiative possible within the tightly knit structure. Government and leadership have been a source of strain in Mormon history, as shown by the apostasy and grumbling that accompanied all Mormon efforts. Yet the movement always kept a favorable balance between consensus and coercion. Perhaps only in Nauvoo was it momentarily threatened, but here the brutal murder of Joseph Smith further consecrated the legitimacy of leadership.

Plural Marriage and Change of Doctrine

Perhaps the second most important source of strain for Mormonism in the last century was polygamy. The new marriage and family forms demanded attitudes toward and relations between husbands and wives for which the background of the people had ill-prepared them, and as a result the new institution went against the grain for many. This was, perhaps, especially the case with the women, but both men and women in the last analysis accepted it because they believed it to have been divinely commanded. Brigham Young often reproved the women for grumbling, and the church preached plural marriage as a duty.

Plural marriage did not show an increase throughout the years in Utah corresponding to the growth of the church. This may in part be accounted for by the poorer situation of new immigrants and settlers, but it is also indicative of at least a passive and perhaps often unconscious resistance. Church campaigns and periods of tension between Mormons and gentiles or the federal government saw increases in the rate of plural marriage, but at other times such marriages fell off seriously. The Mormon Reformation of 1856–57 and the related Utah Mormon War of 1857 marked one such period. In fact, plural marriages never again reached the height of these years, although the membership of the church

grew greatly. A decade later, in response to the agitation for autarchy and the campaign of the revived Utah version of the
School of the Prophets to defend local self-sufficiency through
large-scale co-operation, the number of polygamous marriages
again increased. Yet the number performed in the years 1868–69
was only about half those of the Reformation period, despite the
doubled membership of the church. In general, the curve of plural marriages declined after 1857. There was some relative increase
in the days of the final struggle after the passage of the Edmunds-
Tucker Law.

Exactly how many persons lived in polygamy is not easy to say.
The church at one time estimated some 10–15 per cent, while
non-Mormons visiting Utah often put the figure as high as 50 per
cent. In 1890 Joseph F. Smith estimated that there were about
3,000 polygamous families and, before the congressional committee investigating Reed Smoot in 1904, he suggested 4,000. Since
about two-thirds of the plural families involved two wives and
another 20 per cent three wives and since the fertility rate seems
to have been lower among plural wives, the average size of a
polygamous family—husband, wives, and children—was probably
around seven. This would make the number of Saints living in
polygamy in the years 1890–1904 something like 21,000–28,000.
With church membership between 200,000 and 250,000 in those
years, this would make the polygamous segment of the church between 10 and 11 per cent. On the basis of these figures it would
appear that something like 8 per cent of the families were plural
families. This would accord with the partial studies that have
placed the figure for polygamous husbands around 7 per cent, although one such study suggested 15 per cent. The percentage of
polygamists rose sharply with importance in church organization,
since polygamy was the ideal form according to church teachings.
Mormon polygamy had this in common with other polygamous
societies: while plural marriage was the ideal, it could be practiced by only a few. It is suggested that among the Saints the
hangover of older attitudes was an important factor in keeping
this minority small.

Plural marriage was not only a source of strain in the obvious
sense that it came to be the bone of contention of the fierce conflict of the second half of the nineteenth century. It was also a
source of strain for those who practiced it. The accounts of apos-

tates often give a dark picture of the way the institution func-
tioned. A recent study based upon a sample of less than 200 families, but a sample probably not too far from typical of the whole,
found that over half the families were "highly" or "moderately"
successful, while a quarter were in a middle category, and a final
quarter were found to show considerable conflict.[8]

Since there was no imbalance in the Utah sex ratio, Young
indicates that a pattern began to take shape which made it incum-
bent upon polygamous suitors to withraw when a single man had
already established courtship relations with a young woman. This
is a far cry from some of the stories told by apostates and repeated
by hostile critics. On the whole, no stable patterns of polygamous
behavior with regard to status among wives, rules of residence,
priority of children, and the like had time to form before the
federal offensive drove the practice underground. The advantage
taken by the first wife (the only legal wife in civil law) and her
children in matters of inheritance and the difficulties of the church
and the husbands in trying to bring equity into such situations
were an important source of strain in the new institution. The
carry-over of monogamous attitudes, the relative status of wives
within the family, temperamental differences among wives, economic hardship (despite the formal requirement that a man must
have church approval and be able to support additional wives
before entering upon a plural marriage), and unconscious guilt,
which was increased after the 1890 manifesto[9]—all these Young
found to be causes of trouble. He found actual cases of "resentment if not downright disbelief in the system" as well.[10]

After the official declaration of Wilford Woodruff in 1890,
some church leaders took additional wives, and the peculiar institution became a cause of strife within the church. It nearly caused
a resurgence of Mormon-gentile conflict in the Smoot case of
1904. And when church leaders testified without complete candor
and counseled such testimony, it caused inner stress for some members. Moreover, an excommunicated polygamous tradition continues to plague the church today.

Despite the changed attitude of the Mormon church, plural
marriage continues to be practiced in Utah. This represents not
only the continuation of the older tradition but also is itself a
challenge of the right of the church to change and revise basic
articles of belief. The *Doctrine and Covenants* issued in 1835

revised important sections of the older revelations in the *Book of Commandments*. It is, however, held by Latter-day Saints that this revision was divinely inspired. Evidently it did not cause any serious difficulty for the church or its leadership. However, the attempt to change basic doctrine or at least its practical implications in the case of polygamy had more serious effects. The original promulgation of polygamy not only contradicted the general beliefs of the Mormon people, which as converts they had brought into the church with them, but actually contradicted definite statements in the *Book of Mormon* that were unambiguous in their sanction of monogamy as the only proper form of Christian marriage.[11] The result was conflict and secession and finally the establishment of the Reorganized Church.

Having weathered this change in belief, one that could be explained in Mormon terms as a later revelation clarifying earlier ones, the church after 1890 faced a conflict caused by the revision in the reverse direction. The position of Wilford Woodruff's manifesto in the *Doctrine and Covenants*, part of the canon but not numbered, suggests the ambiguous status of the utterance itself. Was it inspired or wasn't it? There was conflict in Mormon minds and within church councils for some years. Even after the complete victory of antipolygamy forces within the church, there remained the Mormon Fundamentalists, those who refuse to accept the church's surrender on this question. The writings of the late Joseph Musser are the best example of such an attitude.

An excommunicated and proscribed polygamous tradition has survived and gains adherents on a small scale within Mormondom. The recent arrest of members of the polygamous community at Short Creek, Arizona, offers a prominent example. It has been estimated that there are several thousand polygamists in Utah today, and some have estimated as many as 20,000, a figure that includes women and children in plural families. These polygamists are excommunicated, but they often live within the general communities in larger towns and in some cities. These Fundamentalists claim that President John Taylor, who made such a stubborn last-ditch fight on this issue, called together seven men just before his death and told them that polygamy must not be allowed to disappear from the earth. His counsel is apparently held by the Fundamentalists as a revelation, since Taylor was president of the church. Hence these people continue to assert an older Mormonism, despite the wishes and measures of the church government.

The Fundamentalists appear to have some kind of secret organization, although no one outside knows just what it is and how it functions. They appear to be a strongly knit group, capable of united action. The Short Creek community owned much large farm equipment that must have been costly and required a sizable group to finance. The continuation of this proscribed tradition is a considerable embarrassment to the church and to those middle-class Mormons who desire respectability; yet it is a genuine, grass-roots continuation of the old tradition. It is, however, largely cut off from the main body of Mormons as far as influence is concerned. It arouses both sympathy and indignation from various groups among the orthodox.

Family Ideals versus Equality of Women

While plural marriage is the aspect of Mormon life that has become best known to outsiders, it is nevertheless an important fact to note that Mormonism early came very close to accepting the equality of women with men. Yet this was done while accepting patriarchal ideals of family organization. These ideals were most obvious during the days of plural marriage, but they remain important as part of Mormon family ideals, despite the disappearance of polygamy itself among church members. The father, according to Mormon teaching, is "the legislator, the judge, the governor" in the family.[12] "The father is the head, or president, or spokesman of the family. This arrangement is of divine origin."[13]

Yet Mormonism recognized that women are not basically inferior to men. The doctrine of the equality of women is to be seen in the Utah territorial laws, which granted women the right to vote in 1870; and women voted in Salt Lake City in the municipal election of February of that year and the general election in September. This was one year before the first election in Wyoming in which women voted, although the Wyoming law was passed in December, 1869.[14] Granting suffrage gave rise to an anomalous situation, in that eastern feminists—in their opposition to polygamy—joined forces with other antipolygamy groups to achieve the repeal of woman suffrage in Utah,[15] finally accomplished in 1887. Brigham Young held that women would "make just as good mathematicians and accountants as any man" and could "do the business of any counting house."[16] Joseph Smith "recognized man as the head of the family, but did not countenance an overlordship on his part."[17]

Mormon women have at times been counseled not to resent the priesthood privileges of the men, in which they do not themselves participate. "When the Priesthood is understood and exercised righteously there can be no 'sex antagonism.' "[18] Women as well as men are eternal intelligences in Mormon doctrine, but women are dependent upon men and upon marriage for exaltation in the afterlife and are subordinate to men on this earth within the family. Yet there is a genuine equality in many respects between the sexes.

This apparent contradiction in doctrinal emphasis has been a source of strain in the past, but, since the abandonment of polygamy, it has become unimportant. The emphasis on the equality of women found in earlier Mormon attitudes and teachings has been accentuated by the more general attitude prevalent in the country. Today, practically no difficulty arises from this problem. Mormon women have a great degree of equality, and the differences between rural and urban areas are about the same as those found among non-Mormons. Women are still not admitted to the priesthood, nor will they be; but the auxiliary organizations activate women to an extent that makes them feel very much a part of the church.

Progress versus Agrarianism

Another source of strain for Mormonism has been its emphasis both upon progress and upon the preferability of agriculture. Mormon teaching holds man to be intelligent and free and defines the significance of his existence both in this world and in the world to come in terms of progress. The strong this-worldly emphasis of the Mormons has rendered this belief in progress applicable to the present life. As a result, Mormons have been open to innovation in technical and social as well as religious matters. It is significant that they have eschewed those peculiarities of dress and behavior that have characterized so many sects. Yet together with this emphasis upon progress has gone an emphasis upon agriculture as the proper basis of Mormon community-building and as the ideal way of life for the Mormon family. Such an agrarian orientation was not necessarily in conflict with a dedication to progress in the earlier days, when the development of Utah into a region capable of supporting a stable population was the general task. But since the integration of Utah into the larger national economy, such an orientation becomes less appropriate. Even earlier, Brigham Young's policies give one example of this problem. He had opposed the development of mining on a scale beyond the requirements of domestic territorial needs; yet the progress of the national economy necessitated the exploitation of Utah's resources. The conflict around this problem was one factor in the secession of the Godbeite "New Movement." Mormon orientations toward mastery over the environment and their related dedication to progress were, however, contained within an agrarian context. As a result, the more prosaic virtues of hard work, responsibility, thrift, and getting ahead were concretely perceived in rural terms. It is ironical that, driven by conflict and persecution, the Mormons would seek to build their agricultural utopia in a region which, from the point of view of farming, was most unpromising, while at the same time most favorably endowed with mineral wealth. The result was, however, Mormon neglect and gentile development of mining, with the consequence that in the last years of the Mormon-gentile conflict the wealth was on the gentile side while the Mormons had the numbers.

With the urbanization of Utah, a city middle class emerged that has considerable influence in the church and in community life generally. This middle class is of recent rural origin and has carried with it into the new urban setting concrete forms of Mormon beliefs and attitudes developed in a rural environment. It is for this reason that Mormon professional and business people get such enjoyment out of Welfare Plan farm work. Moreover, the lack of large-scale industry in Utah until recently has kept these rural orientations somewhat appropriate to urban life.[19] The Mormons, as a result of their own history and the general forms of church teaching, possess what may be called an "agrarian ideology"; that is, they perceive and define social problems and personal goals with an outlook that took concrete shape in terms of a way of life based upon farming. Hard work on the farm led to success, and this fitted in with the Old Testament emphasis of the Mormons upon this-worldly rewards for virtue. This in time overcame the egalitarianism of the Law of Consecration. Their belief in progress came to be at the same time an acceptance of wealth as a prestige symbol. With urbanization, such norms continue, and today probably a majority of the church membership is not engaged in agriculture, and there is great occupational differentiation even in the larger villages.

There are two results of this persistence of agrarian ideology in the urban situation. One is that it is freed from the context of the farm and even of the church and prepares the urban Mormon to take part successfully in the competitive modern society and economy. The individualism of agrarian life is projected into the city occupations and especially into those areas where the church does not command or evoke co-operation and thus makes for an even more aggressive version of competitive middle-class mores. The second result of the agrarian ideology is that the church officialdom does not come to terms with contemporary problems in a contemporary way. Modern industrial relations, limitation of hours of work in factory and office, and the inhibition of the businessman's quest for wealth by social regulation—all brought into existence by a complex, highly differentiated, and interrelated industrial society—tend to be seen from the older, agrarian viewpoint.[20] While Catholic and Protestant bodies have concretized Christian teachings with regard to industrial society and its problems, the Mormon leadership has failed to meet this new situation.

The result has been that some Mormon leaders seek refuge in conservative politics. Yet conservative politics, attractive because they at least pay lip service to the older agrarian virtues, are not the natural development of the Mormon position. The fact that some Mormon leaders have left politics alone while preaching the agrarian virtues and that others, like Brigham H. Roberts, were attracted by the New Deal would indicate as much. It would also imply that all three positions recognize, albeit implicitly, that the Mormon church is no longer an agency of major social action or reform. The fact of accommodation is expressed in taking any one of these three positions.

Yet politics, conservative or otherwise, offer no solution to the conflict engendered by the twin orientations to progress and to agriculture, now expressed in terms of an urban middle-class outlook dedicated to success in the world of business and the professions combined with earlier agrarian attitudes toward newer social problems—a position that may assume the form of laissez faire attitudes in economics and rigid, escapist conservatism in politics. This was demonstrated most convincingly in the early 1940's, when the Mormon church failed to face up to the problem of the migration of large industry to Utah.

The agrarian suspicion of large-scale industry was to be seen in the Mormon fears when Big Steel came to Utah at the beginning of World War II. The church leaders felt that industry would disorganize the rural communities upon which the church had been established. Mormons at first, presumably at the tacit bidding of their leaders, resisted the coming of the Geneva Steel Company, a subsidiary of United States Steel, to Utah. Discussions between the president of the company, Dr. Walther Mathesius, and J. Reuben Clark, Jr., of the First Presidency of the church dispelled many of these suspicions, and the church from then on took a co-operative attitude. Actually, Geneva Steel has been a boon to Utah County and has improved the condition of small-scale farming through supplementing the farmers' incomes. Far from undermining agriculture as the Saints feared, the amount of land farmed by owner-operators increased in the years following Geneva's advent. The success of Geneva in winning the Mormon leadership and population was a tribute to the sensitivity of the company executives to the nature of the problem.

The Mormons finally submitted to the coming of Geneva Steel and found after a while that they rather liked having the company settle in Utah. Yet, at first, their reactions were negative, and their original acceptance was a bowing to inevitability. The church was as thoroughly unprepared, so far as any well-thought-out policy was concerned, in this regard as were the rural Mormons employed at Geneva, who at first thought certain safety regulations an interference with their personal freedom. The carry-over of agrarianism from country to city conditions resulted in a conflict between the orientation to progress accepted by the Mormons, but hardly possible today without industry, and the preference for agriculture and the agrarian ideology that has come to characterize the Mormon outlook. Will the Mormon church be better prepared for similar developments another time?

Political Conservatism versus Social Idealism

The tendency of some Mormons to accept political conservatism indicates the existence of another conflict within the Mormon group. Social idealism versus political conservatism is a very real conflict in Mormonism. The idea of the gathering, the ethic of co-operation, and the notion of property as subservient to social considerations are all firmly held components of the belief system of the Latter-day Saints. The importance of this orientation can be seen in the response to such problems as water distribution, the coming of the railroad, and more recently the depression, responses that involved the evolution of co-operative forms for meeting the challenge. The enthusiastic reception of the church call for Welfare Plan volunteers and for local Welfare Plan activity demonstrates the vitality of the social ideals of Mormonism in the contemporary situation.

In the conditions of Mormon reintegration back into the larger general community, it would be surprising if such social idealism did not spread over denominational boundaries and become identified with larger projects, involving the co-operation of both Mormons and gentiles for the ends of the general community. Such, indeed, has been the case. Some important men in the church, the late Brigham H. Roberts, for example, and many intellectuals, became strong supporters of New Deal measures. In fact, J. Reuben Clark, Jr., in 1939 felt it necessary to correct socialistic interpretations of the United Order. "There is a growing—I fear it is growing—sentiment that communism and the United Order are virtually the same thing, communism being merely the forerunner, so to speak, of a reestablishment of the United Order. I am informed that ex-bishops, and indeed, bishops, who belong to communistic organizations, are preaching this doctrine." This reference to communism probably is not to be interpreted as referring to the Soviet or Comintern variety but rather to secular co-operativism and socialism. And, even so, perhaps President Clark's fears were exaggerated. Yet a tendency toward embracing secular social ideals going somewhat in a socialistic direction was real and had real roots in the Mormon tradition, although, as President Clark showed, extremes were not warranted by official revelations.

On the other hand, Mormon accommodation to the general community has been accompanied by a lessening of social experimentation. Said Geddes: "Having given up the utopian struggle and having re-entered American society, the reunion was so thorough-going that in economic matters religious leadership espoused the cause and became a bulwark of the existing capitalistic system, giving it sanction by example and precept."[21] Moreover, Mormon leadership has become politically conservative, and such conservatism increases the strain and conflict. That both these viewpoints are obvious developments out of Mormon ideology and Mormon experience is plainly to be seen. Yet this very division also testifies to the inability of Mormonism to give its own peculiar answer to the general social problems of our time. Mormon social values play but little part in aiding the church in its confrontation with the gentile world today. The conflict between the social idealism born of Mormon beliefs and political conservatism remains a real one.

Patriotism versus Particularism

Mormon answers to economic problems have been based upon the Mormon social tradition, but they have been restricted in significance to the Mormon group. This is so despite the fact of Mormon reintegration into the general community. Mormon exclusiveness remains, and not only in the church Welfare Plan. It is also symbolized by an insistence upon teetotalism with regard to tobacco, tea, and coffee and, of course, alcoholic beverages. Yet Mormons feel themselves very much to be Americans. Patriotism and a belief in the peculiarity and divine character of America and American institutions have been greatly emphasized by the church in recent decades. It would seem that two emphases of this kind contain a possibility of strain and conflict. This was definitely the case in earlier days; yet the attitudes were always compromised, as may be seen in the failure of Mormon separatism to gain the upper hand in the last century. These two orientations are accommodated to each other today in terms of parallelism. The Latter-day Saint is active in both communities. The Saints are both gathered and scattered. The Mormon will engage in cooperative enterprises within the church while he pursues laissez faire methods in the secular sphere.

Yet the Mormon definition of themselves as a group apart offers at least a possibility of conflict with full participation in the secular, gentile world. So far, parallelism has worked well, but one wonders whether or not it will divide the Mormon psyche, setting up parallel loyalties, attitudes, and convictions which, if they are ever brought to confrontation around a basic issue, will result in inner psychological struggle and conflict within the Mormon group.

Belief versus Environment

Not only have the Mormons identified themselves with America, they have also felt an unusual concern with the Indian. In this they have been unusual among settlers in this country. Basing themselves upon the *Book of Mormon*, they set out early in their career to bring the gospel to the aborigines. In Missouri, in frontier conditions, their talk of the Indians joining them in the task of building Zion was a contributing factor to the hostility they met among the gentiles. In Utah, although four Indian cattle thieves were killed in a skirmish in the first months of settlement, the Black Hawk War was fought in 1867, and the Indians were often a minor problem, the relations between settlers and Indians were better than in most places. Brigham Young had said that it was better to feed them than to have to fight them, and Jacob Hamblin spent a career as apostle and peacemaker among the Indians of southern Utah. Moreover, in the Utah War of 1857, the Indians in the southern region of the Territory joined with the Mormons against the "Mericats" (whom they distinguished from Mormons), as may be seen in the Mountain Meadows Massacre.

Yet the Mormons, like all settlers, were usurpers of Indian lands, although the sparse Indian population in the Great Basin mitigated this problem to a considerable extent. Moreover, the conditions of settlement and the result of contact of such widely differing cultures were such that Indians were looked down on and suspected. Thus, although the Mormon attitude was more friendly than that of many other groups, the Saints also developed what we may call a "pioneer attitude" toward the Indian, while their religious precepts told them they were bound in conscience to aid in the reclamation of their Lamanite brothers. This conflict has largely vanished, although in some areas where Mormons and Indians live close together, as in the Southwest, it is still a real source of strain.

This conflict between a missionary and a pioneer attitude toward the Indian is not the only instance of a disjunction between Mormon beliefs and the actual environment of Mormon settlement. Earlier we noted the irony of the Mormon orientation to agriculture in the midst of so much mineral wealth. Other implications of Mormon beliefs, when acted upon, have caused difficulty for the Saints. The very notion of a gathered and peculiar people has antagonized neighbors, and the attempts to build Zion have evoked active hostility. Peculiarity of beliefs and institutions has aroused prejudice and suspicion and called forth fear and aggression.

Such problems persist to the present day. This may be seen in the conflict situation set up by the Mormon emphasis upon large families in an environment where its realization must lead to migration from the agricultural villages, which cannot sustain any large increase in the adult population. The result is a migration of youth from the state.[22]

Since many Mormons do not like to leave the Mormon region, this necessity to move is a source of dissatisfaction. Yet it has its positive results also, in building the church elsewhere throughout the country, especially in urban areas. There is some indication that migration can lead to apostasy and thereby create further problems for the church. Yet against this predisposition to apostasy must be placed the opposite tendency—the tendency for removal to kindle or awaken a new sense of belonging and loyalty and to promote activity in the local Mormon groups established outside Utah. This final problem, deriving from Mormon familism in the Utah situation, raises the issue of possible apostasy in a personal confrontation with the non-Mormon world, the same question that our initial problem of education and the encounter with modern learning raised in such sharp and threatening form. But in connection with migration, one feels that Mormonism has made a more adequate response. The church is gradually developing the ability to live as part of the non-Mormon community outside Utah and, in fact, even outside the United States.

On the whole, it must be said that Mormonism has successfully handled the dilemmas with which history has confronted it. It has not found a final solution to some of them, but many have been outlived by a successfully operating church. What really remains is that problem with which we started this chapter—the encounter of Mormonism with secularism. What the final outcome of that confrontation will be, no one can say.

CHAPTER TEN

Epilogue

Mormonism, in developing a peculiarly American religion, also established a peculiarly American subculture that has survived fierce opposition and surmounted tremendous obstacles. In the final analysis, it has achieved its striking successes because it was able to answer for its adherents the fundamental questions of "Why?" and "Whither?" Yet these are perennial questions, which take new forms in new conditions, and they arise again today within the very heart of Mormondom and the very texture of Mormonism. The destruction of the semi-isolation of the last half of the nineteenth century, the growth of the gentile population in the intermountain West, the progress of modern thought, the dispersal of the Saints eastward—in short, the reintegration of Mormondom into the parent culture and the accommodation and compromises that it involved—raise once more these old questions.

The issues take varied, concrete forms in different circumstances and for different persons. The way they affect the Mormon church has been put most strikingly and also perhaps most exaggeratedly by those of its critics who see its present situation as a long twilight, a repose following upon victory but at the same time an anticipation of death. The plateau visible in contemporary Mormon life is, for these observers, a subtly inclined plane leading to extinction. The religious outlook of Mormonism, they say, met the needs of men of the first half of the last century, embodying for them meaningful and challenging ideals that inspired their undoubted heroism. These ideals and the action they infused combined with the circumstances of westward movement to evolve the greatly proliferated Mormon organization, which settled and civilized the intermountain West. The church and its institutions became a perfected expression of the needs of a pioneering co-operative community, a mighty instrument for taming the desert. The extreme activism, the orientation toward mastery over the environment, the intricate organization, and the complex co-operativism that characterized the movement found an appropriate outlet in pioneer agriculture and settlement and were an ideal weapon for vanquishing the difficulties presented.

Now, say these critics, Mormondom has defeated its foes, but it has been frozen in the posture of combat and cannot relax and meet the new situation that victory brings into existence. It stands today, advocating and acting out the highly organized behavior that was both the product of and the tool for dominating older pioneer situations. In short, it is their contention that the Mormon church is obsolete, that it has been the strategic weapon for conquering the wilderness, but that the measure of its success is at the same time the index of its obsolescence. The church, these critics claim, is an elaborate pioneering mechanism, a vast socio-logical apparatus, nicely modeled for tasks now finished, leaving it functionless.

Such observers interpret the intense activity and organization of the Latter-day Saints today either as a reflex continuation of old habits surviving beyond their usefulness or a diversionary attempt to keep from facing the crisis of reorientation that the new conditions have created. Mormonism, they assert, still offers a meaningful way of life to many, but its sands are running out. Its fundamental *raison d'être* is gone, and the consequent absence of function will soon permeate into Mormon consciousness every-where. The hyperactivity of today—the streamlined modern organization of the church and its auxiliary bodies—is activity for activity's sake, organization for organization's sake. It is not without significance that recent Mormon contributions have been in the field of recreation, in the opinion of these critics, for play is the most important activity left to a complex institution whose vital functions have disappeared.

Before turning to consider the merits of such criticism, it should be noted that the undoubted crisis of transition that lurks beneath the surface of Mormon life, which these critics perceive in perhaps a somewhat astigmatic manner, is but a Mormon expression of a general American situation. The nation as a whole has conquered the wilderness, integrated the immigrants, and solved many of the most pressing problems of industrial and agricultural production. Consuming has become a dominant domestic concern, and play and recreation a national activity, a large-scale industry. Americans have entered the consumption era, they have become a "people of plenty," and many are seeking values and standards by which life in the new circumstances may be rendered significant. Older attitudes formed in older situations are being shed as no longer appropriate, and a search for new meaning and a deeper significance may be discerned throughout the land. Our critics would undoubtedly agree that Mormonism here, as in so many other of its historical expressions, is both typically American and peculiarly itself. But they might allege that in the Mormon case the hardening of older patterns of relationships and expectations into stable and highly organized religious institutions and highly explicit religious and theological doctrines makes reorientation more difficult than for the general community. The tougher the skin, the tougher the molting. It is claimed that the crystallization of institutions and attitudes limits flexibility and narrows the arc of possible innovation.

The same arguments have been put in other ways. Some have suggested that the millennial Zionism and social idealism of the Mormon movement served in the past to elicit profound human responses and to bring out in men profoundly humane values. Today, however, with the completion of the tasks in terms of which such responses were made concrete in action, what is required is a new cause to evoke heroism. Moreover, while the older cause separated men from the larger community, what is needed today, these observers declare, is a cause that will unite men across creedal divisions. Or again, it has been said that Mormonism answered the intellectual needs of the common man in the middle of the nineteenth century and was an indication of and answer to his search for truth; but today, say these critics, its point of view is rendered obsolete in the face of modern science, and it succeeds only in causing suffering and confusion to its youth who seek knowledge in modern educational institutions.

What shall be said of such criticisms? Is the Mormon church indeed obsolete?

There is one outstanding fact about the history of Mormonism that might give pause to the prophets of doom. If there is anything demonstrated by the experiences of the Mormon movement, it would seem to be viability. Mormonism has been a hardy movement. Yet the reply of the critics cannot be completely disregarded—Mormonism has never before had to face the problems of ultimate success and long-term prosperity.

It also seems that the observers who see Mormonism as obsolete underestimate its contribution to character formation and the moral life and the importance of its strictly religious tenets in the eyes of its adherents. Mormonism has always ultimately rested upon its religious appeal, and that would still seem to offer meaningful content to many.

There is some reason to believe that the extreme Mormon emphasis upon this-worldliness and activism increases the problem involved here. Yet the present construction of temples in Europe and the residence of Mormon groups in eastern cities of the nation both imply a new recognition by Mormons that there is a way of life, Mormon in its spirit, that does not require literal removal to Utah and concrete participation in a sociogeographical entity. The gathered may now be gathered in spirit, and Zion need not be literally in the mountain tops of Deseret. This new emphasis may also be seen in the cultural activities of the church, the most striking of which has recently been the 1955 European tour of the Tabernacle Choir.

The Mormon movement may be on the eve of its Diaspora, which would not mean that its central city would cease to be central but that belongingness would no longer be exclusively identified with a specific place. After all, the Jewish Diaspora long antedated Trajan's destruction of the Temple, and the Jews long ago showed that dispersion was quite reconcilable with the existence of a central city. In the Mormon case, such a shift in emphasis implies a recognition of the more intangible and more contemplative aspects of the religious life. Such a turn would be of the utmost importance for Mormonism, since the typically this-worldly spheres of activity that Mormonism has emphasized and in which it has hitherto excelled are precisely those areas of human action where more inclusive, more secular, and less peripheral organizations can make a more attractive appeal to the consciences and idealisms of men. Governmental or voluntary, such organizations seem the appropriate context for contemporary this-worldly accomplishments.

Only in the field of recreation has Mormonism been able to meet the challenge involved here, and even in that field Mormon security is not unequivocal. To concentrate the efforts of a religious movement in this area as a means of meeting or avoiding the crisis of reorientation could mean accepting only a residual position in the areas more strategic to the determination of events. It would seem that the religious man must participate in the larger, more inclusive, civic activities of the day or surrender any idea of affecting modern life or any genuine engagement in its vital problems.

Moreover, it would seem a grave mistake for a religious movement to concentrate its attention on this-worldly activities, since it is precisely this-worldliness and activism that modern man appears to be finding inadequate. For organized religion to offer competition in spheres of life in which non-religious organizations do better—spheres themselves inadequate to the facing of deeper human problems—is to be found wanting. The basic need of Mormonism may well become a search for a more contemplative understanding of the problem of God and man. And it is precisely here that the intellectuals—the products of Mormonism's great valuation of education—may make important contributions.

It is a tremendous presumption to attempt to judge the future of a movement like Mormonism. Yet it is my suspicion that those who emphasize the obsolescence of Mormonism, those who see the end of the movement in a stereotyped lack of creativity and a routine running down, who believe that this Mormon world will end not with a bang but a whimper, are wrong. There is still too much vitality—the characteristic Mormon vitality—remaining for such a prognosis to be likely.

I once put this problem to a group of Mormon students, many of them graduate students in the natural and social sciences and the humanities, at an esteemed eastern university. I asked them what they really thought. The result was more persuasive than any analysis could possibly be. They took the suggestion maturely. They did not react with a counterfire of stereotypes. They showed thoughtfulness and an awareness of what was involved. Some, of course, thought the question completely outlandish. Others saw the possibility of flexibly reinterpreting and developing old values in the new situation. Most important, they showed the kind of will that makes such reorientation possible. They demonstrated that Mormonism was meaningful to them, who were in some ways Mormondom's young elite—those sent east to bring learning and higher degrees to Utah. Their testimony must be admitted as eloquent.

Strains, yes; conflict, perhaps; but strains and conflict are both signs and sources of vitality. The fact is that the Church of Jesus Christ of Latter-day Saints is still a vital institution. Conflict and strain have not been sufficient to prevent its orderly functioning over the last many decades. It may not be so well adapted or prepared to meet new problems as it was at times in the past; yet all transitions and all reorientations are difficult. That its values still provide a meaningful context to great numbers of its adherents cannot be denied. Its flexibility in the past and its viability under the most adverse conditions do not augur badly for its future.

Notes

CHAPTER ONE

1. This account can be found in Joseph Smith, *History of the Church of Jesus Christ of Latter-day Saints*, ed. B. H. Roberts (Salt Lake City, 1902), Vol. I, chaps. i–vi, pp. 1–59, and chap. viii, pp. 71–80.

2. The principal biographical sources used for this discussion are, in addition to Joseph Smith's own writings, Fawn M. Brodie, *No Man Knows My History* (New York, 1945); William Alexander Linn, *The Story of the Mormons* (New York, 1902); Eber D. Howe, *Mormonism Unveiled* (Painesville, Ohio, 1834), republished as *History of the Mormons* (1840); Lucy Mack, *Biographical Sketches of Joseph Smith the Prophet and His Progenitors for Many Generations* (Liverpool, 1853); I. Woodbridge Riley, *The Founder of Mormonism* (New York, 1902).

3. Whitney R. Cross, *The Burned-over District: The Social and Intellectual History of Enthusiastic Religion in Western New York, 1800–1850* (Ithaca, N.Y., 1950), p. 142. This is an important source for background on the religious situation and general conditions of western New York at that time.

4. *Ibid.*, p. 82.

5. *Ibid.*, p. 140.

6. The general picture of the religious situation presented in this chapter is drawn, in addition to the sources cited previously, from the following works: Lowell L. Bennion, *Max Weber's Methodology* (Paris, 1933); Arthur E. Bestor, *Backwoods Utopias: The Sectarian and Owenite Phases of Communitarian Socialism in America, 1663–1829* (Philadelphia, 1950); Henry Bettenson (ed.), *Documents of the Christian Church* (New York and London, 1947); Crane Brinton, *Ideas and Men: The Story of Western Thought* (New York, 1950); Catherine Cleveland, *The Great Revival in the West, 1797–1805* (Chicago, 1916); Wesley M. Gewehr, *The Great Awakening in Virginia, 1740–1790* (Durham, N.C., 1930); George Godkin, *The Great Revivalists* (Boston, 1950); Charles R. Keller, *The Second Great Awakening in Connecticut* (New Haven, 1942); David M. Ludlum, *Social Ferment in Vermont, 1791–1850* (New York, 1939); C. H. Maxson, *The Great Awakening in the Middle Colonies* (Chicago, 1920); Perry Miller, "Jonathan Edwards to Emerson," *New England Quarterly*, XIII (1940), 589–617; H. Richard Niebuhr, *The Social Sources of Denominationalism* (New York, 1929); Charles Nordhoff, *Communistic Societies of the United States* (New York, 1875); Robert E. Park and Ernest W. Burgess, *Introduction to the Science of Sociology* (Chicago, 1921); Talcott Parsons, *The*

Structure of Social Action (New York, 1937); William Warren Sweet, *Religion in the Development of American Culture, 1765–1840* (New York, 1952), *The American Churches* (New York and Nashville, Tenn., 1947–48), *Revivalism in America: Its Origin, Growth, and Decline* (New York, 1944), *Religion in Colonial America* (New York, 1942), and *The Story of Religion in America* (New York and London, 1930–39); R. H. Tawney, *Religion and the Rise of Capitalism* (New York, 1926); Ernst Troeltsch, *The Social Teachings of the Christian Churches*, trans. Olive Wyon (New York, 1931); Joachim Wach, *The Sociology of Religion* (Chicago, 1944), and *Types of Religious Experience* (Chicago, 1951); and Max Weber, *The Protestant Ethic and the Spirit of Capitalism*, trans. Talcott Parsons (New York, 1931).

7. Niebuhr, *op. cit.*, p. 84.

8. Frederick Jackson Turner, *The Significance of the Frontier* (New York, 1920), p. 37. His *Rise of the New West, 1819–1829* (New York, 1906) was also consulted in the preparation of this chapter. In connection with the economic background, Harold F. Williamson (ed.), *The Growth of the American Economy* (New York, 1944), was consulted.

9. Sweet, *Religion in the Development of American Culture, 1765–1840*, p. 197.

10. Linn, *op. cit.*, p. 47.

11. *Doctrine and Covenants*, 20:1–4.

12. Parley P. Pratt, *Key to the Science of Theology* (Liverpool, 1855), pp. 76–77.

CHAPTER TWO

1. Although there seems very little doubt today as to Joseph Smith's authorship of the *Book of Mormon*, there was a time when the controversy over this subject generated some degree of heat. Those interested in such not-quite-solved historical problems will find the following titles useful: George B. Arbaugh, *Revelation in Mormonism* (Chicago, 1932); Fawn M. Brodie, *No Man Knows My History* (New York, 1945); Whitney R. Cross, *The Burned-over District: The Social and Intellectual History of Enthusiastic Religion in Western New York, 1800–1850* (Ithaca, N.Y., 1950); Eber D. Howe, *Mormonism Unveiled* (Painesville, Ohio, 1834), republished as *History of the Mormons* (1840); William Alexander Linn, *The Story of the Mormons* (New York, 1902); Walter F. Prince, "Authorship of the Book of Mormon," *American Journal of Psychology*, XXVIII, No. 3 (July, 1917), 373–89; George Reynolds, *The Myth of the Manuscript Found* (Salt Lake City, 1883); B. H. Roberts, "The Origin of the Book of Mormon," *American History Magazine*, Vols. III and IV (1908–9); Theodore Schroeder, "Origin of the Book of Mormon," *American History Magazine*, Vols. I and II (September, 1906–May, 1907); and "Authorship of the Book of Mormon," *American Journal of Psychology*, XXX (January, 1919), 66–72; C. A. Shook, *The True Origin of the Book of Mormon* (Cincinnati, Ohio, 1914).

2. I. Woodbridge Riley, *The Founder of Mormonism* (New York, 1902); Eduard Meyer, *Ursprung und Geschichte der Mormonen* (1912).

3. Perhaps the study which best represents this more reasonable point of view is Brodie, *op. cit.* It has, however, been criticized from an orthodox Mormon point of view. For such a criticism see "Appraisal of the So-called Brodie Book" in *Church News* (*Deseret News*), May 11, 1946. This review was republished as a pamphlet by the Church of Jesus Christ of Latter-day Saints.

4. Brodie, *op. cit.*, p. 47.

5. *Ibid.*, p. 46.

6. The close connection of righteousness and prosperity is found in the following verses of the *Book of Mormon:* I Nephi 13:15, 17:37, 38; II Nephi 1:20, 32, 3:2, 4:4; Jarom 9; Omni 6, 7; Mosiah 2:22, 31, 36, 7:29, 23:19, 20, 25:24, 27:7; Alma 9:13, 36:1, 30, 37:13, 38:1, 44:4, 45:6, 7, 8, 48:15, 50:20–22; Helaman 3:20, 4:13, 15, 16, 26, 11:20, 12:1; and Ether 7:26, 10:16.

7. The central message of "repentance" is to be found in the following verses of the *Book of Mormon:* I Nephi 10:18, 14:5, 6, 7, 22:28; II Nephi 2:21, 5:22, 6:12, 9:24, 28:17, 19, 31:13, 17; Jacob 3:3, 8, 6:5, 11; Mosiah 2:38, 4:10, 11, 11:20, 21, 25, 29, 16:12, 18:7, 20, 26:29, 30, 35, 29:19, 20; Alma 5:51, 54, 6:3, 7:3, 9, 8:16, 29, 9:25, 10:20, 22, 23, 12:15, 24, 33, 34, 13:21, 27, 30, 16:13, 17:16, 19:36, 21:6, 22:6, 16, 23:15, 24:11, 26:22, 35, 29:2, 32:13, 34:15, 16, 17, 31, 33, 34, 35, 36:24, 37:22, 26, 31, 33, 41:6, 42:4, 16, 17, 22, 24, 28, 31, 48:19, 49:30; Helaman 4:15, 5:19, 29, 32, 41, 7:17, 22, 28, 8:7, 10:11, 14, 11:4, 7, 9, 14, 15, 12:22, 23, 24, 13:2, 6, 8, 10, 11, 13, 39, 14:9, 11, 13, 15:1, 7, 14, 17; III Nephi 1:23, 3:25, 4:33, 5:4, 7:23, 8:25, 9:2, 22, 10:6, 11:23, 32, 37, 38, 12:19, 18:16, 32, 20:20, 21:20, 22, 23:5, 27:16, 20, 30:2; IV Nephi 1; Mormon 2:8, 10, 3:2, 13, 22, 4:10, 5:2, 22, 24, 7:3, 8; Ether 2:11, 15, 4:18, 5:5, 7:26, 9:28, 34, 35, 11:20, 13:17, 20, 15:3; and Moroni 6:7, 8, 7:31, 34, 8:10, 16, 24, 9:3, 22.

8. The following verses of the *Book of Mormon* directly affirm the doctrine of free will: II Nephi 2:16, 26, 27, 10:23–24; Alma 13:3; and Helaman 14:30.

9. That man will be judged according to his works is set forth in the following verses: II Nephi 29:11; Mosiah 3:24, 5:15, 16:10; Alma 3:26, 27, 5:16, 41, 42, 52, 7:24, 9:28, 11:41–44, 12:12, 26:22, 32:20, 34:37, 40:21, 41:3, 5, 42:23–27; Helaman 12:24–26; III Nephi 26:4–5, 27:14–15; and Mormon 3:20, 6:21.

10. The availability of mercy and grace to all men and the universal application of the Atonement are set forth in the following verses: I Nephi 3:7, 7:12, 17:35; II Nephi 2:4, 9, 6:14, 9:5, 7, 21, 25, 10:2, 25:16, 23, 26:24, 25, 26, 27, 28, 30, 31:19, 33:12; Mosiah 3:11, 12, 16, 18, 21, 13:28, 15:11, 12, 19, 16:12, 28:3, 4, 7; Alma 3:19, 5:37, 38, 48, 9:17, 11:40, 12:15, 22:14, 26:16–20, 29:4, 32:22, 27, 33:23, 34:4, 12; and Moroni 7:15, 16.

11. The presence of prophecy is to be seen in the following texts:

I Nephi 4:6, 5:2, 3, 4, 10:17, 11:11; II Nephi 28:1; Jacob 4:15; Jarom 4; Mosiah 21:34; Alma 5:46, 7:26, 8:24, 10:12, 12:7, 9, 17:3; Helaman 6:5; III Nephi 3:19; and Ether 12:5.

12. The importance of obedience to the commandments is set forth in the following verses: I Nephi 2:20, 22, 4:14, 15:11, 22:31; II Nephi 1:20, 32, 3:2, 4:4, 9:27; Enos 10; Jarom 9; Omni 6; Mosiah 1:11, 2:4, 13, 22, 31, 33, 36, 41, 4:6, 30, 12:33, 27:33; Alma 7:23, 8:15, 9:8, 13, 12:32, 30:3, 31:9, 36:1, 30, 37:13, 35, 38:1, 45:7, 48:15, 50:20–22; Helaman 5:6, 15:5; and III Nephi 12:20.

13. The following verses affirm the present life as a probationary state: II Nephi 2:21, 9:27; and Alma 12:24, 42:10–13.

14. See n. 6.

15. The importance of perseverance is stated in the following verses: I Nephi 13:37; II Nephi 31:15, 16, 20; Omni 26; Mosiah 2:41, 4:6, 30; Alma 5:13; and III Nephi 15:9.

16. Reference to "plainness of the gospel" is to be found in the following verses: I Nephi 13:29; II Nephi 25:7, 20, 28, 28:3–6, 31:2, 32:7; Jacob 2:11, 4:14; Enos 23; Mosiah 2:40; and Alma 5:43, 13:23, 14:2.

17. The necessity of knowledge for culpability is established in the following texts: Mosiah 3:11–22, 15:24–27; Alma 9:16, 19, 23, 24:30, 29:5, 32:19; Helaman 7:24, 8:24, 14:19; III Nephi 6:18; Ether 3:13; and Moroni 8:10–15, 22, 29.

18. The theme of America as a promised land may be seen in the following verses: I Nephi 2:20, 5:5, 12:4, 13:12, 30, 14:2, 17:13, 14, 42, 18:8, 22, 23; II Nephi 1:3, 5, 24, 3:2, 9:2, 10:19, 20; Enos 10; Alma 46:17; Helaman 7:7; and Ether 1:42, 2:7, 9, 10, 15, 6:5, 8, 12, 7:27, 9:20, 10:28, 13:2.

More specific reference to the United States (not named) is to be found in I Nephi 22:7–8; II Nephi 1:7, 11, 10:10–12; Jacob 5:43; III Nephi 20:22, 21:4; and Mormon 5:9, 19.

19. The democratic sentiments of the *Book of Mormon* may be found in Mosiah 7:9, 22:1, 27:3, 4, 29:1–11, 25, 26, 27, 32, 38, 39; Alma 1:17, 2:3, 43:48, 49, 46:35, 36, 48:11, 51:7, 16, 17, 20, 21; and Helaman 5:2.

20. Antimonarchy sentiment is expressed in the following verses: II Nephi 5:18; Mosiah 2:14–18, 6:7, 23:6–14, 29:13–18, 23, 30, 31; Alma 43:45, 46:10, 51:5, 8; III Nephi 6:30; and Ether 6:22–26.

21. The oppressiveness of taxation is set forth in Mosiah 11:3, 6, 13; and Ether 10:6.

22. Antilawyer sentiment may be seen in Alma 10:14, 15, 17, 27, 32; and III Nephi 6:21.

23. The obligation of clergymen to work may be seen in Mosiah 18:24, 26, 27:5; and Alma 1:3, 5, 26, 30:33.

24. Reference to "the abominable church" may be seen in the following verses: I Nephi 13:4–9, 26, 27, 28, 14:3, 9–17, 22:13, 14; and II Nephi 6:12, 28:18.

25. Cross, *op. cit.*, pp. 83–84, 231–33.

26. Brodie, *op. cit.*, pp. 59–60.

27. Cross, *op. cit.*, p. 233.

28. Antisecret-society sentiment, usually believed to be a reflection of current anti-Masonic attitudes, is to be seen in the following verses: II Nephi 10:15, 26:22; Alma 37:29; Helaman 2:8, 3:23, 6:18, 19, 21–26, 30, 38, 39, 7:4, 25, 8:1, 28, 10:3, 11:2, 10, 26, 27; III Nephi 2:11, 3:9, 5:6, 7:9, 9:9; Mormon 1:18, 8:27; and Ether 8:15, 16, 18, 19, 22, 24–26, 9:5, 6–7, 10:33, 11:15, 22.

29. The doctrine of the gathering of the Jews is to be seen in I Nephi 10:3, 14; II Nephi 3:5, 10:5–9, 20:22, 21:12, 25:11; III Nephi 16:4, 5, 20:11–19, 28, 29, 33, 46, 21:1, 22, 29; Mormon 5:14; and Ether 13:10, 11.

30. The following verses contain definite antipolygamous doctrine: Jacob 1:15, 2:23, 24, 27, 28, 32, 35, 3:5; Mosiah 11:2, 4, 14; and Ether 10:5.

31. The Mormon church today accepts baptism for the remission of sins and requires it for admission into the church (see *Doctrine and Covenants*, § 13; 19:31, 33:11, 55:2, 68:27, 76:51–52, 84:27, 74, 107:20).

32. Linn, *op. cit.*, pp. 95, 97–98.

CHAPTER THREE

1. *Doctrine and Covenants*, 57:2. This is a collection of the reported revelations of Joseph Smith. It will be referred to hereafter in the text as "*D & C.*"

2. Joseph Smith, *History of the Church of Jesus Christ of Latter-day Saints*, ed. B. H. Roberts (Salt Lake City, 1902), I, 375.

3. Quoted from Fawn M. Brodie, *No Man Knows My History* (New York, 1945), p. 203.

4. *Document containing the Correspondence, Orders, Etc., in relation to the disturbances with the Mormons: and the Evidence . . .* (Fayette, Missouri, 1841), The Governor to General Clark (October 27, 1838), p. 61, and The Governor to General Clark (November 1, 1838), pp. 76–77 (Coe Collection, Yale University Library).

5. Quoted from William Alexander Linn, *The Story of the Mormons* (New York, 1902), p. 237.

6. Quoted from George Q. Cannon, *The Life of Joseph Smith* (Salt Lake City, 1888), p. 348.

7. Smith, *op. cit.*, IV, 241–42.

8. Joseph Smith, *The King Follett Discourse*, ed. B. H. Roberts (Salt Lake City, 193?), pp. 8–21.

9. Brigham Young, *Journal of Discourses* (Liverpool, 1854–75), III, 266.

10. Quoted from Brodie, *op. cit.*, p. 287.

11. Quoted from Linn, *op. cit.*, p. 292.

12. Smith, *History of the Church*, V, 85.

13. *Ibid.*, VI, 222.

14. *Ibid.*, pp. 275–77.

15. Matthias F. Cowley, *Wilford Woodruff* (Salt Lake City, 1909), p. 184.

16. Quoted from Linn, *op. cit.,* p. 351.

To the sources listed above and those given in the previous two chapters, the following are to be credited in connection with this chapter:

BANCROFT, HUBERT HOWE. *History of Utah.* San Francisco, 1891.

BENNETT, JOHN C. *The History of the Saints; or an Exposé of Joe Smith and Mormonism.* Boston, 1842.

BENNION, MILTON LYNN. *Mormonism and Education.* Salt Lake City, 1939.

DURHAM, G. HOMER. *Joseph Smith: Prophet-Statesman.* Salt Lake City, 1944.

ERICKSEN, EPHRAIM E. *The Psychological and Ethical Aspects of Mormon Group Life.* Chicago, 1922.

FORD, THOMAS. *History of Illinois.* Chicago, 1854.

GEDDES, JOSEPH A., and FREDERICKSON, CARMEN D. *Utah Housing in Its Group and Community Aspects.* (Bull. 321, Agricultural Experiment Station, Utah State Agricultural College.) Logan, Utah, 1945.

GOODWIN, S. H. *Mormonism and Masonry: A Utah Point of View.* Salt Lake City, 1925.

HYDE, JOHN, JR. *Mormonism: Its Leaders and Designs.* New York, 1857.

KELLEY, CHARLES, and BIRNEY, HOFFMAN. *Holy Murder: The Story of Porter Rockwell.* New York, 1934.

LARSON, GUSTIVE O. *Prelude to the Kingdom.* Francestown, N.H. 1947.

LEE, JOHN D. *Mormonism Unveiled.* Omaha, Neb., 1891.

MCGAVIN, E. CECIL. *Nauvoo the Beautiful.* Salt Lake City, 1946.

MCNIFF, WILLIAM J. *Heaven on Earth.* Oxford, Ohio, 1940.

NELSON, LOWRY. *The Mormon Village: A Pattern and Technique of Land Settlement.* Salt Lake City, 1952.

Ohio WPA Guide.

Pearl of Great Price. Mormon scripture which contains the Books of Abraham and of Moses and some additional fragments.

RANDALL, EMILIUS O., and RYAN, DANIEL J. *History of Ohio.* Vol. III. New York, 1912.

ROBERTS, BRIGHAM H. *A Comprehensive History of the Church of Jesus Christ of Latter-day Saints.* Salt Lake City, 1930.

TAYLOR, HARRIET UPTON, and OTHERS. *History of the Western Reserve.* Vol. I. Chicago and New York, 1910.

WERNER, MORRIS R. *Brigham Young.* New York, 1925.

YOUNG, LEVI EDGAR. *The Founding of Utah.* New York, 1923.

CHAPTER FOUR

1. Morris R. Werner, *Brigham Young* (New York, 1925), p. 5.

2. *Ibid.,* p. 9.

3. Quoted from Brigham H. Roberts, *The Mormon Battalion: Its History and Achievements* (Salt Lake City, 1919), p. 5.

4. Executive Document No. 60, letter of Secretary of War to General Kearny, marked "Confidential" (1846), quoted *ibid.*, p. 5.

5. [Benson J. Lossing], "The Mormons," *Harper's Magazine*, VI, No. 35 (April, 1853), 616.

6. Dale L. Morgan, *The Great Salt Lake* (Indianapolis, 1947), p. 199.

7. Andrew L. Neff, *History of Utah, 1847–1869*, edited and annotated by Leland H. Creer (Salt Lake City, 1940), p. 98.

8. Thomas Nixon Carver, in the *Westerner*, April 9, 1930, quoted from Milton R. Hunter, *Brigham Young the Colonizer* (Salt Lake City, 1943), p. 350.

9. Chauncy D. Harris, *Salt Lake City: A Regional Capital* (Chicago, 1940), p. 111.

10. Quoted from William Mulder, "Mormonism's 'Gathering': An American Doctrine with a Difference," *Church History*, XXIII, No. 3 (September, 1954), 5, n. 11.

11. *Ibid.*, p. 4.

12. Hunter, *op. cit.*, p. 110.

13. William Mulder, "Through Immigrant Eyes: Utah History at the Grass Roots," *Utah Historical Quarterly*, January, 1954, p. 49.

14. Charles Dickens, *The Uncommercial Traveller*, chap. xii, "Bound for the Great Salt Lake."

15. James Linforth, *Route from Liverpool to Great Salt Lake Valley* (Liverpool, 1855), pp. 17–18.

16. T. B. H. Stenhouse, *Rocky Mountain Saints* (London, 1874), p. 578.

17. Dickens, *op. cit.*

18. Quoted *ibid.*

19. William E. Berrett, *The Restored Church* (Salt Lake City, 1944), pp. 401–2.

20. Gustive O. Larson, *Prelude to the Kingdom* (Francestown, N.H., 1947), p. 118.

21. Stenhouse, *op. cit.*

In addition to the sources listed above and those given in the previous chapters, this chapter is indebted to the following works:

ANDERSON, NELS. *Desert Saints*. Chicago, 1942.

BILLINGTON, RAY ALLEN. *Westward Expansion*. New York, 1949.

BROOKS, JUANITA. *The Mountain Meadows Massacre*. Stanford, 1950.

———. "St. George, Utah: A Community Portrait," Utah Academy of Sciences, Arts and Letters, 1952.

CLAYTON, WILLIAM. *The Journal of William Clayton*, comp. by KATE B. CARTER. Salt Lake City, 1944.

DAWSON, C. A. *Group Settlement: Ethnic Communities in Western Canada*, Part III, "The Mormons." ("Canadian Frontiers of Settlement," Vol. IX.) Toronto, 1936.

ELY, RICHARD T. "Economic Aspects of Mormonism," *Harper's Magazine*, April, 1903.

EVANS, RICHARD L. *A Century of Mormonism in Great Britain.* Salt Lake City, 1937.

JENSEN, ANDREW. *History of the Scandinavian Mission.* Salt Lake City, 1927.

McCLINTOCK, JOHN M. *Mormon Settlement in Arizona.* Phoenix, 1921.

MILLS, ELIZABETH H. "The Mormon Colonies in Chihuahua after the 1912 Exodus," *New Mexico Historical Review,* XXIX, No. 3 (July, 1954), 165–82.

MULDER, WILLIAM. "Mother Tongue, 'Skandinavisme,' and 'The Swedish Insurrection' in Utah," *Swedish Pioneer Historical Quarterly,* VII, No. 1 (January, 1956), 2–11.

———. "Mormons from Scandinavia, 1850–1900: A Shepherded Migration," *Pacific Historical Review,* XXIII, No. 3 (August, 1954), 227–46.

SELLERS, CHARLES COLEMAN. *Lorenzo Dow.* New York, 1928.

SHANNON, FRED A. *The Farmer's Last Frontier, Agriculture, 1860–1897.* ("Economic History of the United States," Vol. V.) New York, 1945.

SMITH, JOSEPH FIELDING. *Essentials in Church History.* 4th ed. Salt Lake City, 1928.

STEGNER, WALLACE. "Ordeal by Handcart," *Collier's,* July 6, 1956.

TYLER, DANIEL. *A Concise History of the Mormon Battalion in the Mexican War.* Salt Lake City, 1881.

WIDTSOE, JOHN A. *How the Desert Was Tamed.* Salt Lake City, 1947.

CHAPTER FIVE

1. Howard Stansbury, *An Expedition to the Valley of the Great Salt Lake of Utah* (Philadelphia, 1852), p. 131.

2. Morris R. Werner, *Brigham Young* (New York, 1925), p. 397.

3. Milton R. Hunter, *Brigham Young the Colonizer* (Salt Lake City, 1943), p. 120.

4. Brigham Young, *Journal of Discourses* (Liverpool, 1854–75), IV, 53–54.

5. John D. Lee, *Mormonism Unveiled* (Omaha, Neb., 1891), p. 284.

6. Juanita Brooks, *The Mountain Meadows Massacre* (Stanford, Calif., 1950), p. 16.

7. Lee, *op. cit.,* p. 388.

8. *Reynolds* v. *United States* (Supreme Court of the United States), 98 U.S. 145 (1878).

9. Kimball Young, *Isn't One Wife Enough?* (New York, 1954), p. 368.

10. James G. Blaine, *Political Discussions, Legislative, Diplomatic and Popular, 1856–1886* (Norwich, Conn., 1887), p. 432.

11. Quoted from Robert J. Dwyer, *The Gentile Comes to Utah* (Washington, D.C., 1941), p. 227.

12. *Doctrine and Covenants,* following § 136.

In addition to titles listed in the notes above and given in the previous chapters, this chapter draws upon the following:

ASHTON, WENDELL J. *Voice in the West*. New York, 1950.

BASKIN, ROBERT N. *Reminiscences of Early Utah*. Salt Lake City, 1914.

DAINES, FRANKLIN D. "Separatism in Utah, 1847–1870," in *Annual Report of the American Historical Association for the Year 1917*, pp. 333–43.

Deseret News, September 14, 1852 (Coe Collection, Yale University Library).

JENSEN, THERALD N. *Mormon Theory of Church and State*. Chicago, 1940.

O'DEA, THOMAS F. "Mormonism and the Avoidance of Sectarian Stagnation: A Study of Church, Sect, and Incipient Nationality," *American Journal of Sociology*, LX, No. 3 (November, 1954), 285–93.

CHAPTER SIX

1. Quotations, in order, are from the following: Orson Pratt, *A Series of Pamphlets on the Doctrines of the Gospel* (Chattanooga, Tenn., 1899), p. 10; Parley P. Pratt, *Key to the Science of Theology* (Liverpool and London, 1855), p. 44; and John A. Widtsoe, *Rational Theology* (Salt Lake City, 1915), p. 13.

2. Widtsoe, *op. cit.*, p. 13.

3. Quotations, in order, are from Orson Pratt, *op. cit.*, p. 11, and Widtsoe, *op. cit.*, p. 13.

4. Quoted from the *Pearl of Great Price*, a standard work of the Mormon church, the two chief books of which are the Book of Moses and the Book of Abraham. Hereafter referred to in the text under those two titles. The present quotation is from Moses 1:38.

5. Widtsoe, *op. cit.*, pp. 19–20.

6. Orson Pratt, *op. cit.*, p. 10.

7. See Joseph Smith, *The King Follett Discourse*, ed. B. H. Roberts (Salt Lake City, 193?); and chap. iii, above, pp. 54–55.

8. Joseph Smith, *Lectures on Faith*, ed. John A. Widtsoe (Salt Lake City, 1943), p. 35.

9. T. B. H. Stenhouse, *Rocky Mountain Saints* (London, 1874), p. 485; Brigham Young, *Journal of Discourses*, I, 50–51.

10. John Hyde, Jr., *Mormonism: Its Leaders and Designs* (New York, 1857), p. 198.

11. Brigham H. Roberts, *Mormon Doctrine of Deity: The Roberts–Van Der Donckt Discussion* (Salt Lake City, 1903) p. 42.

12. Widtsoe, *op. cit.*, pp. 23–24.

13. See George B. Arbaugh, *Revelation in Mormonism* (Chicago, 1932), p. 103 and *passim*, where Campbellite influence is quite probably exaggerated and rendered impossibly exclusive and unique.

14. Parley P. Pratt, *op. cit.*, pp. 33–34.

15. Widtsoe, *op. cit.*, pp. 23–25.

16. Quoted from Lowell L. Bennion, *The Religion of the Latter-day Saints* (Salt Lake City, 1940), p. 43, and Widtsoe, *op. cit.*, p. 14.

17. Bennion, *op. cit.*, p. 43.

18. See *Deseret Sunday School Songs*, No. 181.

19. James E. Talmage, *Articles of Faith* (Salt Lake City, 1901), p. 33.

20. Widtsoe, *op. cit.*, p. 16.

21. Parley P. Pratt, *op. cit.*, p. 32.

22. Talmage, *op. cit.*, p. 54.

23. Parley P. Pratt, *op. cit.*, p. 64.

24. Widtsoe, *op. cit.*, p. 33.

25. Talmage, *op. cit.*, p. 57.

26. *Ibid.*

27. Widtsoe, *op. cit.*, pp. 16 and 22.

28. Talmage, *op. cit.*, p. 71.

29. "Articles of Faith," from Joseph Smith, *History of the Church of Jesus Christ of Latter-day Saints*, ed. B. H. Roberts (Salt Lake City, 1902), IV, 540.

30. Widtsoe, *op. cit.*, pp. 34–35.

31. Smith, *History of the Church*, IV, 588.

32. Quotations are from Smith, "Articles of Faith," in *History of the Church*, IV, 541; Talmage, *op. cit.*, p. 90; Widtsoe, *op. cit.*, pp. 35 and 34; Talmage, *op. cit.*, p. 94.

33. Talmage, *op. cit.*, p. 94.

34. Widtsoe, *op. cit.*, p. 25.

35. Quoted from Parley P. Pratt, "Materiality," in Roberts, *op. cit.*, p. 254; and James E. Talmage, "The Philosophy of Mormonism," *Improvement Era*, IV (1901), 464–65.

36. Widtsoe, *op. cit.*, p. 25.

37. Orson Pratt, *op. cit.*, pp. 225, 227.

38. Ephraim E. Ericksen, *The Psychological and Ethical Aspects of Mormon Group Life* (Chicago, 1922), p. 15.

39. The following references to the "gathering" may be found in the *Doctrine and Covenants*: 6:32; 10:65; 27:13–18; 29:2, 7, 8; 33:6–8; 38:31; 42:9, 36; 45:43, 64–71; 57:14–15; 58:56; 63:36; 84:2; 101:64–70; 110:11; 115:6; 133:4–14.

40. Joseph Smith, "Articles of Faith," in *History of the Church*, IV, 541.

41. Newell Knight, *Journal* (Salt Lake City, 1882), pp. 52–53.

42. Parley P. Pratt, *op. cit.*, p. 163; cf. Orson Pratt, *The Bible and Polygamy* (Salt Lake City, 1874).

43. Stenhouse, *op. cit.*, p. 485.

44. Quotations, in order, are from Adam S. Bennion, *What It Means To Be a Mormon* (Salt Lake City, 1917), p. 169; Widtsoe, *op. cit.*, p. 146; Talmage, *Articles of Faith*, p. 457; Widtsoe, *op. cit.*, p. 146.

45. Talmage, *Articles of Faith*, p. 456.

46. William E. Berrett, *The Restored Church* (Salt Lake City, 1944), pp. 666, 667, 665, quoted in that order.

47. Widtsoe, *Rational Theology*, p. 147.

48. Joseph Sudweeks, *The Principles and Practice of Genealogy* (Salt Lake City, 1949).

49. Quotations from Joseph F. Smith, *Gospel Doctrine* (Salt Lake City, 1929), p. 260; and Bryan S. Hinckley, *Mormonism and Daily Life* (Salt Lake City, 1931), pp. 2–3.

50. George Stewart, Dilworth Walker, and E. Cecil McGavin, *Priesthood and Church Welfare* (Salt Lake City, 1939), p. 250.

51. Quotations, starting with "In obedience to . . . ," are from Widtsoe, *op. cit.*, pp. 167 and 168–69; Brigham Young, *Discourses of Brigham Young*, ed. John A. Widtsoe (Salt Lake City, 1925), p. 462; and Widtsoe, *op. cit.*, pp. 168–69.

52. Widtsoe, *op. cit.*, p. 56.

53. Rex A. Skidmore, *Mormon Recreation in Theory and Practice: A Study in Social Change* (Philadelphia, 1941), p. 5; *MIA Activities Manual* (Salt Lake City, 1933), pp. 46 ff.

54. These statements are supported by census figures of the last three decades. For example, see Edward L. Thorndike, "The Origins of Superior Men," *Scientific Monthly*, May, 1943, and also *Science News Letter*, August 31, 1943.

55. Ericksen, *op. cit.*, p .98; see also John A. Widtsoe, *Joseph Smith as Scientist* (Salt Lake City, 1908), and Nels L. Nelson, *Scientific Aspects of Mormonism* (New York and London, 1904).

The chief sources for this chapter besides the works given in the notes and listed in previous chapters are as follows:

Older versions of the standard works: *Book of Commandments* (Zion [Independence, Mo.], 1833) (Coe Collection, Yale University Library). Four editions of the *Doctrine and Covenants* (Kirtland, Ohio, 1835; Nauvoo, Ill., 1844; Nauvoo, Ill., 1845; and Nauvoo, Ill., 1846).

BERRETT, WILLIAM E., BENNION, LOWELL L., and LYON, T. EDGAR. *Contributions of Joseph Smith*. Salt Lake City, 1940.

CHASE, DARYL. *Christianity through the Centuries*. Salt Lake City, 1944.

HARRIS, F. S., and BUTT, N. I. *The Fruits of Mormonism*. New York, 1925.

MIA activities handbooks, especially the 1933 edition, and other MIA materials.

OAKS, L. W. *Medical Aspects of the Word of Wisdom*. Salt Lake City, 1929.

POULSON, M. WILFORD. *Word of Wisdom Background*. Provo, Utah, 1930.

PRATT, ORSON. *Divine Authority of the Book of Mormon*, a series of pamphlets published in 1850–51.

ROBERTS, BRIGHAM H. *A New Witness for God*. Salt Lake City, 1895.

SMITH, JOSEPH FIELDING. *The Progress of Man*. Salt Lake City, 1949.

TALMAGE, JAMES E. *The Great Apostasy*. Salt Lake City, 1915.

WIDTSOE, JOHN A., and WIDTSOE, LEAH D. *The Word of Wisdom: A Modern Interpretation*. Salt Lake City, 1938.

CHAPTER SEVEN

1. Oliver Cowdery, "Defense in a Rehearsal of My Grounds for Separating Myself from the Latter-day Saints," quoted from Charles A. Shook, *The True Origin of the Book of Mormon* (Cincinnati, Ohio, 1914), pp. 50–54.

2. Wesley P. Lloyd, *The Rise and Development of Lay Leadership in the Latter-day Saint Movement* (Chicago, 1939), p. 11.

3. Joseph Smith, *History of the Church of Jesus Christ of Latter-day Saints,* ed. B. H. Roberts (Salt Lake City, 1902), IV, 287.

4. M. M. Quaife, *The Kingdom of Saint James* (New Haven, Conn., 1930), p. 36.

5. The text of the *D & C,* § 134, differs somewhat from that in the 1835 Kirtland edition where it is chap. cii.

6. Joseph Smith, *op. cit.,* VI, 318–19.

7. Joseph Fielding Smith, *Essentials in Church History* (4th ed.; Salt Lake City, 1928), pp. 626–27.

8. Lowell L. Bennion, *The Religion of the Latter-day Saints* (Salt Lake City, 1940), p. 147.

9. Joseph Smith, *op. cit.,* I, 39 ff.

10. Lowry Nelson, *The Mormon Village: A Pattern and Technique of Land Settlement* (Salt Lake City, 1952), p. 57.

11. *Ibid.,* p. 62.

12. Richard T. Ely, "Economic Aspects of Mormonism," *Harper's Magazine,* April, 1903, p. 668.

Other sources not listed in the notes or in the previous chapters include the following:

DURHAM, G. HOMER. "A Political Interpretation of Mormon History," *Pacific Historical Review,* XIII (June, 1944), 136–50.

MORGAN, DALE L. "A Bibliography of the Church of Jesus Christ of Latter-day Saints (Strangite)," *Western Humanities Review,* V, No. 1 (Winter, 1950–51), 43–114.

MUSSER, JOSEPH W. *Celestial or Plural Marriage.* Salt Lake City, 1944.

ROSE, ARNOLD M. "The Mormon Church and Utah Politics: An Abstract of a Statistical Study," *American Sociological Review,* VII, No. 6 (December, 1942), 853–54.

WHITNEY, ORSON F. *Popular History of Utah.* Salt Lake City, 1916.

CHAPTER EIGHT

1. Joseph Smith, *History of the Church of Jesus Christ of Latter-day Saints,* ed. B. H. Roberts (Salt Lake City, 1902), I, 146–47.

2. Elmer T. Clark, *The Small Sects in America* (New York, 1937).

3. *Book of Commandments,* 44:26–30; cf. *Doctrine and Covenants,* 42:30–35.

4. "Stewardship Lease," in Smith, *op. cit.,* I, 367.

5. Leonard J. Arrington, "Early Mormon Communitarianism: The Law of Consecration and Stewardship," *Western Humanities Review,* VII, No. 4 (Autumn, 1953), 352.

6. Quoted from *ibid.,* p. 353.

7. Smith, *op. cit.,* I, 367.

8. See Arrington, *op. cit.,* p. 353, n. 41. Cf. *Doctrine and Covenants,* 51 : 5–6, which was supposedly given in 1831 but was not published until 1835. Whether or not it was changed before publication or whether such were the rules of the order at Thompson, Ohio, is not known (see Arrington, *op. cit.,* p. 346, n. 16).

9. *Book of Commandments,* 51 : 6; and *Doctrine and Covenants,* 51 : 3.

10. Smith, *op. cit.,* I, 364–65.

11. Joseph A. Geddes, *The United Order among the Mormons (Missouri Phase): An Unfinished Experiment in Economic Organization* (Salt Lake City, 1924), pp. 31–32. J. Reuben Clark, Jr., taking this 1835 statement as definitive, emphasizes the importance of private ownership in the Mormon ethic: "The fundamental principle of this system was the private ownership of property. . . . The United Order is an individualistic system, not a communal system" (*Church Welfare Plan* [Salt Lake City, 1939], p. 30).

12. Hamilton Gardner, "Communism among the Mormons," *Quarterly Journal of Economics,* XXXVII (November, 1922), 147.

13. J. Reuben Clark, Jr., *The United Order and the Law of Consecration as Set Out in the Revelations of the Lord* (Salt Lake City, 1945), p. 29; cf. *Doctrine and Covenants,* 101 : 6 and 105 : 3–4.

14. Arrington, *op. cit.,* pp. 359–60.

15. *Journal of Discourses,* II, 307.

16. Smith, *op. cit.,* III, 63–64, speaks of these co-operatives.

17. Gardner, *op. cit.,* pp. 151–52.

18. *Ibid.,* p. 173.

19. Smith, *op. cit.,* IV, 472–75.

20. Joseph F. Smith, "Address," in *Reports of the April Semi-annual Conference* (Salt Lake City, 1900), p. 47.

21. Lowry Nelson, *The Mormon Village: A Pattern and Technique of Land Settlement* (Salt Lake City, 1952), p. 63.

22. Leonard J. Arrington, "Property among the Mormons," *Rural Sociology,* XVI, No. 4 (December, 1951), 343–44.

23. *Ibid.,* pp. 345, 347, and 350.

24. Charles H. Brough, *Irrigation in Utah* (Baltimore, 1898), pp. 12–13.

25. Hamilton Gardner, "Co-operation among the Mormons," *Quarterly Journal of Economics,* XXXI (May, 1917), 497.

26. *Ibid.,* pp. 497–98. See Evon Z. Vogt and Thomas F. O'Dea, "A Comparative Study of the Role of Values in Social Action in Two Southwestern Communities," *American Sociological Review,* XVIII, No. 6 (December, 1953), 645–54, for a smaller, somewhat more controlled, study, which points to the same conclusion; also see Amos G.

Warner, "Three Phases of Cooperation in the West," *American Economic Association Publications* (1887), II, No. 1, 118–19, who attributes Mormon success to this religious factor.

27. Frederick Jackson Turner, *The Frontier in American History* (New York, 1921), p. 258.

28. Vincent Ostrom, "The Social Scientist and the Control and Development of Natural Resources," *Land Economics*, XXIX, No. 2 (May, 1953), 105–16.

29. *Ibid.*, pp. 106–7. For an interesting treatment of the problem of co-operation in the West see Walter Prescott Webb, *The Great Plains* (Boston, 1931). The book by Teague quoted by Ostrom is C. C. Teague, *Fifty Years a Rancher* (Los Angeles, 1944), p. 134.

30. Hubert Howe Bancroft, *History of Utah* (San Francisco, 1891), p. 722.

31. George Thomas, *The Development of Institutions under Irrigation* (New York, 1920), p. 27.

32. This is often given as a definition of riparian doctrine. It is also stated as "the right of the full natural flow of the stream subject to the reasonable use of other riparian owners." For an interesting treatment of water problems under western conditions see Vincent Ostrom, *Water and Politics* (Los Angeles, 1953). The new doctrine that replaced the riparian-rights doctrine provided water rights to lands not actually located on the banks of streams. Evidently, the practices of miners in handling claims played some role in the development of the western doctrine.

33. Ray Allen Billington, *Westward Expansion* (New York, 1949), p. 542.

34. Title 100, Utah Code, Annotated (1943).

35. Orson W. Israelsen, J. Howard Maughan, and George P. South, *Irrigation Companies in Utah* (Bull. 322, Agricultural Experiment Station, Utah State Agricultural College, Logan, Utah [1946]), p. 3.

36. *Ibid.*, pp. 11–13; cf. Title 100, Utah Code, Annotated (1943), 18-2-7, 10, 46; see also Wells A. Hutchins, *Mutual Irrigation Companies in Utah* (Bull. 199 [1927]), and W. Preston Thomas and George T. Blanch, *Drainage and Irrigation, Soil Economics, and Social Conditions, Delta Area, Utah* (Bull. 273, Agricultural Experiment Station, Utah State Agricultural College, Logan, Utah [1936]); two federal government bulletins, *Mutual Irrigation Companies* (U.S. Department of Agriculture Technical Bull. 82 [1929]) and *Mutual Irrigation Companies in California and Utah* (U.S. Farm Credit Administration, Cooperative Division, Bull. 8 [Washington, D.C., 1936]).

37. *Journal of Discourses*, XVII, 43 and 57.

38. Gardner, "Communism," pp. 163, 164, and 165.

39. Leonard J. Arrington, *Orderville, Utah: A Pioneer Mormon Experiment in Economic Organization* ("Utah State Agricultural College Monograph Series," Vol. II, No. 2 [March, 1954]), p. 6.

40. Gardner, "Communism," p. 165.

41. Edward M. Webb, secretary of the United Order at Orderville, manuscript, quoted from Andrew Jenson, "An Experiment in a Communistic System, Called the 'United Order,' " in *Utah Historical Records Survey, Miscellaneous* ("W.P.A. Historical Records Project"), pp. 55–59 (manuscript in Public Library, St. George, Utah); see also Mary Ann Hafen, *Recollections of a Handcart Pioneer* (Denver, 1938), pp. 57–58 (privately printed and distributed).

42. Webb, *op. cit.,* pp. 55–59.

43. Emma Carroll Seegmiller, "Voices from Within: The Story of the United Order," from *Utah Historical Records Survey* ("W.P.A. Historical Records Project"), p. 30 (manuscript in Public Library, St. George, Utah).

44. Arrington, *Orderville,* p. 15.

45. Andrew Karl Larson, "Agricultural Pioneering in the Virgin River Basin" (unpublished M.A. thesis, Brigham Young University, 1946), p. 231; also cf. Mark A. Pendleton, "The Orderville United Order of Zion," *Utah Historical Quarterly,* VII, No. 4 (October, 1939), 141–59, and Emma Carroll Seegmiller, "Personal Memories of the United Order," *Utah Historical Quarterly,* VII, No. 4 (October, 1939), 160–200.

46. Arrington, *Orderville,* p. 15.

47. *Ibid.,* p. 31.

48. Seegmiller, "Voices from Within," p. 4.

49. Arrington, *Orderville,* p. 41.

50. Joseph Fielding Smith, *Essentials in Church History* (4th ed.; Salt Lake City, 1928), p. 531.

51. Leonard J. Arrington, "The Transcontinental Railroad and Mormon Economic Policy," *Pacific Historical Review,* XX, No. 2 (May, 1951), 143–57.

52. Gardner, "Cooperation," p. 484.

53. Leonard J. Arrington, "Zion's Board of Trade: A Third United Order," *Western Humanities Review,* V, No. 1 (Winter, 1950–51), 20.

54. Joseph A. Geddes, *Institution Building in Utah* (Logan, Utah, 1949), p. 14.

55. *Ibid.,* p. 22.

56. Brigham Young, *Discourses of Brigham Young,* ed. John A. Widtsoe (Salt Lake City, 1925), p. 423.

57. Albert E. Bowen, *The Church Welfare Plan* (Salt Lake City, 1946), p. 27.

58. J. Reuben Clark, Jr., *Church Welfare Plan* (Salt Lake City, 1939), pp. 7–8.

59. The most important of these subcommittees are: Finance, Correlation, Building, Agriculture, Industries and Projects, Processing, Cooperatives, and Storage and Storehouses. In all, over 40 members serve on these.

60. Bowen, *op. cit.,* p. 130.

In addition to the books cited in this chapter, the following works were found useful:

ARRINGTON, LEONARD J. "The Deseret Telegraph—a Church-owned Public Utility," *Journal of Economic History*, XI, No. 2 (Spring, 1951), 117–39.

BLEAK, JAMES G. "The Annals of the Southern Utah Mission," Archives of the L.D.S. Church Historian, Salt Lake City.

DURHAM, G. HOMER. *Joseph Smith: Prophet-Statesman*. Salt Lake City, 1944.

FOX, F. Y. "The Consecration Movement of the Middle Fifties," *Improvement Era*, XLVII (February, 1944), 80 ff., and (March, 1944), 146 ff.

TAYLOR, FRED G. *A Saga of Sugar*. Salt Lake City, 1944.

THOMAS, GEORGE. *The Development of Institutions under Irrigation*. New York, 1920.

WIDTSOE, JOHN A. *Principles of Irrigation Practice*. New York, 1914.

CHAPTER NINE

1. A director of one of the L.D.S. Institutes of Religion with whom I raised some of these problems pointed out to me that the threat of apostasy, while very real, was not the only effect on the Mormon student of going away to school. He said that many students who took their religion for granted while at home were awakened to the real worth of Mormon values for the first time when they got away from home and went outside the Mormon community.

2. See Hugh Nibley, "Lehi in the Desert," *Improvement Era*, Vol. LIII, Nos. 1–10 (January–October, 1950), and Sidney B. Sperry, "New Light on the Great Apostasy," *Improvement Era*, Vol. LIII, No. 9 (September, 1950).

3. See Joseph Fielding Smith, *Signs of the Times* (Salt Lake City, 1942), in which the author speaks of the literal fulfilment of Bible and *Book of Mormon* prophecy in our day. The author is immensely popular as a writer with the rank-and-file membership of the church.

4. Maurine Whipple, *This Is the Place* (New York, 1945), p. 176.

5. Lowry Nelson, *The Mormon Village: A Pattern and Technique of Land Settlement* (Salt Lake City, 1952), p. 269.

6. *Doctrine and Covenants* (1950 ed. of the Reorganized Church), p. 308.

7. *Ibid.*, pp. 308–9.

8. Kimball Young, *Isn't One Wife Enough?* (New York, 1954), pp. 57, 157, 165.

9. *Ibid.*, pp. 212, 222, 237, 138, 291–92, 406–8, 440–41.

10. *Ibid.*, p. 237.

11. Jacob 1 : 15, 2 : 23–24, 27–28, 32, 35, 3 : 5; Mosiah 11 : 2, 4, 14; Ether 10 : 5.

12. John A. Widtsoe, *Priesthood and Church Government* (Salt Lake City, 1939), p. 82.

13. *Ibid.*, pp. 80–81.

14. Susan Young Gates and Leah D. Widtsoe, *Women in the Mormon Church* (Salt Lake City, 1926), p. 9.

15. Robert J. Dwyer, *The Gentile Comes to Utah* (Washington, D.C., 1941), pp. 190 ff.

16. Widtsoe, *op. cit.*, p. 87.

17. T. Edgar Lyon, "Concept of Marriage," from William E. Berrett, Lowell L. Bennion, and T. Edgar Lyon, *Contributions of Joseph Smith* (Salt Lake City, 1940), p. 97; cf. also William E. Berrett, "The Place of Women in Society," in Berrett, Bennion, and Lyon, *op. cit.*, pp. 54 ff.

18. Widtsoe, *op. cit.*, p. 87.

19. Cf. John A. Widtsoe, *How the Desert Was Tamed* (Salt Lake City, 1947).

20. Nelson, *op. cit.*, p. 280.

21. Joseph A. Geddes, *Institution Building in Utah* (Logan, Utah, 1949), p. 14.

22. Joseph A. Geddes, *Migration: A Problem of Youth in Utah* (Bull. 323, Agricultural Experiment Station, Utah State Agricultural College, Logan, Utah [1946]).

Index